C0-AVO-464

WHAT WILL BE TAUGHT—THE NEXT DECADE

WHAT WILL BE TAUGHT—

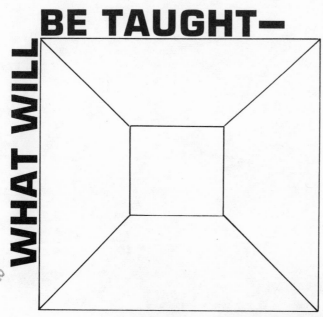

THE NEXT DECADE

MARK M. KRUG
University of Chicago

F. E. PEACOCK PUBLISHERS, INC. Itasca, Illinois

36880

Copyright © 1972
F. E. Peacock Publishers, Inc.
All rights reserved
Library of Congress
Catalog Card No. 77-174167
Printed in the United States of America

CONTENTS

v

36880

36880

The reader of this book will find toward the end of the chapter on Science a gentle exchange between Simplicio and Salviati that has profound meaning for anyone interested in projections of curricular trends in the next decade. They are discussing the future science curriculum, and disagree about what the role of subject-matter should be: Is it a means toward the goal of teaching the student how to inquire? Or is scientific knowledge an end in itself? Finally Simplicio says, "It is rather doubtful that we shall come to an agreement on this issue." Salviati replies, "I don't think it would be hard if you gave up your fixations about designing structured sequences for groups of students, placing students on an almost inviolable learning continuum, and planning primarily for efficiency." Simplicio: "These are not my fixations, my dear Salviati. They are the fundamental basis on which the Science curriculum of the next decade must stand."

Aside from the debaters' civility, a courtesy not often encountered in contemporary discussions of the issue, and aside too from its specific application to science, this exchange can stand as a fair indication of the central issue around which controversy now swirls in the practical world of elementary and secondary curricula. Is the education of children like the programming of computers, or can we encourage and nurture inquiring minds? Subject-matter specialists have dominated curricular decisions throughout the past decade, making the structure of knowledge in their field determine the scope and sequence of instruction, and selecting as content not only what was useful to students, but also what was interesting to themselves, a proper contribution for scholars to make. Teachers and administrators, at the same time, have been busy for most of this century standardizing programs for groups of students and routing their charges through uniform learning schedules, for this approach to instruction increases efficiency, protects institutional structures, and assures that the clientele necessary to support the teaching force will require the services the school is prepared to render.

Now in the decade ahead we anticipate a steady decline in enrollments, and we live with rising popular protest about the quality of education. Perhaps the time is right for broadening our discussion, dampening down for a while the scholar's enthusiasm for promoting his field, the administrator's penchant for efficiency, and the teacher's drive for security, and restore to preeminence the needs of children and the needs of society. This book should be helpful, as it raises many of the right questions and suggests some orderly ways to pursue a few of them toward the right answers.

DR. H. THOMAS JAMES
President, The Spencer Foundation
Former Dean, School of Education, Stanford University

INTRODUCTION

The general public and even professional educators usually see or examine a fragment or a portion of the school curriculum. Parents get some idea about mathematics instruction or other courses when they are either elated or concerned by the rate of progress made by their child in a particular subject matter. High school teachers, depending upon the school in which they teach, may be involved, to one degree or another, in the formulation of the curriculum and the selection of teaching materials in their particular discipline. They do that in committee sessions or in department meetings, but they seldom, if ever, have an opportunity to get an in-depth look into the total curriculum in their own schools. They know even less about the national trends in the instruction of other disciplines than their own. This is regrettable, because common sense would dictate that in order to understand the total child in a school setting, or to comprehend the effectiveness of the school as an institution of learning, one must look at the total curriculum. That in essence is the purpose of this book. We hope to give the readers, lay and professional, an overview of the present high school curriculum and to indicate the trends for the future.

It may be helpful to explain the assignment given to the contributors. Each of them was asked to assess the present situation in his respective field, and to indicate the discernible future trends. Very importantly, the contributors were also asked to *evaluate* the directions in their respective subject matter areas.

According to Professor C. Baird Shuman, the central question facing English educators and teachers is whether it is possible to devise basic programs in English that are sequential and cumulative from kindergarten through the graduate schools. The trend to seek a structure in English to find the answer to the question, "What is English?" will continue, Shuman concludes, even if one is never found.

Art instruction must become "Visual Instruction," argues Professor Kenneth Marantz. Visual instruction must include in addition to the traditional "appreciation" of great paintings and sculpture, free interaction of students with new art forms like photography, architecture, films and multimedia happenings. Art education must, according to Marantz, get out of the classroom and operate in the "mainstreams of human existence."

Professor Leopold Klopfer has used an ingenious way to discuss the future of science education. His chapter is a dialogue, with a cast of participants who have first appeared in Galileo Galilei's *Dialogue Concerning the Two Chief World Systems,* published in 1632. Using this device, the author discusses the best ways to teach scientific literacy to all children and the task of training scientists and engineers needed for our highly advanced technological society.

Professor Roger Pillet traces the great progress made in foreign language instruction during World War II in special programs developed in the U.S. army and the impact of N.D.E.A. institutes for foreign language teachers. He deplores the halt in the trend toward introduction of foreign language courses in elementary schools, but is greatly heartened by the more enlightened appreciation in secondary schools of foreign language study as a significant feature of respective world cultures.

The "new mathematics," widely hailed and welcomed in schools, has not fulfilled its high promise, says Professor Max Bell. In spite of the excellent new materials and new conceptual approaches and in spite of the phenomenal rise in the use of mathematics and mathematical models in natural sciences and in the social sciences like economics and political science, "most school mathematics experience is still very poor." Bell explores the reasons for this failure and suggests ways to deal with the dilemma.

Professor Mark Krug describes the "revolution in social studies," which occurred in the last decade and assesses its impact on social studies instruction. In spite of the progress made in developing new rationales and new materials, Krug concludes, that the social studies field is in trouble because of the massive alienation of young people who view United States history and our political system with great doubts and often with outright distrust.

Teachers are largely trained, not made, says Professor Kevin Ryan, and progress or lack of progress in schooling depends to a large extent on the effectiveness of the pre-service and in-service teacher training. Generally, the new trends in teacher education include great emphasis on academic preparation and clinical training which involves microteaching simulation and sensitivity training. That is all to the good, but what is needed, according to Ryan, is the evolvement of a meaningful philosophy of teaching which would give the teacher a sense of purpose and direction.

The most revealing aspect of this birds-eye view of the curricular trends in secondary education in the next decade is the large area of common agreement among the contributors.

It is clear that the ideas of Jerome Bruner on the structure of the disciplines and on sequential teaching of interrelated concepts and generalizations have had a significant impact on the entire high school curriculum. All authors list among the future trends, more attention to student interests and to student involvement in curriculum making. And finally, there is a common agreement that schools must become more humane, more free and less rigid and less structured institutions and that more opportunities must be provided for student self-development and for individualized instruction.

Ogden Dunes, Indiana   MARK M. KRUG, EDITOR
   June, 1971

R. BAIRD SHUMAN
Duke University

I THE TEACHING OF ENGLISH IN THE DECADE AHEAD: THE 1970'S

In his *Letters to a Young Poet,* Rainer Maria Rilke observes that "The future enters into us, in order to transform itself in us, long before it happens." Actually, it is extremely difficult to talk about the future, and even more difficult to predict what it will hold, largely because time is a continuum in which past, present, and future are necessarily parts of a single entity, each impinging upon each, each substantially affecting each. Rilke's statement is both true and false; or, more accurately, perhaps, neither true nor false; or still more accurately, possibly, incapable of proof. For whenever one begins to meditate on the future, he in some way affects that future; and, as Rilke suggests, the future does enter into us long before it happens and is, indeed, perhaps always in us, for the past must always be the most salient force in shaping the future.

Certainly the most available and intelligent bases for writing about the teaching of English in the decade ahead are to be found in the past, largely in the decade or so immediately prior to the juncture at which

1

we now find ourselves. Probably the most sweeping changes in education in this century have occurred since the Russian launching of Sputnik I in 1957; and, while teachers of English have been part of a smaller revolution than teachers of mathematics, basic sciences, and foreign languages, both revolutionary and evolutionary changes have been afoot in the profession and English teachers have had to make many basic adjustments in the face of these changes. The changes of the seventies will, in many cases, be a continuation and intensification of the changes which began to take place shortly after the shock of Sputnik I caused Americans to take a very critical and searching look at their educational system.

This chapter then must be deeply concerned with the immediate past as well as with the future of English teaching. It must also be concerned with the profession of teaching as it relates to the English teacher and as the English teacher relates to it.

THE BEGINNINGS OF DRASTIC CHANGE

Even before the Russians leaped dramatically ahead of the United States in the exploration of outer space in 1957, a widespread disaffection with progressivism was beginning to be felt in educational circles. Even staunch supporters of John Dewey were appalled by the frequent misinterpretations and misrepresentations of his educational theories when they were transformed into practice by those who were not fully conversant with them. To some, progressivism sanctioned their own lack of preparation and enthusiasm for teaching. All too many progressive English teachers emphasized a rather nebulous life adjustment approach to the teaching of their subject area, often to the neglect of teaching students the basic rudiments which are required for literacy. Tales abounded of high school graduates who could not spell, who could not read simple materials with any ease, and who could not tell a complete sentence from a fragment. Industry had to retrain numerous high school students in areas of basic literacy, and colleges and universities in many cases had to staff more sections of noncredit remedial English than of the regular freshman composition course.

Those teachers who were most concerned about their professional problems, which were now reaching the critical stage, demanded through their professional organizations a thoroughgoing review by a competent professional body of the status of the teaching of English. Responsive to their professional constituencies, the American Studies Association, the College English Association, the Modern Language Association, and the National Council of Teachers of English, supported largely by a grant from the Ford Foundation, arranged that 28 teachers, all of them members of one or more of the four sponsoring organizations, participate during 1958 in three three-day conferences and come together in a final meeting to draft a preliminary version of a report of the conferences. In the following year, 1959, the essence of this seminal report was published under the title *The Basic Issues in the Teaching of English*[1] and marked a significant turning point in the teaching of English.

The *Basic Issues Report* was more concerned with posing questions with which those involved in English should be concerned than it was with providing answers. The answers were to come later from many sources. The 35 questions posed were wide-ranging and most of them avoided quite scrupulously begging the question. The report also provided a compelling rationale for the study of English and particularly for the study of literature: "The reader of literature gets from it a vicarious experience which is of the first importance in teaching him something of his identity as a human being. . . . of all the arts, the most accessible would seem to be the literature written in one's own language."[2]

This report pointed out the extent and diversity of the high school English teacher's job, both curricularly and extracurricularly. It asked thoughtful questions about the responsibilities of English teachers; but perhaps the question which has elicited the most fruitful and extensive response, presaging as it did Bruner's *The Process of Education*, was, "Can basic programs in English be devised that are sequential and cumulative from the kindergarten through the graduate school?"[3] A large proportion of the curriculum centers later established under Project English were more vitally concerned with this question than with any other. Certainly very little that was done in the direction of bringing about change in the teaching of English during the decade of the sixties can be said to be unrelated to the *Basic Issues Report*, which engendered the sort of thinking and self-appraisal from which salutary change usually springs.

PROJECT ENGLISH

If the *Basic Issues Report* set the stage, surely it must be conceded that the government's funding of some 25 Study and Demonstration Centers in English, which began in 1962, provided the means by which those most vitally concerned with the teaching of English could test their hypotheses under the most ideal circumstances and were provided with the means of making their findings available to the profession at large through government-sponsored publications giving detailed accounts of the work of each center.

The major thrust of most of these centers, whether they were primarily concerned with the teaching of literature, the teaching of grammar, the teaching of composition, or the teaching of all three of these, whether they were concerned with the teaching of the culturally disadvantaged or the culturally advantaged, with the teaching of slow learners or the academically gifted, was to make the teaching of English a reasonable and intelligently structured pursuit. But even more importantly, most of the centers were consciously concerned with making the learning of English a pursuit in which the learner could see direction and reason. Of course, as students come to see a valid purpose in what they are doing, they have fewer motivational problems in learning how to do it well.

The Oregon Curriculum Center at Portland, concerned with developing a sequential curriculum in literature, language, and rhetoric from grades 7–12, enunciated principles which more or less characterized the thinking of those working in curriculum and demonstration centers throughout the country: ". . . in the classroom, an awareness of purpose should be present in every assignment. Far too many English textbooks ignore this fact."[4] They chose examples from conventional textbooks dealing with the presentation of how to write complete sentences, pointing out that in a statement such as "To write well, one must follow the rules," the silent, and probably in many cases incorrect, assumption is that everyone wants to write well. It is suggested that it is far more effective to let the student discover the usefulness of writing effectively and then to learn how to write as effectively as possible.

The Northwestern University Project English Center headed by Wallace Douglas was concerned primarily with the teaching of composition. Professor Douglas and his colleagues examined very carefully the present status of the teaching of composition and found it to be artificial and very much unrelated to reality. Further, the Northwestern team found that most teachers in grading writing are looking for errors to correct rather than strengths which the student should be urged to develop and refine. This center suggested that the child as much as possible be permitted "to do his own experimenting with his own grammatical and stylistic patterns and transformations."[5] It has not been easy for teachers of English, who often view their major role to be that of pointing out errors, inconsistencies, and barbarisms in other people's writing, to stand back and let youngsters develop naturally and with little negative motivation in the form of red marks on papers, low grades, and endless repetitions. The Northwestern group found that the average composition class not only failed to provide an atmosphere in which writing as an art could flourish, but that it probably served to stifle the very elements which might encourage one to write well, imaginatively, and vitally.

The report of this group outlined nine essential steps to good writing: (1) analyzing the assignment; (2) searching for an idea; (3) examining one's knowledge of the topic; (4) gathering information; (5) organizing the information gathered; (6) writing the paper in actuality; (7) revising the first version or rough draft; (8) copying and carefully proofreading the final draft; and (9) conferring with the teacher about the paper. The center avoided having youngsters write according to the basic forms of formal discourse as much as possible, capitalizing on the students' ability to use language as a meaningful and effective means of communication, and encouraging them to write as naturally as possible, at least until they had gained confidence in their ability to get their thoughts down on paper.

Many English classes in the United States still proceed oblivious to the suggestions of the curriculum and demonstration centers, although everywhere one finds that the centers have made some impact either directly or indirectly—and probably will continue to do so for years to come—for those who worked in these centers are the people who, in many cases, are now training teachers, writing or editing textbooks, planning curriculum, and in one way or another influencing both school administrators and parents.

When one reads, for example, that Kenneth Koch, a gifted poet and Columbia University professor of English who teases verse out of the students in Manhattan's P.S. 61, begins a class by saying, "Hi there, poets. How about a Christmas poem today? Like what would the ocean do if it really cared about Christmas? Or the eagles, sparrows and robins —what would they do?"[6] it becomes clearly apparent that the spirit of the centers is alive in unexpected precincts. And the fact that Koch has published a delightful book of his students' work testifies to the success and effectiveness of his method.[7] Perhaps the centers served no greater purpose than to remove the restraints from many good teachers who, before the centers questioned prevailing teaching methods and suggested more adequate and imaginative ones, did not feel that they could go it alone.

THE NDEA INSTITUTES

The work of the curriculum and demonstration centers was effectively disseminated among elementary and secondary school teachers by the institution of a far-ranging program of summer institutes for teachers, supported by the College Entrance Examination Board and later by the federal government. These institutes were directly related to the teaching of English, often stressing the usual tripod of grammar, literature, and composition. Some focused on one leg of the tripod, others on all three. Some institutes emphasized the teaching of English to the culturally deprived, others to nonnative speakers, others to academically gifted students, some even to special groups such as the deaf. These institutes, although receiving less government support currently than they did in the mid-sixties, continue to the present day and their contribution has been incalculable.

Most of the institutes were aimed at average teachers. They were available to everyone in the profession, not alone to those who had outstanding undergraduate records. The aim was to afford classroom teachers of English the opportunity to improve themselves in highly practical ways without removing them from their classrooms for training during the regular school year. Literally hundreds of English institutes, most of them running for six or eight weeks, have been held in all of the 50 states as well as in our territorial possessions.[8] Teachers attending them are not charged tuition and are paid a stipend for each week of attendance plus an additional stipend for each dependent. The response to the NDEA Institutes has been almost overwhelming, and the results highly encouraging. Without such institutes, it is highly doubtful that the new grammar would have made the inroads that it has

in elementary and secondary education; indeed, the widespread introduction of transformational grammar into school curricula has come
about largely through the efforts of teachers who have attended summer institutes and have explored through them new ways of making the
study of grammar something more than the prescriptive routine that
it had come to be through the years.

The NDEA Summer Institutes of 1967 were provided with the
reports of most of the curriculum and demonstration centers, and the
fresh and stimulating materials presented in these reports were carried
back to the classroom by many hundreds of the participants in the
institutes that summer.

THE STRUCTURE OF THE DISCIPLINE

Teachers deeply concerned with their subject matter have probably always been very much interested in knowing how their substantive fields are put together, how the materials which go into making up
their substantive fields cohere and interrelate. In a sense, Aristotle's
four causes, Hegel's triad of thesis, antithesis, and synthesis, and Leib-
niz's monads are forerunners in spirit of Jerome Bruner's structuralism
which was enunciated most clearly in *The Process of Education,*[9] certainly one of the two or three most influential books to be produced in
the field of education during the sixties. Bruner, acknowledging the
staggering proliferation of information which was coming available to
man at a time in history when it was estimated that quantitatively
knowledge was doubling every decade, stressed the necessity for young
people to learn and understand the structures of their discipline rather
than to commit to memory endless processions of facts which would
probably become obsolete within a short period. Most teachers who
read and examined Bruner agreed that students needed an operational
understanding of the structure of a discipline along with a factual
knowledge of that discipline.[10]

As teachers of English came increasingly to accept Bruner—and
even those who had not read him were to imbibe much of his philosophy through their contacts with people who had read him and through
the use of textbooks which were increasingly taking him into account
—the teaching of English began to show signs of moving from the
lecture-memorize stage to the explore-discover stage. The transition is

not yet complete, and, indeed, it may never be; however, at the present time, more teachers in more places are engaging their students imaginatively in a new process of learning in which, their basic analytical apparatus sharply honed, they set out independently on uncharted courses and work more independently than has ever been the case before.

How does the new process operate? In literature, for example, each student in a class may read different books. Perhaps one student will explore a single major author, another will explore a theme such as the literature of protest, and yet another will proceed with a chronological study of the development of the American novel. In grammar, the student whose teacher accepts the modern view of the discipline does not learn countless rules which prescribe how people shall speak and write, but rather is encouraged to develop a sensitivity to varieties of English and to describe how the real functioning language operates. For example, rather than learning that the predicate nominative is correct, the student sets about discovering how people answer the question, "Who was it?" If he finds that more people say "It was him" than "It was he," he concludes that "It was him" is standard among the people who make up his sample. He makes no moral or social judgments about this, but simply records his findings.

Most schools are still a long way from approaching the teaching of English from such a point of view; however, the fact that system-wide adoptions of such modern textbooks in grammar as the *Roberts English Series*[11] are widespread indicates that change is afoot in many areas. There is no way to teach Roberts from a traditional base. If teachers are to use the texts, their methods must change.

The emphasis on the structure of the discipline is manifested in scores of articles and books about the teaching of English written during the sixties.[12] Before Bruner's rise to such great popularity, the *Basic Issues Report* had sparked teachers and professors of English to search for a sequential pattern in their discipline and this had caused them to reconsider the overall structure of English. Many teachers who had thought they knew what English was now pondered the question, "What is English?" and were amazed at the diverse answers that the question prompted.[13] It became apparent to many people in the field that (1) the English teacher was the jack-of-all-trades in many schools and that (2) any faculty member, regardless of training or background, was thought by most administrators to be competent to teach English.

THE TEACHER OF ENGLISH

The mere recognition of these problems certainly has not diminished them very much. English teachers are still involved in the teaching of literature, composition, grammar, drama, speech, reading, journalism, creative writing, business English, debating, literary criticism, and other areas too numerous to mention. Many English teachers do not know what they will be teaching until the day that school starts, hence their preparations must necessarily be day-to-day.

Who are the paragons who are able to undertake such an awesome variety of teaching tasks? Usually they are people with a little work beyond a bachelor's degree in English. Most of them have been trained primarily in literature. Only about 5 percent have had a course in advanced composition, yet most of them will be teaching composition more often than literature, for at both the elementary and secondary levels, the major emphasis is on teaching students written communication. In a typical school district, fewer than 10 percent of all English teachers will have had a college course in grammar and fewer than 5 percent will have had a course in the history of the language, yet most will be expected to teach grammar for at least 30 percent of their teaching time each year.[14]

English teachers are regularly expected to work with the yearbook and newspaper staffs in their schools, yet only a handful of them have had any course work in journalism. Newspaper and yearbook assignments often go to new teachers who, in many cases, are also expected to teach the slower classes. Obviously, in such a situation it is difficult for the beginning English teacher to build the sort of self-esteem and self-assurance which would serve to make him an effective teacher. Many of the most conscientious do not last through the first year of teaching, and this is not surprising. Many of those who do last give up what to them seems the losing battle to achieve excellence in their teaching because the odds against excellence are too great.

The fact remains that most English teachers have not had the training to perform in the variety of areas which English encompasses. They struggle heroically to fill in the gaps in their training, but they often function inefficiently and ineffectively in two thirds or three quarters of their teaching on account of lack of specific training.

As the study of grammar has become increasingly specialized, it has become clearly apparent that the time should be upon the profession to make a clear differentiation between teachers of literature and teachers of grammar. Most of the people teaching grammar are not teaching grammar at all in the sense that the modern linguist uses the word nor could they do so without considerably more specialized training in linguistics than most English teachers now have. The student is subjected to something glibly called "grammar" during substantial portions of each of his 12 years in public schools. This something is generally highly repetitious, distressingly contradictory, and little related to the way people actually use language. Those students who enjoy this part of the English course, often enjoy it—or want it to be included year after year—because the rules of grammar which are taught are specific and absolute; when tests are given on the material, the studious and obedient student can often perform well. He will not necessarily be able to speak or write more effectively as a result; but if grades are of fundamental importance to him, as they are apparently to most students, he can rest assured that he will have a respectable grade in his grammar units.

The truly analytical student, who has a genuine desire to know how language really operates, will not necessarily do well in a traditional grammar unit because he will ask unanswerable questions, point out contradictions which his teachers have bypassed successfully for decades, and intrude into areas in which the average English teacher has little knowledge.

The English teacher often fails to realize that by the time a child is three or four years of age, he has mastered nearly all of the syntactical complexities of his language. His natural speech is grammatical even though it may not be standard. He masters the many confusing prepositions which give unity to speech, and he does so without much specific instruction. He knows that school starts *in* a week, that he woke up *at* seven o'clock, that it gets dark *before* six o'clock and that he has played *for* an hour. He can easily make transforms from simple sentence to interrogative sentence; he uses compound and complex sentences with ease long before he knows what they are. Even though he probably cannot pick out the various types of sentences in print, he goes on using the full range of structures available to him, babbling on unself-consciously at five or six, generally consistent in his use of the language, be it standard or nonstandard.

Many teachers feel that it is their duty to make moral judgments about their students' level of usage, to correct them and make them speak more nearly as members of the teacher's own social class speak. This sort of teacher—and he is not a vanishing breed—attempts presumptuously to superimpose a major part of his own value system, as reflected by usage, upon his students. He often rejects the language of his students, only to consider them unteachable if they reject his particular brand of the same language. The less training the English teacher has in grammar, the more dogmatic he is likely to be in trying to teach it. His own insecurities may destroy his effectiveness as a teacher. Perhaps one would not go so far as Harold Allen who says that English is "the study of the English language and of its use as a medium of communication,"[15] but it is difficult to deny the fact that language is central to most of the communicating that people engage in, particularly on the written and spoken levels, and that it is therefore undesirable for the teacher to be so much concerned with demanding standard usage that he stifles the word flow of his students.

The teacher who has been exposed to such seminal works as Bloomfield's *Language,*[16] Fries's *American English Grammar,*[17] Marckwardt's *American English*[18] and his later *Linguistics and the Teaching of English,*[19] Whorf's *Language: Thought and Reality,*[20] Cassirer's *Language and Myth,*[21] and Joos's *The Five Clocks*[22] will not be picky and pedantic about English usage but will approach the teaching of grammar with a messianic vigor and high excitement. He will appreciate the linguistic diversity of his students and will infect them with an enthusiasm for and curiosity about language which will make the study of grammar a high point for them. Such a teacher will approach student writing with the same sort of positive attitude which he brings to the teaching of grammar and will encourage expression by discussing what is good in student writing and what should be capitalized on and developed rather than reading each student effort in order to find in it the errors in spelling, punctuation, and usage which will undoubtedly occur in most student efforts.

The only problem is that very few English teachers have been well trained in modern grammar. Perhaps in schools of the future, the teaching of grammer will be separated from the teaching of English and will be undertaken by specialists. If this were to happen, the student would not study grammar during each of the 12 years of elementary and secondary school. He would learn something about usage and mechanics from his regular English teachers. But he would study grammar for a semester or a year much as he now studies algebra or physics or

European history. His teacher might have a degree in English; however, he would be just as likely to have a degree in anthropology, linguistics, or in some foreign language. The outcome of a course in grammar would be that the student would learn to appreciate the miracle of how language operates. He would come to understand in part the mysteries of the broad tapestry of dialects which he encounters almost daily in a society as mobile as ours. He would learn how to use dialects different from his own, but he would not be asked to replace his own with a dialect foreign to him. The study of grammar would be a most humanizing experience, a major benefit of which would be that the student might come to understand men better through understanding how they communicate with one another.

THE ENGLISH TEACHER AND SPECIALIZATION

In the ideal school of the future, perhaps English teachers will be encouraged to become specialists in some segment of their major field. Broadly, they might essentially be teachers of literature, composition, grammar, or speech and drama. Even a small move in this direction would bring about a world of improvement over existing conditions. However, in large school districts—and with consolidation, they are easy to find even in thinly populated areas—still further specialization might be encouraged. The literature teacher, while able to teach a survey course, might well be a specialist in Shakespeare or in the 18th-century novel. The composition teacher might be a specialist in creative writing or in critical exposition. This may seem like a highly idealistic hope, but it really is not. Even small colleges and universities, when they are about to hire someone in the English department, go out to find someone in a specific subarea, although the person hired may be teaching partially outside that subarea.

To date, few secondary schools have looked for specialists, and teacher-training institutions have largely turned out generalists. High school teachers with bachelor's degrees in English are asked to teach in a much broader field than are their college and university counterparts who nearly always have master's degrees and often have doctorates. And in the face of this, we still wonder why so much high school teaching in the field of English is ineffective. I can only stand aside and marvel that the high schools are doing as good a job as they are in view of the way they waste specialized human resources. In the average high school today, the organization of the program is not conducive to good teaching, and most high school English teachers are so overworked and overloaded with paper work that they have little time or desire to grow professionally.

Under the *rotating unit* approach to the teaching of English, increased specialization on the parts of teachers would be encouraged.[23] This approach, which is most effectively used in English departments of 10 or more people, breaks the English curriculum down into its various components. Students register for three or four English courses, each running for from 9 to 12 weeks, during each school year. Lower division (grades 9 and 10) and upper division (grades 11 and 12) courses are offered.

During each school year, the student is required to register for one skill course such as expository writing, public speaking, or the writing of poetry, one substantive course such as the development of the English novel or modern grammar, and one appreciation course such as the early poetry of Robert Frost or T. S. Eliot's *Four Quartets*. Some courses would have prerequisites; a student probably could not enroll for any elective skill course until he had completed the basic course in expository writing. A student who could not satisfy the requirements of one of his courses would be required to take a substitute course, in many cases not the same course as the one for which he received no credit.

Under such a system, student motivation should be improved since a broad range of electives could appeal to a broad variety of interests and backgrounds. For the weak student, a failure in a course would be easier to make up than would the failure of an entire year of English. Teachers would be able to concentrate on preparing smaller segments of material than they are now able to do, hence they might be expected to gain some depth in their coverage. Hopefully, beginning teachers would not be called upon to teach survey type courses if more experienced teachers were available to handle them.

Some modest beginnings have been made in a few school districts toward implementing the rotating unit approach to the teaching of English. The beginnings have not been without some disappointment. Some teachers have complained that in a 9- or 12-week unit, they never really come to know their students. Others have found that the units offered were not encompassing enough to fill nine weeks. One teacher, for example, was nearly driven to distraction trying to think of ways to keep her nine-week unit on the business letter going. She finally had to give up and teach other things for two or three days every week; and she used good judgment in doing so, because both she and her students had exhausted the possibilities of the initial unit in a relatively short time. The lessons to be learned from this are that (1) the unit should be substantial enough to fit legitimately into the time available and (2) the teacher should use judgment in deciding whether or not to stick with a unit which seems to be palling, provided, of course, that the material to be included in the unit has been covered. It is really too soon to be able to make any judgments about the success of the rotating unit approach; however, it does provide some interesting alternatives to English departments that are seeking to move in new directions.

The school that wishes to take an initial step toward encouraging teachers of English to specialize will probably be well advised to make a distinction between literature teachers, grammar teachers, and composition teachers. Once this has been done, it might be advisable for it to move toward the rotating unit approach or something similar. The farsighted school district will give the chairmen of its secondary school English departments a strong voice in the selection of teachers and will encourage them to build departments which seek to employ specialists.

THE ENGLISH STUDENT

Many English teachers teach as though all of their students were planning to progress to doctorates in the field. Most English teachers still teach a book-centered curriculum, McLuhan notwithstanding. Some of the more conservative ones still boast that they do not watch television, although this breed is vanishing.

Students have never, as a group, been better informed than they are today. When they enter high school, most of them have clocked from 10,000–15,000 hours of television viewing. Regardless of the quality of what they have watched, it must be admitted that they have been exposed to a tremendous amount of oral English, much of it relatively standard, and that they have been deluged with ideas on as broad a spectrum of topics as has ever been available to young people. To those who have been exposed to the moral issues faced by Dr. Welby in his practice of medicine, by Perry Mason in his practice of law, by the voyagers in "Star Trek," *Silas Marner* is going to seem like an interminably plodding novel that has little meaning for modern people. Perhaps young people should view *Silas Marner* and other such works in a more reverential light, but the fact remains that they generally do not. If teachers cannot make English as interesting as television, many of their students will not respond to it. For better or worse, this is a fact of life with which English teachers are learning to live.

Many teachers are discovering quite happily that students who are interested and involved do not cause discipline problems. The first step toward making students be interested and involved comes when the teacher abrogates some of his duties and responsibilities. In many British primary schools, the role of the teacher has changed drastically from that of an imparter of knowledge to that of a facilitator of learning activities.[24] In these schools ". . . there is a special attitude toward children and how they learn. There is a sense of pace, a commitment to the dignity of children, and an exciting confidence in the spontaneous."[25]

Students today are an active lot of people. The teacher who fails to treat them as such will not be able to communicate well with them. The National Council of Teachers of English realizes this and at its 1970 convention passed the following resolution regarding students' rights:

1. Freedom implies the right to make mistakes and thus students must at times be permitted to act in ways which are unwise from an adult point of view so long as the consequences of their acts are not dangerous to life and property, and do not seriously disrupt the academic process.
2. Students in their schools should have the right to live under the principle of "rule by law" as opposed to "rule by personality," and, to protect this right, rules and regulations should be assented to by those who would be bound by them and should be in writing.

*   *   *   *   *

3. Deviation from the opinions and standards deemed desirable by the faculty is not *ipso facto* a danger to the educational process.[26]

At all levels, more attention is being given to the student as an individual, and the trend is bound to continue as school discipline becomes more flexible, as grades are de-emphasized, and as increased opportunities for independent study at every stage of education become more commonplace.

THE TEXTBOOK SITUATION

As the death knell began to be sounded for progressive education, teachers began to take a close look at the textbooks available to them, and often found an appalling dearth of texts which really were English-oriented, even though they were clearly identified by their publishers as "English Texts." Books of readings particularly seemed to stress the nonliterary, apparently in an attempt to entice the reluctant reader.

James J. Lynch and Bertrand Evans, sponsored by the Council on Basic Education, began a close investigation of school texts in English and published their well-documented and completely shattering report, *High School English Textbooks: A Critical Examination,* in 1963.[27] In summarizing their findings about literature texts, they especially objected to the fact that selections were altered, often quite drastically, by editors. They found that "perhaps three-fourths of the volumes examined appeared to have been organized before their content was determined."[28] They were distressed by the "dismissal of the past" which was obvious in most of the books examined which gave "relatively little space to anything written before 1900 or even 1933."[29] Lynch and Evans suggested that publishers of literature anthologies commit themselves to (1) drastically reducing the size of their books but being most selective, and (2) admitting into school anthologies only works of high literary distinction.[30] This, of course, becomes a risky business and in effect makes editors and publishers much more the arbiters of public taste than many qualified people think they should be. Also, if a student is not exposed to a broad range of literature—excellent, good, mediocre, and poor—, he may never develop the literary judgments which he will find necessary in later life, if he is to be a discriminating reader or even a discriminating viewer of film and television plays. Many English educators argue in favor of presenting students with a broad range of materials and are appalled only that too many teachers attempt to teach every selection in an anthology as though it were the finest work of a consummate artist.

In turning to textbooks in grammar and composition, Lynch and Evans found that endless repetition of material from one level to the next became, in their words, "suffocating."[31] Added to this difficulty was the fact that most of the books examined were padded with materials not directly related to the matter at hand. Further, most of the grammar and composition textbooks neglected "literature as a source and center of activities."[32] In a later book, Evans and his collaborator, James Knapton, argued convincingly for using literature as the center of English programs.[33] Every other part of the English curriculum would move centrifugally from it but would always be tied to it. They quote Tolstoi as saying, "The business of art is not instruction but infection,"[34] and their case for the centrality of literature is based essentially on this philosophy.

Lynch and Evans feel that the convention of the four-volume series has a stifling effect upon textbook writers and that the usual practice of having separate literature and composition series is pedagogically unsound.[35]

Writing about textbooks during the period preceding Sputnik I, Michael Shugrue avers, "If textbooks in English had been outstanding, the plight of the English classroom would have been less precarious. Well-intentioned authors, however, had ignored the linguistic and critical discoveries of the scholarly community . . . and produced . . . textbooks for the schools which were outmoded, timid, and intellectually unsatisfactory."[36] Certainly in the years that have passed since the Lynch-Evans study, most significant strides have been made by textbook publishers, partly because of demands from the profession, but largely because of the competition which inexpensive, easily available paperback books have provided.

The upgrading of the profession in the past decade has left its mark on the textbook scene. Hans Guth, himself a highly successful writer of high school and college texts, is quite correct in his assertion that "publishers provide the textbooks they can reasonably expect teachers to adopt. If substandard books continue to be published and used, the reason is not necessarily that publishers do not believe in quality. Rather, they have learned from sad experience that books of high quality do not always sell well."[37] Publishers obviously have to be interested in sales. They are aware of public pressures and other such threats to the success of textbooks, and they must act in the light of all the hazards they have been able to identify in a highly competitive market. As a result, most high school texts even today are aimed at conservative, middle America. In English, many are written so that they can be taught reasonably well by teachers with minimal training in English, since in this area more than in any other, teaching out of field is a commonplace.

Nevertheless, in recent years, as larger numbers of teachers have been better trained both at the collegiate level and through in-service education and NDEA Institutes, the demand for more up-to-date textbooks has increased, and the publishers have begun to meet the challenge. Recent books have also taken into account, more than ever before, the ethnic diversity of the people using them, and series such as Ginn and Company's Voices in Literature, Language, and Composition,[38] Macmillan and Company's Gateway Series,[39] and the SRA packets have provided teachers with a richness of material quite unprecedented in the history of English teaching. Simon and Schuster introduced an exciting new concept, remarkable for its flexibility, in its Papertexts. This graded series offers as individual fascicles a broad range of short stories, each with varied apparatus, which fit into a three-ring binder. In effect, the teacher using Papertexts can make up his own anthology.

In 1966, Harcourt, Brace and World published Paul Roberts' landmark series of grammar texts which offers a sequential program of transformational grammar from grades 3 through 12; and more recently, McGraw-Hill has published Guth and Schuster's American English Today Series, a sequential grammar program for grades 7 through 12.[40] As such series are adopted, the whole teaching of grammar must change and will, hopefully, be more in keeping with the results of recent research in the field.

Fader and McNeil have produced a realistic view into the reading preferences of young people in *Hooked on Books,*[41] and Ned Hoopes has produced several books of readings aimed at alienated young people, the most usable of these being *Who Am I?*[42] Holt, Rinehart and Winston have published a highly appealing group of readers in its Impact Series which is aimed primarily at students who have reading problems.

It is certainly undeniable that some splendid books are currently available to teachers of English. However, some of the best books are under attack by local pressure groups and, in some cases are being withdrawn from the schools for which they were purchased. For example, the public schools of Rocky Mount, North Carolina, yielding to pressures from members of the Twin County Fundamentalist Ministerial Association, have withdrawn from their schools two series, New Worlds in Literature, probably as significant a series in literature as has appeared for some years, and Voices in Literature, a series very popular among poorly motivated students (see above). The reasons that the pressure group in question set forth for objecting to these books have nothing to do with literary quality. The major objections are (1) that the books contain stories written by Communists or, if not by Communists, by people who are "pretty far out";[43] (2) that "the books contain outright curse words,—like 'damn' ";[44] and (3) that the young people in some of the stories do not show proper respect for their elders. In the face of such actions as these, many teachers throw up their hands and either leave the profession or settle down to teach only the vapid, innocuous works which will offend no one, and which will certainly inspire few students ever to read for pleasure.

THE QUESTION OF CENSORSHIP

This leads us to one of the thorniest problems in the profession today, that of censorship. If the English classroom is to be a vital place and if the teaching of English is to have valid outcomes, then English departments must be given considerable latitude in selecting the books to be taught. Presumably English teachers are responsible people. They do not choose their texts in order to sway students to the ways of life depicted in the books which are being read.

Any community which permits outside pressure groups to dictate curriculum will soon have a deteriorating school system, just as it would have a deteriorating medical situation were it to permit the local PTA or WCTU to prevent its physicians from prescribing certain drugs or giving certain types of approved treatment. Certainly there are restraints upon physicians, lawyers, and other professionals; however, these restraints come essentially from the profession itself through such professional organizations as the American Medical Association or the American Bar Association.

In most censorship cases involving English teachers, the teacher is acting within limits which have been defined by the National Council of Teachers of English in such publications as *The Student's Right to Read*[45] and *Meeting Censorship in the Schools: A Series of Case Studies.*[46] The National Council of Teachers of English asserts that "because of outside pressures many English teachers cannot carry out their central responsibility: teaching the cultural heritage of Western Civilization."[47] The Council lists some of the books which have caused teachers difficulties, some so severe that the teacher has virtually been drummed out of the profession: *Huckleberry Finn, The Scarlet Letter, Catcher in the Rye, Brave New World, 1984,* and *The Grapes of Wrath.*[48] To this list may be added scores of well-known works including *To Kill a Mockingbird; Good Morning, Miss Dove; Crime and Punishment; The Merchant of Venice; Oedipus Rex; Demian;* and *Death in the Family.*

08808

Censorship does not prevent young people from reading material which might, in the eyes of the censors, threaten their innocence. Rather, it makes it necessary for them to read questionable books without any mature direction or discussion of what is in them. If there lurks any danger in the books that youngsters read—and most people who understand literature and psychology quite well feel that there does not —the danger lies in a child's being exposed to an inflammatory book and having no one to talk it over with.

Kenneth Donelson suggests that the time has come for English teachers to be more on the offensive than on the defensive in regard to the problem of censorship. He contends that "English Departments have too long sheltered students from reality, and in their noble efforts have made clear that there are two worlds—the real world and the world of the English class."[49] As the most imaginative and effective English teachers and curriculum planners in English move toward relevancy, many nonliterary pressure groups are pulling in the opposite direction and are making of the teacher's job a mockery.

When such groups succeed at one level, as has the Twin County Fundamentalist Ministerial Association in Rocky Mount, it usually moves on to the next level. In this particular case, the pressure group, having succeeded in getting two excellent series banned from the Rocky Mount Public Schools, has moved on to a meeting with the governor, the lieutenant governor, and the state superintendent of public instruction in an attempt to have the two series in question banned from the entire state of North Carolina.[50]

When one teaches literature, he covers the whole range of human experience; this is a fundamental purpose for teaching it. Guth quite correctly notes that "great literature is typically more searching, revealing, or disturbing than literature designed to confirm existing standards. As a result, the works the teacher finds most satisfying are the most likely to give offense to the self-righteous."[51] The teacher who cannot teach the broad range of quality literature available to him becomes a professional eunuch.

In 1959, Harry E. Hand urged teachers to be cautious in selecting books for class use, implying that safety should be a major factor governing book selection.[52] While nearly everyone writing on the subject feels that much is to be lost in heated censorship fights,[53] most current writers urge teachers to exercise judgment, to have a rationale for teaching every work they require students to read, and to select the works most

36880

appropriate to what they are teaching. The most important factor in the whole censorship question is probably that of keeping open lines of communication between the schools and the community. Donelson's fifth responsibility which he lists for English departments is "To communicate to the public and to our students what is going on in the English classroom and why it is going on."[54] The *why* of this statement is of particular importance; most pressure groups know at least a part of *what* is going on but have little idea of *why* it is.

Donelson insists that English departments must "establish and maintain a nucleus of English teachers who know literature well and who understand what constitutes literary merit and adolescent appeal in any work."[55] He further urges teachers to know arguments for and against censorship so that they can do intelligent combat against pressure groups when necessary. Certainly his fourth responsibility for English departments is most rational in its suggestion "to prepare a rationale or defense for any book to be taught in any class by any teacher."[56]

Students are coming more and more to demand literature relevant to their times and situations. They are not overprotected when they go to the films or tune in on a television program. It seems absurd that the school should be forced by minority pressures from within the community into playing the sort of paternalistic role which all too many school districts have come to play.

PROFESSIONALISM AND THE TEACHER OF ENGLISH

Teaching at all levels is generally referred to as a profession; yet, in view of what has been written above, one is tempted to ask whether the English teacher is, indeed, viewed by the community as a professional. Would pressure groups get as far attacking lawyers or physicians as they do when they attack teachers?

What are some of the identifying characteristics of a profession? To begin with, those in a profession generally have extensive, specific training for that profession; and until they have satisfactorily completed this training, they are not viewed as professionals nor may they practice the profession. For example, no matter how great is the shortage of physicians within a community, a housewife with a bachelor's degree cannot be given an emergency certificate to practice medicine. In such a situation, even a pathologist with a Ph.D. but without an M.D., although highly qualified in medicine, cannot be granted permission to practice. To suggest such a thing would be unthinkable. Nevertheless, in the same community, the housewife, sometimes even without a degree, can be given an emergency certificate to teach and the pathologist, were he to desire to teach, would probably be much sought after whether or not he had had any specific training for teaching. This is not necessarily a bad situation, but it does cause one to question whether teaching qualifies as a profession on this particular count.

In regard specifically to English teaching, there is even a greater question, for, as we have said, any certified teacher is thought by many school administrators to be capable of teaching English. Indeed, if a survey were made of all high school teachers with 20 years of service or more, probably more of them would have taught English at one time or another than would not have done so.

Generally the professional is privy to an extensive body of specialized information which the untrained public is unable to understand and to use. The English teacher, if he has been trained properly, will have insights into grammar, writing, literary criticism, and teaching skills which are not held by the average layman. However, many people who do not have these insights *are* English teachers, and this is one major factor in weakening the profession. The physician who does not keep up with developments in his profession will soon lose his clientele; however, the English teacher who does not know a morpheme from a metaphor is usually protected by tenure and goes on for three or four decades, as Henry Adams said, telling lies to the young. Certainly in most school districts there is little external impetus for the teacher to keep himself current. The weak teacher with a master's degree and 20 years' experience receives the same salary as the spectacularly good teacher with equal qualifications, so that generally the only reason for wishing to achieve excellence is that of knowing the satisfaction which comes from outstanding teaching.

Another criterion of a profession is that it is self-regulating; that is, it sets the standards for practitioners, it admits to the profession those who meet the standards, and it enforces the standards diligently. Those who are most competent to make judgments make them; the pediatrician is judged by fellow pediatricians, the ophthalmologist by fellow ophthalmologists. However, in the schools, the English teacher, even the chairman of the department, often does not have a voice in the hiring and/or retention of fellow English teachers.

In view of these few criteria—and one might cite many more—it seems apparent that the English teacher is at best a semiprofessional, nor is this situation indefensible. The English teacher may be certified in most states after only four years of higher education, whereas the physician, lawyer, or college professor is usually in school for at least twice that time. The lifetime earning potential of a teacher with a bachelor's degree does not compare unfavorably in many parts of the country with that of people of equal training—nurses, engineers with only a bachelor's degree, accountants, and librarians.

The distressing fact is that most high schools are not able to accommodate the professional because the professional requires a sort of autonomy which most bureaucratically organized school systems are unable or unwilling to provide. Some showcase school districts have risen above this and have attracted professionals to the ranks of their faculties, but the average school district drives professionals away and in so doing seeks its own level which is mediocrity.

If schools as we know them are to be a potent force in the future —and in view of what one reads in the writings of Paul Goodman[57] and others, one is forced to consider at least the very real possibility that schools will become a diminishing force within our society—certainly some drastic restructuring of them will need to be done. In English, it would certainly seem desirable for secondary schools to have in residence at least one professional, an experienced teacher with a doctorate or close to it, assigned to a given secondary school and paid a salary commensurate with his training, whose chief function would be to help plan curriculum and supervise teaching. Teachers as we know them, semiprofessionals, would do much of the teaching, although they would be assisted by trainees or interns who would have substantial teaching responsibilities. Paraprofessionals would handle much of the routine work—keeping the register, grading objective tests and some essays, typing, running the mimeograph machine, supervising study halls and lunchrooms in schools where such supervision seems necessary, in general, freeing the teaching staff to do its teaching well and giving it time to prepare materials and to grow professionally.

The inevitable question of meeting the cost of such a program arises. There is no reason that a reorganization of this sort should be prohibitively expensive. While the senior or master teacher would be paid a high salary, regular teachers would be paid at their regular salaries, and the teaching interns would be at the lowest rung of the salary ladder. Paraprofessionals would probably be paid an hourly wage, but in most school districts, such people are already being employed, so this should not add considerably to the operating budget. The important consideration in educational matters must ultimately be the quality of instruction available. Certainly, under the proposed change, teachers could function more effectively, and better teachers would be lured into the profession.

Under such a program, all hiring of English teachers would be done in consultation with the English department, which would try to achieve a balance by carefully selecting teachers whose interests are complementary. Also, ideally, most teachers would have 11-month contracts and would spend the summer working on curriculum and planning for the year ahead. This might be combined with some summer school teaching.

The climate seems right for a growing professionalism among English teachers. Certification requirements are being strengthened so that more academic preparation is demanded than has ever been demanded previously. The National Council of Teachers of English (NCTE), with a membership of well over 100,000, is becoming a powerful force in American schools and is yearly producing a wealth of materials which are readily available to the classroom teacher who would improve his teaching skills. The NCTE provides English teachers with their greatest opportunity of articulation with other members of the profession. The Modern Language Association, although smaller than NCTE and traditionally more college-oriented than school-oriented, has also begun to enroll in its ranks large numbers of school people and has worked coöperatively with NCTE in planning many valuable school-oriented activities. Among these are the Dartmouth Seminar and the Vancouver Conference.

THE DARTMOUTH SEMINAR AND THE VANCOUVER CONFERENCE

The British and the Americans are said to be two peoples separated by a common language. Certainly the articulation between the secondary schools of the two peoples had not been great up until the mid-sixties. However, in 1966, at the instigation of the National Council of Teachers of English, the British sister organization, the National Association for the Teaching of English, and the Modern Language Association, the Carnegie Foundation sponsored a month-long seminar at

Dartmouth College attended by about 50 educators, half from Britain and half from the United States.[58] The seminar also brought in 23 well-known consultants from both sides of the Atlantic for short periods to discuss specific topics in the teaching of English. Besides this, each of the participants had prepared a position paper prior to the seminar, and these papers, totaling over a thousand pages, were read and discussed by all of the participants.

All levels of education were represented at the Dartmouth Seminar, whose invited members were chosen in such a way as to assure a great diversity of viewpoints. The ultimate aim was to have the members pool information about the aims and methods of education. The outcomes were many. Two books have been produced which describe the seminar. Herbert J. Muller's *The Uses of English*[59] is aimed at intelligent laymen while John Dixon's *Growth Through English*[60] is a report for those professionally engaged in the teaching of English. Besides this, numerous articles have been written by various participants about the seminar.

One participant—a senior researcher, E. Glyn Lewis from the University of Wales—identified some of the chief differences between the American and British approach to the teaching of English. He writes that "in Britain, English is seen as a *process*—a process of discovery, or of self-expression, of creative response. . . . It is one of the last vestiges in aesthetics as applied to teaching."[61] He comes very close to the heart of the difference in the two approaches when he writes that the American "believes in actually teaching and would not deny that he has been known even to instruct. The teacher in Britain, represented at Dartmouth, on the other hand, pins his faith to the 'sunburn principle,' to exposure. It is the conflict of the Brunerian approach . . . and the Piagetian principle, concerned to emphasize the concept of readiness, of judiciously waiting for the appearance of a propensity and for the spark from heaven to fall."[62]

Actually, the American is more comfortable with Bruner than with Piaget or even Montessori, and the Dartmouth Seminar made this clear to most of the participants. The American is concerned with quantity, with fitting all that is deemed essential in a subject into manageable structures. This is one reason that American teachers have latched onto sequential programs and to modern grammar, particularly the transformational grammar described by Chomsky in *Syntactic Structures*[63] and adapted to school use in the Roberts English Series. Apparently the

American temperament requires a framework which, to the typical British teacher, would seem repressive and unnecessary.

Americans were amazed at the role of the teacher in British English classes where little formal teaching is done and where the master is more a clearinghouse for student activity than an instructor. Much has been learned from the British particularly about the uses of improvised drama as a central school activity in English classes. Around the time of the Dartmouth Seminar, the tide was beginning in some quarters to swell against overstructuring. James Squire, former executive secretary of the National Council of Teachers of English, points out that "the Huntington Writers Conference called for the abandoning of rigid conformities of all prescribed and structured programs."[64]

Out of the Dartmouth Seminar grew a call for careful attention to the following matters:

1. The centrality of the pupil's exploring, extending, and shaping experiences in the English classroom.
2. The urgency of developing classroom approaches stressing the vital, creative, dramatic involvement of children and young people in language experiences.
3. The importance of directing more attention to speaking and listening experiences for all pupils at all levels, particularly those experiences which involve vigorous interaction among children.
4. The wisdom of providing young people at all levels with significant opportunities for the creative uses of language: creative dramatics, imaginative writing, improvisation, role-playing, and similar activities.
5. The significance of rich literary experiences in the educative process and the importance of teachers of English restudying particular selections to determine their appropriateness for reading at different levels.
6. The need to overcome the restrictiveness of rigid patterns of "grouping" or "streaming" that limit the linguistic environment in which boys and girls learn English and that tend to inhibit language development.
7. The need to negate the limiting, often stultifying, impact of examination patterns that direct attention of both teachers and pupils to aspects of English which are at best superficial and often misleading.
8. The compelling urgency of improving the conditions under which English is taught in the schools: the need for more books and libraries, for better equipment, for reasonable class size, for a classroom environment that will make good teaching possible.
9. The importance of teachers of English at all levels informing themselves about the results of pertinent scholarship and research so that their classroom approaches may be guided accordingly.

10. The need for radical reform in programs of teacher education, both pre-service and in-service.
11. The importance of educating the public on what is meant by good English and what is meant by good English teaching.[65]

The thrust of most of these matters puts the learner in a central position, and the suggestions are very much in keeping with those of such influential recent writers as Carl R. Rogers,[66] Herbert Kohl,[67] George Dennison,[68] Charles Silberman,[69] and Neil Postman and Charles Weingartner.[70] In a society as egalitarian as ours attempts and professes to be, the schools are the most significant equalizing force and, in a very real sense, the English classroom becomes the most equalizing area within the school as students work toward achieving a stake in the common fund of their cultural heritage through literature and language.

In the decade ahead, the emphasis will be increasingly on the learner, largely as a reaction against the dehumanizing effects of an overcrowded and highly technological society. In this regard it is significant that a recent volume of the yearly publication *Classroom Practices in Teaching English*[71] is entitled *Humanizing English: Do Not Fold, Spindle, or Mutilate.* One has but to read through the selections in a volume such as Ronald and Beatrice Gross's *Radical School Reform*[72] to come to the conclusion that education is becoming less subject-centered and more student-centered. This trend is especially true in English where more independent study is presently carried out than in any other subject field in the curriculum. In the decade ahead, it is probably safe to predict that in many districts, no student will pass through the last four years of secondary school without being exposed to some independent study in English.

The Dartmouth Seminar and its aftermath of exciting publications has caused many English teachers to reexamine what they are doing, and, as more teachers are able to participate in international meetings and to see schools abroad and in various parts of their own country in operation, self-examination and healthy self-criticism will increase.

The next step after the Dartmouth Seminar came during the following year when a somewhat larger group of teachers, this time from the United States and from many parts of the British Commonwealth, including Australia and New Zealand, met for a conference in Vancouver, British Columbia. Also, Canadian and British teachers have been increasingly involved in the National Council of Teachers of English and have been active participants in its annual meetings. Whether this

sort of interchange will increase as rapidly as it should during the
decade ahead depends largely upon the amount of financial support
available for it. Such support would usually have to come from foundations and from the federal government, so the overall economic state
of the nation will have a great bearing on how internationally involved
the profession will be able to become. Immense international involvement is now technologically feasible, so the only real barrier to it is a
financial one.

ENGLISH TEACHERS AND THE NEW TECHNOLOGY

To write about the future of the new technology is a very risky
business. A decade ago, schools were undergoing great changes as programmed learning, teaching machines, and language laboratories were
being adopted at an unprecedented rate and at enormous cost to school
districts. In many of the same schools today, teaching machines have
been packed up and put away, language laboratories—if they are still
operational—are used only by the brave, and learning packets are
boxed in chaotic order in the library storeroom.

Some of the equipment of the new technology is still being used
and will continue to be used. Self-contained language laboratories,
those that are set up in each language teacher's individual classroom,
are still used extensively, but most language teachers have rebelled
against having to move a class of students to a language laboratory for
a whole period when the laboratory part of the lesson occupies just a
portion of the period. From this fact, one can assume that teachers will
make use of technological aids which allow them flexibility.

Similarly, motion-picture projectors seem firmly entrenched in
most high schools and are used extensively by English teachers. Most
teachers will be more likely to use films if they can show them in their
own classrooms than if they have to conduct youngsters to another part
of the school for film viewing. Therefore, English classrooms need sufficient electrical outlets, a motion-picture screen, and shades or draperies
which can be pulled to darken the room. All sorts of projection equipment will receive more use if it may be used within the classroom.

Both television and phonograph equipment is seen more frequently in classrooms than ever before. It is not unusual for the teacher
to work toward achieving a mood for writing or for studying poetry by

using background music. Closed-circuit television is used quite extensively, although it is generally not popular among teachers or students. The chief objection to it is that the student is being lectured at and has no opportunity to question or respond as the program progresses. However, a new and exciting use of television will grow during the coming decade as it becomes possible to record and store programs for later showing. The equipment for doing this has been quite costly, but the price is now coming within easier range for many school districts to purchase the necessary equipment.

School libraries will probably be much more extensive in the future as an ever-increasing body of material becomes available inexpensively on microfiche cards. Each card would cost, at present rates, 25 cents and would hold up to 60 pages of printed material. Inexpensive microfiche readers are now available, and the price will probably go down much more as they come to be mass produced. Other photoduplicating processes will make it possible for students anywhere to have at their fingertips primary resource materials which were, even 15 years ago, available generally only to the scholar who could travel to the library which had them. English teachers already have at their disposal an almost unbelievable array of resources through NCTE/ERIC,[73] and most NCTE publications contain in every issue reports of ERIC materials which have become available.

The computer will have a profound effect upon all teaching in the decade ahead, but probably its impact on the teaching of English will be less direct than will be its impact in some other disciplines. One effect which will be felt very soon—if it has not been felt already—will be in the increased use of modular scheduling so highly individualized that most students will have a new schedule for every week that they attend school. Some schools have already gone over to this sort of scheduling, and by 1980 it will likely be a more common practice than that which is predominant now.

Experiments have been made with the machine grading of student writing. It seems extremely doubtful that machines that are presently available will be able to make dependable judgments about anything so subjective as style, although some machines may be programmed to pick out errors in writing. However, the tendency in theme grading seems to be away from picking out errors, so the machine is not likely to take over in this province no matter how devoutly teachers might pray that it be possible for it to do so.

Schools with large concentrations of youngsters who have severe reading problems may find it desirable to take the lead of Sister Bede Sullivan, chairman of the English department of Lillis High School in Kansas City, and to institute extensive film appreciation programs. In Lillis High School, every Monday morning is spent viewing and discussing a film. The English program during the week is related to the film, and the film is viewed again on Friday. The faculty at this school has found that this is one way to deal with mature literary concepts such as imagery, symbolism, simile, metaphor with students who are virtually nonreaders. The school, of course, offers instruction in reading, but while this is going on, students are being exposed to mature ideas and are being constantly challenged by these ideas. This makes them more eager to learn to read.

Considerable experimentation has been done in recent years with student-made films, and this device is likely to grow in popularity. When students plan films and write scenarios, they are directly involved in a composing process which to most of them has more vitality and interest than theme writing.

One effective technique which is promising for the future is that of putting a class into contact with an author or some other prominent person by telephone hookup. Some classes have spent an hour interviewing a person who has interested them. Recently, for example, an American Literature class at San José State College conducted by Professor Martha H. Cox held a telephone interview with Nelson Algren in Chicago, and a number of high schools have done similar things.

As exciting as some of the new technology is, some of it will be oversold and school districts will find themselves in possession of costly equipment which will not be used once the novelty has worn off. Therefore, it is desirable for schools to rent much of its equipment until it is sure that teachers really will use it consistently. In some cases, part of the rent can be applied toward purchase.

DISCIPLINE

Through the years the school has come to serve essentially a custodial function. At the beginning of each school year, school superintendents, officers in PTA chapters, class presidents, and other functionaries make speeches outlining the lofty ideals of free, public education. But usually there is no significant public outcry if these ideals are not met or even approached. Large outcries are heard when schools contemplate going over to four-and-a-half day weeks so that each teacher will have a planning period in every week. If the schools do not run for the conventional five days, working parents have to make arrangements to have their children looked after, and this becomes inconvenient and expensive.

The school generally serves its custodial function much as a prison serves its. Youngsters are usually required to be in some specified, assigned place for every hour of the school day. Often they are even marched to a lunchroom where they must sit under supervision during lunch periods. Free periods are still often spent in study halls which are an abomination to students and teachers alike. Those who try to maintain an open classroom are often considered to lack control, since noise pervades their classes.

Silberman has written a scathing report about American schools in which he is especially critical of the regimentation which characterizes them. He contends that students are not disruptive essentially but rather that schools are disruptive of childhood.[74] Silberman, Kohl, Dennison and others like them support much of what came out of the Dartmouth Seminar and the Vancouver Conference, and they appear to be the wave of the future.

Hopefully the seventies will see the demise of the formal classroom as we know it today. Discipline problems will decrease as rules become less numerous. Teachers have for too long made it a sin for a child to be thirsty in the middle of a class period, to have to go to the lavatory during class, to forget to bring a pencil, to talk with another student, to act in any way like a human being during those sacred hours when school is in session. As the list of mortal sins within the classroom diminishes, so will many problems which have been tied up with the enforcement of rules.

Already the trend in schools is much away from memorization and toward the development of understandings. This attitude will reduce such discipline problems as cheating, since there will be less and less reason for students to cheat. Rather, especially as grade pressures decrease, they will work to learn because they will realize that there is excitement in learning.

The Melbourne (Florida) High School under the direction of B. Frank Brown has grown increasingly away from restrictiveness and the results have been encouraging. As more freedom and self-government have been granted to students, "the need for teachers to monitor in the halls, the cafeteria, and bus-loading areas diminished; finally this problem disappeared completely as an administrative function of the school. . . . The problem of truancy diminished to the point where it eliminated itself."[75] It is noteworthy that the dropout rate which is about 30 percent for the nation at large is only 4 percent for Melbourne High School.

If schools are to exist as fundamental institutions within a democratic society, then students must see democratic processes at work within them. Where they see flagrant violations of such processes, they will rebel against the hypocrisy of those committing the violations. In all classes, in all school dealings, the student must be accorded the rights granted to him by the Constitution. In classes in the areas generally designated "The Humanities," he must be encouraged to develop, but not discouraged from dissenting. The English teacher can probably do more than any other one person in the school to bring students to realize the significance of being an individual.

In many areas, there is a pleasing openness in schools. In some cases, as in Centerville, Ohio, where two junior high schools without walls are functioning very satisfactorily, the openness is physical as well as attitudinal. But openness must begin with a frame of mind rather than with a building, and the English teacher who lacks this frame of mind will probably bring little to his students no matter how much information he has at his command.

BEHAVIORAL OBJECTIVES

It would be impossible to look to the decade ahead without saying a word about behavioral objectives. English teachers will find a valuable source in John Maxwell and Anthony Tovatt's *On Writing Behavioral Objectives for English.*[76] For those who wish to write behavioral objectives for English courses, this is a fine book. Also of help would be Lynn Dieter's article "Behavioral Objectives in the English Classroom: A Model"[77] which deals with writing a set of objectives for Schaeffer's *Shane.*

Hans Guth is very likely close to being realistic when he writes, "No one who knows English teachers will be surprised to find that many of them regard the behavioral objective movement with open hostility." Guth continues, "No doubt, in the long run, the pent-up frustrations of the teacher and the sheer rebelliousness of today's students will defeat the manufacturers of learning modules and performance tests."[78]

The behavioral objective craze is unlikely to have a profound effect upon the teaching of English in the seventies, although it may well continue to have an effect upon the teaching of science and mathematics to which it may be more easily and sensibly applied. In many ways it is closely akin to programmed learning and, in some areas of English having predictable desired outcomes, it can be used effectively. However, in the area of literature, for instance, behavioral objectives tend to box the teacher in. As Guth observes, "We don't teach literature just to produce symptoms,"[79] and it is only symptoms which can be observed objectively that behavioral objectives can really measure.[80]

DIRECTIONS

One must come ultimately to the part of a chapter like this in which he looks into his crystal ball and attempts to predict. In the face of this somewhat awesome task, one can probably be forgiven if he lapses into the first person which is the easiest person to use for prognostication.

Where is the teaching of English going? I must try to answer this question by making a mental division of what I am going to say into two columns, one labeled *Where I hope English is going* and the other labeled *Where English probably is going.* The story is brought to mind of the English teacher who died and, being a marginal sort of person, was given her choice of heaven or hell. She decided to look heaven over first. It was blissfully calm, but she was told that her job in heaven would be to teach English. She was informed that she would have five classes a day with 75 people to a class. She muttered something about Conant, and asked to be shown to hell. Hell lacked some of the accoutrements of heaven, but was not unbearable. She, however, was taking no chances, so she asked her guide what her job would be there. He said that she would do what she had always done, teach English. Warily she asked, "And how many classes will I have?" Her guide answered rather apologetically, "Only two." "And how many students will be in each one?" Again, apologetically he answered, "Probably about ten."

The teacher was amazed and told her guide what she would be called upon to do were she to elect to go to heaven. Not dismayed by this information, he responded, "But, you see, there is no shortage of English teachers here."

If the fruits of the Dartmouth Seminar and the Vancouver Conference are harvested, if the warnings of Kohl, Dennison, Silberman, and a host of other keen observers are heeded, English teachers will move away from the formal classroom and schools will move away from the formal regimentation which now so often characterizes them. In doing this, the chief emphasis will be on the student and on learning theory rather than on rules and structure. This is not to say that the profession should throw Bruner out in order to make way for Piaget; the two can co-exist meaningfully and productively. But if Piaget is permitted to come first, Bruner will be much easier to implement.

I would think that a concomitant of this sort of change would be an increased awareness of student's rights and encouragement from English teachers for students to be directly involved in planning and running the English program. This would mean the demise of citywide or systemwide curriculum guides and other such impressive and costly documents.

In the area of grammar, I think that a new grammar will replace the transformational/generative grammar which now seems to be gaining a foothold. My guess is that teachers will find transformational grammar too drastically different from what they have been used to and that students will generally find the intricate diagrams quite beyond them. Probably the return will be to a modified structural grammar with increased emphasis on semantics in the teaching of both grammar and composition. History of the language will probably receive new attention. Those who produce and sell textbooks cannot allow one form of grammar to become entrenched if their sales figures are to continue high.

Literature teachers are looking for new constructs within which to teach their subject. The "New Critics" have paved the way, and Northrup Frye's *The Anatomy of Criticism*[81] has been enormously influential. My prediction is that new approaches to the teaching of literature, many of them involving the extensive use of media, will bring about great changes in approaches to literature within the schools.

The teaching of composition is already broadening in many schools to include any creative facet of composing. Composing need not always be associated with writing, although writing is one of the desirable outcomes of it. But the student who improvises dramatically or helps plan a class film or takes pictures or dances in reaction to a poem or a story is composing in a very real way, and his creativity should be used as a springboard to writing rather than viewed as an impediment to it.

I fervently hope that teachers will increasingly become professionals in ways which I have outlined in this chapter. I hope that those planning to enter the teaching of English, if departmental structure remains similar to what it is now, will receive training in modern grammar, history of the language, criticism, and advanced composition before they can be certified. Their professional training should involve some exposure to team teaching, to the use of media, and to interdisciplinary studies since many secondary schools will be emphasizing humanities programs. I hope that teachers will be able to depend upon administrative support in censorship matters, and that they will not be judged effective or ineffective on the basis of how much noise is heard when one opens their classroom door. I also hope that somehow teachers will become increasingly humane. Considering the pressures upon them, most of them are remarkably humane now; however, there is still room for improvement.

The federal government, in giving really nominal aid to English in the sixties, contributed more to the teaching of English than any single factor has in the past. The Curriculum and Demonstration Centers funded by Project English produced colossal results, and the NDEA English Institutes have helped to disseminate these results. Sources of federal aid have been diminishing, but should they come available again, the results could be astounding not only for the profession but for society at large since English can be a distinctly humanizing force in a severely troubled society. Much of what is accomplished in the seventies will depend upon how much federal and foundation money the profession is able to attract.

As older school buildings are replaced with new ones, and even as older buildings are remodeled, there will be a trend toward less formal classrooms. Movable furniture, carpeted floors, self-contained audio-visual facilities, and self-contained nuclear paperback libraries of about 500 books will increasingly come to be seen in many English classrooms. Air conditioning will make year-round operation feasible in many places where it is now a hardship.

In short, the schools of the seventies should be better, happier, and more productive places for students and teachers than have been the schools of any other decade in the history of American education.

NOTES

1. *The Basic Issues in the Teaching of English*, Seminar Report (New York, 1959). This report was also published in *PMLA*, Vol. LXXIV (September, 1959), pp. 1-12.

2. "The Basic Issues in the Teaching of English," *PMLA*, Vol. LXXIV (September, 1959), p. 2.

3. *Ibid.,* p. 4.

4. Albert Kitzhaber *et al.,* "A Curriculum in Rhetoric (Grades 7-12)," in Lois Josephs and Erwin R. Steinberg, *English Education Today* (New York: Noble & Noble, Publishers, Inc., 1970), p. 92.

5. Wallace W. Douglas, *Curriculum Study Center in English Composition,* revised. (Evanston, Ill.: Northwestern University, Curriculum Study Center in English, 1967.)

6. *Time Magazine,* December 28, 1970, p. 26.

7. Kenneth Koch, *Wishes, Lies, and Dreams* (New York: Chelsea Publishers, 1970).

8. For example, in the summer of 1965, more than 20,000 English teachers attended 110 federally funded institutes. See Richard Corbin, "NCTE Presidential Address: Poetry and Hard Fact," *English Journal,* Vol. LV (1966), p. 268.

9. Jerome Bruner, *The Process of Education* (Cambridge, Mass.: Harvard University Press, 1960).

10. John J. DeBoer, a past president of NCTE took exception to Bruner and stated that "for school English his idea simply will not work." Quoted in Josephs and Steinberg, *op. cit.,* p. 587.

11. Roberts English Series, stressing transformational grammar for grades 3 through 12, is published by Harcourt, Brace & World, Inc., 1967–1969.

12. See, for example, such articles as Stephen Judy, "Structures in the Teaching of Composition," *English Journal,* Vol. LIX (1970), pp. 213-18; Andrew MacLeish, "Some Structures for Written English," *English Journal,* Vol. LVIII (1969), pp. 877-85; J. L. Walker, "The Structure of Literature," *English Journal,* Vol. LV (1966), pp. 305-15; and Michael Grady, "Structured Structuralism: Composition and Modern Linguistics," *English Journal,* Vol. LIV (1965), pp. 633-39.

13. The question is perhaps best answered in Commission on English, *Freedom and Discipline in English,* a report (New York: College Entrance Examination Board, 1965), pp. 1-3.

14. For an interesting account of the academic preparation of secondary school English teachers in one typical medium-sized city, Portland, Oregon, see Albert Kitzhaber *et al., Education for College* (New York: The Ronald Press Company, 1961), pp. 91 *ff.*

15. Harold Allen, "The 'New English' Anew," *NASSP Bulletin,* Vol. LI (April, 1967), p. 18.

16. Leonard Bloomfield, *Language* (New York: Henry Holt and Company, 1933).

17. Charles C. Fries, *American English Grammar,* English Monograph No. 10, National Council of Teachers of English (New York: Appleton-Century-Crofts, Inc., 1940).

18. Albert H. Marckwardt, *American English* (New York: Oxford University Press, 1958).

19. Albert H. Marckwardt, *Linguistics and the Teaching of English* (Bloomington, Ind.: Indiana University Press, 1966).

20. Benjamin Lee Whorf, *Language: Thought and Reality* (Cambridge, Mass.: The M.I.T. Press, 1956).

21. Ernst Cassirer, *Language and Myth* (New York: Harper & Bros., 1946).

22. Martin Joos, *The Five Clocks* (New York: Harcourt, Brace & World, Inc., 1961).

23. See R. Baird Shuman, "The Rotating Unit Approach to the Teaching of Secondary School English," in Howard C. Zimmerman (ed.), *Educational Comment: Ideal Designs for English Programs* (Toledo, Ohio: University of Toledo Press, 1968), pp. 31-38, and "A Prospectus on Education," *The Clearing House,* Vol. XLIV (1969), pp. 67-71.

24. Ann Cook and Herbert Mack, "The British Primary School," *Educational Leadership,* Vol. XXVII (1969), pp. 140-43. Condensation printed in *Education Digest,* Vol. XXXV (February, 1970), pp. 36-38.

25. *Ibid.,* p. 340; p. 36.

26. An unpublished document entitled "A Resolution Passed by the National Council of Teachers of English at the Sixtieth Annual Meeting, 1970," p. 6.

27. James J. Lynch and Bertrand Evans, *High School English Textbooks: A Critical Examination* (Boston: Little, Brown and Company, 1963).

28. *Ibid.,* p. 410.

29. *Ibid.,* p. 411.

30. *Ibid.,* pp. 416-17.

31. *Ibid.,* p. 419.

32. *Ibid.*

33. James Knapton and Bertrand Evans, *Teaching a Literature-Centered English Program* (New York: Random House, Inc., 1967).

34. *Ibid.,* p. 7.

35. Lynch and Evans, *op. cit.,* p. 424.

36. Michael F. Shugrue, *English in a Decade of Change* (New York: Western Publishing Company, Inc., 1968), p. 23.

37. Hans P. Guth, *English Today and Tomorrow* (Englewood Cliffs, N.J.: Prentice-Hall, Inc., 1964), p. 397.

38. Voices in Literature, Language, and Composition (Boston: Ginn and Company, 1969).

39. A three-year program for disadvantaged youngsters at grade 7 or above. See Gateway Series (New York: The Macmillan Company, 1967).

40. The series, released in 1969, includes *Exploring English, Our Common Language, The Tools of English, The Structure of English, The Uses of Lan-*

guage, and *The Growth of English* (Hans Guth and Edgar Schuster, American English Today Series [New York: McGraw-Hill Book Co., 1970]).

41. Daniel Fader and Elton McNeil, *Hooked on Books* (New York: Berkeley Publishing Corporation, 1966).

42. Ned Hoopes, *Who Am I?* (New York: Dell Publishing Company, 1968).

43. *Raleigh* (N.C.) *News and Observer,* December 14, 1970, p. 2.

44. *Ibid.,* p. 1.

45. National Council of Teachers of English, *The Student's Right to Read* (Champaign, Ill.: The Council, 1962).

46. National Council of Teachers of English, *Meeting Censorship in the Schools: A Series of Case Studies,* ed. by John Hove (Champaign, Ill.: The Council, 1967).

47. National Council of Teachers of English, *The Student's Right to Read, op. cit.,* p. 10.

48. *Ibid.*

49. Kenneth L. Donelson, "Challenging the Censor: Some Responsibilities of the English Department," *English Journal,* Vol. LVIII (1969), p. 869.

50. *Raleigh (N.C.) News and Observer, op. cit.,* p. 1.

51. Guth, *English Today and Tomorrow, op. cit.,* p. 23.

52. Harry E. Hand, "Sex in the Modern Novel: A Teaching Problem," *English Journal,* Vol. XLVIII (1959), pp. 473 ff.

53. See R. Baird Shuman, "Making the World Safe for What?" *Illinois Schools Journal,* Vol. XLVIII (1968), pp. 145-54. Condensation printed in *Education Digest,* Vol. XXXIV (December, 1969), pp. 36-38.

54. Donelson, *op. cit.,* p. 873. See also John F. Symula, "Censorship and Teaching Responsibility," *English Journal,* Vol. LX (1971), p. 130.

55. Donelson, *op. cit.,* p. 871.

56. *Ibid.,* p. 873.

57. Paul Goodman, *Growing up Absurd* (New York: Random House, Inc., 1960), and *Compulsory Miseducation* (New York: Horizon Press, 1964).

58. One educator was from Canada.

59. J. Muller, *The Uses of English* (New York: Holt, Rinehart & Winston, Inc., 1967).

60. John Dixon, *Growth through English* (New York: Modern Language Association, 1967).

61. E. Glyn Lewis, "Postscript to Dartmouth—or Poles Apart," in Josephs and Steinberg, *op. cit.,* p. 621.

62. *Ibid.,* p. 622.

63. Noam Chomsky, *Syntactic Structures* (New York: Humanities Press, Inc., 1957).

64. James R. Squire, "Excellence, Innovation, and the Transformation of the English Curriculum" (the first Mary Angella Gunn Lecture, October, 1968) printed in D. L. Burton and J. S. Simmons, *Teaching English in Today's High Schools* (2d ed.; New York: Holt, Rinehart & Winston, Inc., 1970), p. 5.

65. As reported by Albert H. Marckwardt, "The Dartmouth Seminar," *NASSP Bulletin,* Vol. LI (1967), pp. 104-5. Reprinted with the author's kind permission.

66. See Carl R. Rogers, *Client-Centered Therapy* (Boston: Houghton Mifflin Company, 1965), which has been read by many teachers. Teachers have also found considerable interesting material in Carl Rogers, *Freedom to Learn* (Columbus, Ohio: Charles E. Merrill Publishing Company, 1969).

67. Herbert Kohl, *36 Children* (New York: New American Library, 1967).

68. George Dennison, *The Lives of Children* (New York: Random House, Inc., 1969).

69. Charles Silberman, *Crisis in the Classroom* (New York: Random House, Inc., 1970).

70. Neil Postman and Charles Weingartner, *Teaching as a Subversive Activity* (New York: Delacorte Press, 1969).

71. Edward R. Fagan and Jean Vandell (eds.), *Classroom Practices in Teaching English* (Champaign, Ill.: National Council of Teachers of English, 1970).

72. Ronald Gross and Beatrice Gross, *Radical School Reform* (New York: Simon and Schuster, Inc., 1969).

73. ERIC stands for Educational Resources Information Center which is part of the U.S. Office of Education.

74. As reported in *The Wall Street Journal,* September 21, 1970, p. 7.

75. B. Frank Brown, *The Nongraded High School* (Englewood Cliffs, N.J.: Prentice-Hall, Inc., 1963), p. 62.

76. John Maxwell and Anthony Tovatt, *On Writing Behavioral Objectives for English* (Champaign, Ill.: National Council of Teachers of English, 1970).

77. Lynn Dieter "Behavioral Objectives in the English Classroom," *English Journal,* Vol. LIX (1970), pp. 1259-62, 1271.

78. Hans P. Guth, "The Monkey on the Bicycle: Behavioral Objectives and the Teaching of English," *English Journal,* Vol. LIX (1970), pp. 785-86.

79. *Ibid.,* p. 789.

80. The teacher of English who is interested in behavioral objectives should turn to Carole M. Kirkton, "A Planning Shelf for Curriculum Planning, Part III: Behavioral Objectives," *English Journal,* Vol. LIX (1970), pp. 142-50, which presents a comprehensive view of available materials.

81. Northrup Frye, *The Anatomy of Criticism* (Princeton, N.J.: Princeton University Press, 1957).

KENNETH MARANTZ

The Ohio State University, Columbus

II VISUAL EDUCATION AND THE HUMAN EXPERIENCE

Humanity is not, as once was thought, the end for which all things were formed; it is but a slight and feeble thing, perhaps an episodic one, in the vast stretch of the universe. But for man, man is the center of interest and the measure of importance.

JOHN DEWEY

Education is the guidance of the individual towards a comprehension of the act of life; and by the act of life I mean the most complete achievement of varied activity expressing the potentialities of that living creature in the face of its actual environment.

ALFRED N. WHITEHEAD

The task of the educator is to provide experience.

GEORGE DENNISON

The current American way of life has been depicted as materialistic, technological, grossly unaesthetic, wasteful and antihumanistic in its treatment of minority groups. While this cartoon stereotype may lack the subtleties of a studied portrait it contains the truths that help explain some of the actions which dominate the public stage. The communications media flood our waking hours with reports of striking public servants (police, fireman, and teachers); with articles about the rapid decay of fundamental aspects of tradition like the Catholic church (priests marrying, services in English, ecumenical councils), and conventional morality (removal of censorship boards, openness of homosexuality, huge increase in drug use); with science fictionlike stories of the effects of pollution and population growth; with horrifying accounts of a police-action turned war (massive defoliation, atrocities, soldier revolts); with items from the scientific laboratories that tell us of the creation of life in a test tube and point out the insignificance of man in the cosmos as spaceships and telescopes reach further out into the galaxies; and with the growing seeds of violent social reform as students and blacks and the poor, among others, reach out for a piece of the power structure. Social and economic stability, a characteristic of the decade of the 1950's, has disappeared.

In an important sense this world of ours is a new world, in which the unity of knowledge, the nature of human communities, the order of society, the order of ideas, the very notions of society and culture have changed and will not return to what they have been in the past. What is new is new not because it has never been there before, but because it has changed in quality. One thing that is new is the prevalence of newness, the changing scale and scope of change itself, so that the world alters as we walk in it, so that the years of man's life measure not some small growth or rearrangement or moderation of what he learned in childhood, but a great upheaval.[1] [p. 140]

Any consideration of the functional future of art education must be made in the setting of a society which is unsettled, which must accept uncertainty as a new way of life, and which is gradually resorting its priorities and reordering its values.

Teachers are fortunate to have help in their efforts to sort out the significant from the trivial or, to use a cloying current idiom, to locate the *relevant* issues for study. Our clientele, the youth of this country, have begun to take the lead in mounting a search for irrelevancies in existing curriculum as well as in the greater society. In a real sense, a new subculture is taking shape; a culture founded on discontent, reared on historical ignorance but one which has fundamental humanistic ideals and vast quantities of energy.[2] Some of this energy has gone into developing art forms and rituals necessary for establishing identity and communication. Predominantly the art form of the youth culture is rock music and the poetry inherent in the lyrics.

For the new consciousness this music is not a pastime but a necessity, almost on a par with food and water. Indeed, the new music has achieved a kind of integration of art in everyday life that is probably unique in modern societies. ... Like a medieval cathedral or the carvings in a tribal village, the art of rock is constantly present as a part of everyday life, not something to be admired in a museum or listened to over coffee after dinner and the day's work are done.[3][p. 98]

Visually their expressive aesthetic has been equally an integral part of their life-style. Ignoring the Western tradition of studio art they, as individuals, have become art objects. Hair and clothing (costumes perhaps) are selected and worn to express at the same time a rejection of conventional norms and a statement of collective individuality. Simple home-crafted items combine with second-hand cast-offs to proclaim a disenchantment with a parent culture believed to be captive of a machine-dominated, consumption-oriented technocracy.

In a very brief time the creative energies of the young have developed rituals of dress, music, and celebration. "The essence of any ritual is too abstract and detached from daily experience for it alone to provide the self-sustaining qualities that gave the old Dream its continued relevance, but the search for a new Dream is also attempting to develop new forms, new ways of living, new attempts to deal with the process of life and not with the achievement of redemption."[4] The words of their songs identify their passion for a new and better order. And we are charged, as teachers, *to help them make real* what their ritualistic slogans, marches and community sings have abstracted. Any educational plan which does not listen to the voices of the young as they sing about a world in which the natural and man-made environment is to be made viable and in which constructive human relationships are fundamental concerns is doomed to fail.

By beginning with the education's clientele and their perceived needs, I do not mean to suggest that they have seen the Truth where their elders have failed. Adult society bears the responsibility for leadership and the concerns of the young have been the concerns of their fathers before them. The stupidity of war, the waste of uncontrolled exploitation of resources, the horror of racial antagonisms have been the themes of generations of prophets and poets. But in the past the young seem to have been kept isolated from these concerns and have

not voiced so strong nor so constant a clamor for a future different from
and better than their fathers'. Perhaps their access to knowledge has
frightened them into acting where our ignorance kept us meek. Whatever the cause, the situation we face is a student body, not so innocent
of the world, seeking an education which meets the challenges of a
reality we all share.

Before attempting to develop a rationale for a visual (art) education
for the future I must, if necessarily very briefly, outline the motivating
social conditions which must shape it. An emerging idealistic but somewhat alienated youth culture has already been noted as one factor. The
continuing growth and urbanization of the population must be examined as another. We have had centuries of experience in dealing with
urban problems and yet the massive changes in recent decades seem
to have negated whatever previous skills we may have had in solving
them. When we choose to live in compact anonymity we simultaneously choose to give up some of the freedoms we would have in a
rural context. Although living within the same geographical boundaries, city people group themselves into compact subcultures delineated
by ethnic and/or economic similarities and the divergent needs of these
groups adds another complex of problems. Cities seem more to be
agencies of polarization than mythical melting pots. How is an individual to survive and grow in an environment which is constantly
being disturbed by antagonistic forces? How is institutionalized education going to be structured to support human development in a society
demanding a compromise on individual freedom?[5]

We are custodians who must care for an environment, if we are to continue to
have a safe, pleasing habitat for man. Refusal to respect ecological values has
made many areas on the planet virtually uninhabitable. Our technological
capacity to alter the environment, our concern with speed, profit, labor saving,
expansion, production of goods, is producing the most far-reaching, sudden, and
dramatic upsets of natural conditions which the world has ever seen. With
noise, smog, garbage, sewage, industrial waste, junk autos, spoil banks, bill-
boards, drab and depressing urban sprawls, highways, and pesticides, we have
fouled some of our most desirable natural environments. We have eliminated
species of plants and animals and thus diminished the wonderful biotic variety
of life on earth. On the strength of our knowledge of nature, we have set
ourselves above nature and now presume to alter the environment for any
living creature at whim or for short-term profit.[6]

From the chorus of voices—screaming, cajoling, pleading, damn-
ing, instructing, scolding, prophesying voices—the message cannot be

misunderstood. We are not above nature but part of it. In abusing our environment we destroy ourselves. Can art education shade its eyes from the stinging smoke of garbage fires or the crashing boredom of tract housing or the accelerating disappearance of the landscape and still maintain a sense of integrity?

Clichés of our time: the youth culture, urban sprawl, environmental decay and, one more—increasing specialization. Clichés, because in their persistent presence we have stopped attending to them as a factory worker tunes out the constant din of his machines. The machinist survives, but his hearing is dulled. We, too, survive by sweeping our "social problems" into the public gutter, but our humanity is dulled. We have become objects in a society

. . . that exploits knowledge as it exploits everything else, using even science itself, not as a means for the advancement of civilization and the enrichment of life, but as a ground for gadgetry and invention regardless of the human value of the thing invented, so that the triumph of the epoch makes no distinction between the glories of modern medicine and the horrors of modern war. When a civilization can declare tacitly and even explicitly that whatever *can* be invented *must* be invented regardless of the human consequence, we are already far into that disastrous epoch. . . .[7]

We are treated, or better said, we treat *ourselves* as objects because we sidestep the issues of choice and permit ourselves to be used as specialized extensions of engineering technology. We are increasingly becoming highly trained units of working potential complete with uniform, work hours, and jargonized speech patterns. Although it has been "common to all men at all times in all societies that the living individual might become submerged within his assigned social function,"[8] the demands of mechanization have come very close to objectifying this ever present possibility. ". . . Specialists are people about to be replaced by computers. The main task of the human intellect is to put things together in comprehensive patterns, not to separate them into special compartments."[9] We are more often asked " *What* are you?" than " *Who* are you?" And subcategories within classifications, army style, help determine our status. "Teacher," for example, is *what* I am. But within this general classification is a hierarchy which begins at the preschool level and ends in the clouds with the university professor. The clientele, the training, the disciplines, the jargon, the values are different enough, even within the parameters of this hierarchy to make effective communication difficult, if not impossible. Attend any national conference of educators, for example, at which all "levels" are represented and you will see how rapidly communication is fragmented into the most meaningless units of immediate parochial concerns. *Who* I am as a human being, my unique worth, is a concept which becomes submerged in the activities of my social function.

The results of our clichéd press toward specialization are becoming evident. Communication between members of different vocational specialties becomes increasingly more difficult, and even within broad fields, e.g., physics or education, the subspecialization required for investigating ever-narrower sections of the field makes it hard for workers to communicate effectively. (Note the number of different kinds of journals that proliferate university libraries.) Polarization and alienation from social involvement seem to be products, by-products perhaps, of our fixation on knowledge isolated from significant social utility. We have become rather proficient in creating efficient practitioners like farmers or scholars but are very poor in producing what Emerson has called *Man* on the farm or *Man* thinking. I share Rhinelander's doubt when he wonders "whether intellectual discipline and rational analysis have any relevance to the solution of the pressing problems of the day." Even as daily existence becomes increasingly complex because of population growth and mobility, urbanization, bursts of social revolution, depletion of essential resources and mounting piles of knowledge—or rather *because* of these conditions—it seems an unexamined specialized parochialism and narrow vocational goals are no longer viable supports for general education.

The past few years have seen an increase in written and spoken reaction to the inevitability of a robot society with a computer brain. The age-old question, apparently made obsolete by technology, of the nature of man's humanity has once again become a vital issue. In many of our social institutions the place of man has been shoved aside or been made secondary to the functioning of the institution itself. The call is out to reestablish the essential humanness in social services, in medicine, and in education. That a 1969 publication has to be titled *Humanizing the Secondary School* (ASCD) is evidence enough, for me at least, that human concerns are currently in short supply in the schools. Education, now, is hung up on vocational values, whether the vocational goal is college or jet-engine maintenance. Standardized tests accentuate the value of competition and high scores become the "open sesames" to "higher" education and to better paying jobs. The values imbedded in developing humane qualities are rarely stressed in the curriculums of this country.

"Humaneness is a quality of experiencing or interacting. You cannot be humane all by yourself." It has two themes: enlightenment and compassion. The humane person is one who knows something about himself, the world he lives in and *cares* not only about himself but for others *and* for our "common plight."[10] There are no Waldens to which man can run and Donne's islands have taken on the look of the Bump-Um-Car concession in an amusement park. If the schools are to become institutions for encouraging universal humanism rather than restrictive vocationalism they must reexamine their fundamental values. One "task of the school is to help each individual develop a concept of and a role of self, and to facilitate a continuing enculturation; it is to enable each learner to make individual sense out of a universe of stimuli."[11] Another task evolving out of understanding of one's role will be to develop a responsible personal course of action. Regardless of the way one chooses to earn one's bread, despite the wide range of intellectual, physical, regional, and ethnic variety of our country there are certain common qualities of experience that we all share. Determining one's own identity and reason for being (the nature of one's Freedom) is essential for all of us if we are to find excitement, joy, and contentment in our lives. But also discovering the range of potential human interactions which modify our freedom (the nature of our Responsibility) is essential if we hope to make realistic and constructive choices. Schools will have to learn how to keep the age-old coin of Freedom and Responsibility continually spinning if they expect to meet the demands of fluctuating human relevancy. The "proven" formulas of the past are but grist for the scholar's mill. The human condition is not static nor will it lie quiescent beneath the researcher's glass. The needs of a humane education are to be met only in an ongoing search, devoid of sentimentality, unburdened by aging dogma, and open to the possibilities of new and possibly uncomfortable transient truths. Unless we change our ways we will continue to produce what Goldsworthy Lowes Dickinson, in 1901, characterized as the new English man, a man: "Divorced from Nature but unreclaimed by Art; instructed, but not educated; assimilative, but incapable of thought."[12] Clearly what I would hope for and work for is a human who knows himself as part of nature but is appreciative of art as well, one not only instructed in the necessary skills of social survival but educated in the very process of learning, and one capable of and actively engaged in thinking.

It ought to become clear, also, that I believe vision and the other senses might play a role in achieving these objectives. The task will not be easy for me because we must deal with notions like *art* and *aesthetics* and examine the values which have become so intricately involved with their many meanings. Art is shaped of many different kinds of materials through structural elements like line and color. It has served many functions according to the psychological, ritualistic, decorative or recreational needs of its users. It has been affected by social institutions like commerce, science, and religion. And it plays different social roles depending on one's activity as a creator, critic, teacher, or appreciator. Thus the "isness" and the "oughtness" of that quality of human activity subsumed under the rubric *Art* are matters of profound complexity, heavily laden with normative chains yet exuding a mystery and compelling attraction that has made it a significant human enterprise.

Having made a case for the complexity of analyzing the role of art in man's quest for social and self-definition, I must add another complicating consideration. Some of man's sensory education may derive from responses to or manipulation of objects or events that do not fall neatly into any particular explanation of art. A philosophical conundrum which still vexes some of us concerns two stones presented simultaneously to a viewer. One has been given its form and texture by the action of surf and sand; the other has been shaped by a man's hand. The viewer does not know which is which, and there are no clues that can provide the answer. Is either stone an art object? In what ways will our perception, understanding, and appreciation of the stones change when we are given the "facts"? Is one kind of experience (say, the initial innocent one) more or less valuable than the other? It will be the intent of my exposition to take an amorphous, pluralistic, pragmatic position. The value of naming will be judged by the resultant effect such identification will have on the experience of the human. If such a thing as "situation aesthetics" may be suggested to parallel the current statement of *Situation Ethics*[13] then that will be the frame of reference for my remarks. Aesthetic action, then, should be tailored to fit objective circumstances, the situation.

There may be criticisms for avoiding the crisper speculative skeletons of the psychologists with their learning theories and the philosophers with their aesthetic theories. Yet, we have no Rome, but rather many churches; and if I choose to kneel in different pews, according to my varied needs, I can expect to hear the cry of "Heretic" from those who are valiantly struggling to create a universally applicable theology. But no universal theory of art is needed to appreciate the sensual smoothness of our stone, nor to reflect on its manifold associations with past experiences, nor yet to wonder on the mysteries of its creation. Indeed, depending upon which set of spectacles we set upon our nose, which psychological set we adopt, we can see a world in that stone. If we are sincere in our desire to make the most of human potentials, it would be wasteful to deny any insights because they fell outside some theoretical orthodoxy.

Having sidestepped the issue of developing a coherent theory of art or art education in favor of an eclectic pragmatism, it remains for me to examine the current art scene, to report on movements in the field of visual education and to project my own bias about the directions such education should take. Perhaps, parenthetically, a few words ought to be given to my use of the terms *art* and *visual.* In seeking a modification of existing practice without resorting to the unnecessary invention of new symbols, a new jargon, I will be using *art* and *art education* to describe objects and courses of study as they are commonly used now in the literature. Although no universal definition of *art* seems to be possible, we do have a pretty good idea of what an art museum is, of what is to be found in an art gallery, of the nature of an art history course offered in a university, and of the kinds of statements written in columns of art criticism. Similarly, *art education* is commonly used to describe the kinds of activities children engage in during art classes at school when they make paintings or clay bowls or when they study about paintings or artists. Art education also encompasses those programs of instruction which prepare teachers for these art classes. The introduction of the term *visual* indicates my dissatisfaction with the current state of art education. As described, the field is too narrow, too specialized, too compartmentalized, too tied to an outmoded tradition, too geared to the values of a single subculture to be responsive to the complex of needs inherent in our diversified population. *Visual* education attempts to examine the full range of qualities which can be uncovered or created in the interaction of people and artifacts or events. Obviously many of these qualities will be those already in the domain of art education and there is no intention of denigrating their profound values. But, as will be developed in succeeding pages, there are values relating to personal growth and social need which have not been part of the emerging character of art education and that must be recognized and made a fundamental part of school programs. Visual education, then, is my rubric for this expanded study of the things of this world.

Because visual education is an expanded form of art education and because art education has roots deep within the world of art, an examination of that world ought to give us insights into the riches of this resource as well as clues about the weaknesses in the relationship. In spite of our cultural diversity, art in America stems from a fine arts European tradition. Historically our painters and sculptors (our fine artists) have sought their training in Europe. During our first two centuries this meant that the artist's education was almost totally undertaken abroad and, in more recent times, it meant spending years in England, France, or Italy. Only in the past few decades has it been possible for our artists to achieve a full education at home. Indeed, World War II marks the first significant departure from this traditional rite of passage in its creation of a homegrown approach or style of art conceptualization. Yet the acceptance of indigenous art training and domestic contributions to artistic progress has not markedly altered the value base of the creations nor managed to effectively transform the role the creator plays in society.

For all the furor about the latest aesthetic triumph or outrage (depending on what you read: *The Chicago Tribune* or *Time* or *Art News*) the artists who make the news are generally working within a value structure set some centuries ago in western Europe. They are working for a very select audience—a monied aristocracy, a self-defined cultural elite whose economic status permits them the luxury of connoisseurship or of a feigned sensitivity to whatever objects or ideas are most current. But where the historical patron-artist pattern produced an art, an academic art, which could touch even the relatively uninitiated if they were given the chance to see it, the rise of modernism saw the end of the official academies and the emergence of a kind of aesthetic agnosticism. The artist, freed from the bonds of the Academy, building on his interests in the sciences and psychology turned inward and drew around him a coterie willing to be initiated to his Truth. In a real sense the public was damned to remain ignorant and duly cursed for it. The result of this aesthetic individualism has been the growth of a genuine esoteric art—an art intentionally designed to be a "rejection of a common vehicle of communication between the artist and the majority of the members of his society."[14] The members of a subculture of that society support and presumably appreciate his work but "when artists work only for themselves individually or for a coterie, and disdain the public, the public retorts by ignoring the esoteric artists, and the vacuum thus created is then filled by charlatans."[15] The contemporary "fine arts" in this country not only continue in the tradition of Western elitism but have refined its esoteric base to the point of making the broader society alienated from its potential values.

While my caustic overview of the modern scene may be a bit overdrawn, it does, at least, point out one of the social failings which much of art is subject to. It has produced rapidly changing groups of artifacts and ideas which demand very specialized and new ways of looking to appreciate. Reflect for a moment on the variety of art forms which have sprung, Athenalike, from artists' heads in the past 25 years: Abstract Expressionism, Action Painting, Op, Kinetic Sculpture, Minimal, Hard Edge, Pop, Earth Art, Conceptual Art, Computer Art to name but some of the categories. Like Athena each came on fully armored and ready for battle. And each had its coterie of supporters and struggling array of camp followers. Although some of the ingroup stayed with an idea or style until its natural death there were those hard-edged dogmatists who managed to shrug off last year's mannerisms as a snake sheds skin. The impact on the mass of society, ordinary people who had the end product of a personal process thrust upon them, was and is confusion, hostility, and eventual withdrawal. In a real sense they are given new languages to decipher and very little in the way of instruction or dictionaries or even clues as to any motivation for taking the time to understand them. Confronted with a very large canvas covered with multicolored squiggly lines after a lifetime of looking at representational paintings it seems expected, if sad, that the reaction comes out: "My little girl could do better." Because of the massive assault on the public by an extensive and constantly changing army of exotic art forms the social utility, the potential meaning and human values of these forms, is lost in the babel of war.

Perhaps one of the major impediments to public appreciation is the museum as an institution. The artists in European history we can name like Rembrandt, Giotto, Phidias, Michelangelo produced objects that were simultaneously aesthetic statements and socially useful. If a church required pictures of Christ's life to be constant visual explications of the scriptures the painter went up on his scaffold and produced the necessary frescos. If a temple needed a statue of Zeus or Apollo to objectify divine spirit the sculptor created the necessary marble image. If a family or civic group wanted a visual record of its members, the painter made the portrait. Whether in a church, a guildhall or a home, the art work became a natural part of social interaction—it was something to be lived with, responded to in the course of worship or private contemplation or enjoyed as one walked through the city square. That this mode of artistic function is *not* our way can be noted in a small way in a lending service on this campus called "Art to Live With." Obviously we are being reminded that *some* art, at least, is no longer something to be lived with. The art museum, a creation of the last century, has become a sponge sucking up the altarpieces and stone Madonnas and family portraits from the past and enshrining them in aesthetic temples. Entering the museum one steps out of normal life into an atmosphere of studied reverence. But the artifacts of the Western past are shaped in ways that can be appreciated or at least reasonably approached by the ordinary citizen. The images, if quaint or archaic, are at least consistent with the visual experiences and learnings of modern Western man. Depending upon one's understanding, a kind of dialogue is possible between thing and viewer.

In the museum we find art disassociated from its original life context, and for us this has been the common experience of art. But it is markedly different from appreciating the work in the situation, if not the time, in which it was conceived.

[The act can] provide the rarest of all experiences in art today, at the opposite pole from the commonest, which is the museum experience. It can bring you as close as you are ever going to get to the experience of sculpture [speaking about a Pre-Columbian carving in Guatemala] as an instrument of magical ritual, as all art was before the word "art" was invented and before any consciousness of aesthetic quality was born, an experience similar, but multiplied many times over, to visiting, say, tħe cathedral of Chartres as an architectural monument and then discovering its continuing life in a baptism or wedding being performed in one of its chapels.[16]

Thus the museum has, over the years, become a repository for all kinds of art works and has, simultaneously, set a tone of reverence for them. It has stated that it collects and displays objects which have a certain excellence of design and craftsmanship and that those who come to look may be assured that what they see is "great" art. And the public looking at a Rubens' painting, a Cellini cup, or an engraving by Dürer has no reason to doubt—even when an occasional fake or forgery turns up. They come expecting to respond to great aesthetic qualities and can leave fulfilled. They can leave aesthetically satisfied, even glutted, and return to the "real" world that is totally separated from the qualities inherent in the exhibits. In a sense, a museum visit becomes like a ritualistic bath, a cleansing experience, a necessary periodic inundation that refreshes and even ennobles the spirit.

The museum which either totally devotes itself to modern art or has a section for its display sets up the same kinds of expectations for its visitors as the historical art museum. Physically it is similar, although, because of its newness its architecture may be less classical Greek and more functional modern. There are walls hung with objects and other things, like statues, placed on the floor. There are labels, catalogs, guards, docents, hushed voices, coatrooms, and cafeterias just like the older institutions. But the shock which breaks the expectations comes when one tries to respond to the objects. It is like opening a leather bound edition of Shakespeare only to find graffiti and Chinese ideograms. Because of the reverential atmosphere, the expectation that a museum shows only great art, defense mechanisms take over and the viewer cannot help asking himself about his failure to appreciate. The values of the elite coterie which digs a specific new art form, genuine values perhaps, are not those of the lay public. The initial shock and attendant self-doubt then gives way to "why should I bother"? The values imbedded by his culture in a Gothic crucifix which has become a part of his aesthetic being are nowhere in evidence here. Over the years the "cruderies" of the Impressionists and Expressionists, the "peculiarities" of the Surrealists and even the "eccentricities" of Picasso have become gradually assimilated by him because they seem to have been extensions of the historical tradition. Van Gogh reproductions are commonplace decorator items and the *Guernica* is on a postage stamp. He has come to live with these art forms. But what contemporary art museums now show seem totally alien to his life and he leaves these places unrefreshed and perhaps thankful that the "real" world does not have to live with the things he has seen and rejected. A pile of felt scraps thrown on the floor, photographs of strangely plowed fields, huge single-hued canvases, a wooden replica of a Brillo box, a bank of sputtering television sets—these unexpected items fail to move him in the way a Renoir painting does.

Again, my seemingly negative description of the museum should in no way indicate my wish to see them destroyed. Indeed I believe that they are significantly important institutions and that considerably more support must be given to their maintenance and growth. My remarks are made only to point out a kind of dichotomy existing between elite art which permeates the current art education programs and the aesthetic needs of general society. Ought art education be geared to the appreciation of the exemplars of history which can be appreciated only in the isolation of museums? In what ways can the modern museums be less the institutions of alienation and more the agencies of constructive humanistic growth? At the moment it seems to me that the museum exists as the patron of the modern artist. He creates objects or ideas which have no other function than to be seen in museums. His reputation is made by the number of prestigious institutions that acquire his work; public acceptance, except that of the special wealthy public which supports museums, is apparently of little concern. The museum, in effect, becomes the taste-maker for those interested in what's new. And, apparently, it is what is new that counts most. Museums vie with each other for being the first to discover and exhibit an artist who uses a new material or technology or has a radical idea. The value for society of such gamesmanship has not been clearly defined. The value for art education remains equally obscure.

I believe Oppenheimer summarized the modern artist's condition with respectful sensitivity.

For the artist it is not enough that he communicate with others who are expert in his own art. Their fellowship, their understanding, and their appreciation may encourage him, but that is not the end of his work, nor its nature. The artist depends on a common sensibility and culture, on a common meaning of symbols, on a community of experience and common ways of describing and interpreting it. He need not write for everyone or paint or play for everyone. But his audience must be man; it must be man, and not a specialized set of experts among his fellows. Today that is very difficult. Often the artist has an aching sense of great loneliness, for the community to which he addresses himself is largely not there; the traditions and the culture, the symbols and the history, the myths and the common experience, which it is his function to illuminate, to harmonize, and to portray, have been dissolved in a changing world.

There is, it is true, an artificial audience maintained to moderate between the artist and the world for which he works: the audience of the professional critics, popularizers, and advertisers of art [the museum, for example]. But though ... the critic fulfills a necessary present function and introduces some order and some communication between the artist and the world, he cannot add to the intimacy and the directness and the depth with which the artist addresses his fellow men.

To the artist's loneliness there is a complementary great and terrible barrenness in the lives of men. They are deprived of the illumination, the light and tenderness and insight of an intelligible interpretation, in contemporary terms, of the sorrows and wonders and gaieties and follies of man's life.[17] [pp. 139-40]

The critic, like the museum, lives a somewhat parasitic existence depending upon the products of the lonely artist. He is the extension of the museum label as he mediates between the work and the audience, giving meaning to obscure symbols, explicating hidden structure, showing relationships among works. The critic deals with the new, leaving to the historian the task of illuminating the past. Unlike the historian who can rely on the test of time to identify the significant signposts of civilization, the critic must make judgments without the comfort of an approved position. More like the creative artist he is exposed and lonely as he confronts the new and attempts to set it in its own temporal context. At times the temptation to use the work as a springboard for philosophical flights of fancy is great and the artist is told that he does not really know the meaning of what he has produced. At other times personal definitions of art relegate artists to the aesthetic slag heap. But in all the critic, trained by daily looking at and reflecting on and talking about art, tries to help the less knowledgeable better prepare themselves to take advantage of the qualities of particular objects or events. But like the artist, he too seems to be addressing an audience too separated from the values of the new idiom to understand his meaning. That he too is a taste-maker is inevitable for, as an expert, he is looked to for the judgments the lay public is unwilling or unable to make. In a very logical way the museums and the critics combine to tell us what we ought to like even as they fail to provide adequate paths for us to follow in order to get there by ourselves.

Art museums and art critics are clearly contemporary agents for perpetuating the aesthetic values of a subculture of our society. If art is to be more than a collection of life dissociated objects that have meaning for a limited group, if it is to fulfill the expectations of the multitude of persons who have laid their wreaths at its feet, if it is to have significant meaning as a quality of life itself, then we cannot limit ourselves in schools to the traditional examples or flashy array of modern styles. Rather we must attempt to find aesthetic qualities wherever we look. The artist still remains the key figure in our scene. But I see his role as one paralleling the creative scientist rather than the fashion designer he seems now to be. The ideas he plays with and struggles over and tries out and modifies and builds upon are too important to become the grist of commercial exploitation by galleries, museums, patrons, or critics. No one expects the latest scientific discoveries to be marketed or even understood by the public. True, in medicine, we make rapid use of a new vaccine or surgical technique. But a new insight into the formation of the earth or the nature of life itself cannot be used in these ways. The artist deals in ideas, in emotions, in the process of becoming and shaping experience. You do not have to understand how a medicine works to use it. The *only* way you can "use" a painting is by understanding how it works—understanding can be in the sense of knowing the technique, the formal structure, the iconography: all of these aspects can provide kinds of meaning, but understanding also comes from an emotional response, from rich associations stimulated by the painting, from a sense of excitement and "rightness" about the manner of its being. "Every work of art, every real creation, is a revolt. A revolt first against culture, against its custom of naming and placing and judging. A revolt against aesthetic norms, against existing artistic languages. A revolt in the name of fresh perception, in the name of a tradition ignored by the dominant culture, a revolt which invents new languages, unsuspected forms, surprising juxtapositions."[18] As a revolt, a personal press against the imposition of an unsatisfactory order, we cannot, nor should we want to have a ready and easy acceptance or response. The ultimate *social* value of the scientist's search for causes and new order and the artist's struggle for self-definition is its utility. Art needs no justification as a personal enterprise. The significance for us all in the artist's work is his genius in creating ideas that others can derive new insights from. The great artist seems capable of distilling from his own existence statements that permit others to use to achieve profound emotional gratification—peak experiences.[19] Through his lonely experiments he can show us the way to such experience. However, to make of the artist a Truth *maker* rather than a Truth *seeker* makes his works as granite blocks in the paths of other seekers. If we focus on the making it becomes possible for someone to accumulate answers as one hoards gold bars. The artist's answers in reality become the viewer's questions. What kind of an answer is represented by the statement $E = MC^2$? What kind of an answer is there in the "Winged Victory of Samothrace"?[20]

The artist, the maker of art, through his social agents: the museum and critic and eventually (usually posthumously) the historian determine the *functional* definition of art. The theoretical definition is, of course, a matter for philosophers. To paraphrase T. S. Eliot:

At their desks the scholars sip their tea,
Talking of creativity.

Without doubt these theoretical formulations have had influence upon the kinds of art produced but the public sees only what he is given to see and directed to see.

We have come a long way from the time when art was popularly supposed to be created 'from the gut,' and a fierce inarticulateness was widely assumed to be the mark of a great talent. Nowadays . . . the fount of genius would seem to be the cerebral cortex exclusively, and a generation of young artists appears to have adopted lofty garrulity as its thing, splitting philosophical hairs with Thomistic vigor and swinging footnotes like flails. One used to visit art exhibitions to *look;* now one is increasingly obliged to *read.*[21]

Since the Armory Show of 1913 injected doubt into an American art cosmos that thought it knew the secrets of the universe, there has been a marked reticence among the cognoscenti to fix the path of the stars. Thus it became possible for art to become anything a Duchamp pointed to (a urinal, for example) or a Johns transformed (a bronze light bulb) or, as is today the case, anything he thinks about (the "Conceptual Art and Conceptual Aspects" show reviewed by Schjeldahl above). "The image of the artist has changed radically. Increasingly, it is the artist's *idea,* not his technical prowess, that is important." Art, liberated from academic restraints, then becomes anything and everything and, according to my way of thinking, nothing—or at least nothing special.

The fact that the distinction between "official" and "avant-garde" painting has become meaningless—since all new (or pseudo-new) tendencies are immediately sanctioned by prominent buyers, museums, art critics, etc., whereby they become "official" for the general public—by itself underlines the change which has taken place in the relations between the public and art since the end of World War II.[22]

If everybody's somebody, then nobody's Anybody, to paraphrase Sir William Gilbert. In accepting all comers (selectively perhaps) museums, art journals, and critics—the experts—have divested themselves of the power to delimit art except perhaps to say that only the artists they tentatively pick are to be valued. They have pulled the stinger from the bee's tail and left us with a bunch of interesting notions and objects. But "interesting" means that we pay momentary attention,[23] laugh or get mad or play a game with buttons, and then forget the experience. Contemporary art, or much of it, has become a disposable commodity like a Kleenex to be used and discarded.

What I am suggesting is that the significance of an object or event is not a function of the object alone. "What a work of art communicates can be described only in terms of an interaction between an object and a subject, it communicates nothing at all unless someone is there to look at it. In other words, there are no aesthetic objects, only physical objects, which, when observed, are capable of stimulating an aesthetic event."[24] A gold nugget, a rough diamond tumbling in the stream are not inherently and universally valuable. They acquire value because of their potential to satisfy certain human needs, needs we have identified or created and have, to a lesser or larger degree, cultivated. "A great work of art, in our view, is the potentiality of a vivid and satisfactory human experience. The possibility of that experience lies in the structure of the physical object to which we respond. The condition for our having the experience lies in ourselves."[25] *All* events or objects can be touchstones for some kind of important human experience. When we arbitrarily label a specific thing a work of art what we are saying is that, in our judgment, the thing has a structure which can produce certain kinds of reactions (aesthetic) if we attend to matters of organization, color, shape, and the like. Our aesthetic responses are apt to be greater in observing this object than in others we do not label "art," because the latter tend to be "shallow and trite" and offer only "meager and shoddy rewards."[26]

> Question: If aesthetic experience is the thing we value, does the label "art" extend or limit the probability for such experience?

As I understand it, it is the contention of those education reformers who espouse a shift from current practice to aesthetic education that the label is most important. That is, they believe that "Sufficient commerce with various exemplars of great art to establish the habits of looking to art for the more subtle possibilities of feeling than ordinary routinized experience affords"[27] is one of the basic demands in curriculum reform. The exemplars would be chosen from among those "key monuments" that have passed the test of time by experts. By attending to the inherent aesthetic qualities in the work, students can best come to understand and appreciate aesthetic experience. "Art in all its forms serves to arrest our ordinary activity and to focus our attention on what a piece of experience is in itself rather than on what it might lead to."[28] Through getting with an art work, then, attending to those qualities which need no justification beyond their own presence, their own inner logic and strength of expression, the student ought to be able to transfer the process to non- or pseudo-art works because the aesthetic enterprise is a mode of ordering elements, whether gestures, words, sounds, or colors, which in certain relationships exhibit a form or pattern, what artists call a style. Aesthetic education then seems to be about the business of helping people respond to the style of an object or event, to understand what makes it expressive of that certain coldness, or Baroqueness, or animalness.

Much as I am seduced by the Smiths's scholarship and meticulous clarity of Broudy's arguments I find their position unsatisfying. The problem of eclecticism is not solved. The Smiths apologize for having to pick and choose from among the many existing aesthetic theories to justify their program because no single theory covers enough ground.[29] If aesthetic theory is to be used as the justification, I cannot help wondering about why certain theories were picked or left out. How would an existentialist aesthetic affect the program[30] or one based on Marx?[31] Would not our philosophical point of view influence the inherent aesthetic qualities of a work? And can a program of education be adequately constructed outside of considerations of learning theories? Aesthetic education surely must mean different things to a Skinner and a Bruner.

But these doubts might be appropriately dispelled by extensive discussion with the advocates of the program. A matter not so clearly open to debate is the proposition that historical exemplars of historical high (as opposed to popular or pop) art are the best vehicles for aesthetic education. I have already tried to point out the rapidly changing character of the ingredients of the art world. And Rosenberg suggests one motivating factor in this change in discussing a new "living" art form (Nature Theater of Oklahoma). "The sincerity of 'living art' lies not in its ability actually to become part of nature but in the logic with which it carries on the struggle of earlier twentieth-century art movements against fixed ideas of the aesthetic."[32] If, as mounting evidence seems to support, our ideas about what is aesthetic are changing—indeed, if the dominant view is to reject *any* specific point of view, how can a

study of the past monuments help us better understand our current
visual world? How can one get a Campbell soup can and a Bernini
marble to fit under the same aesthetic umbrella? *Why* should we try to
do so? If the proponents of aesthetic education mean to say that we
should look at the Bernini with a mind that understands something
about the aesthetic values of an educated 17th-century Roman and that
we should look at Warhol's soup can using the frame of reference of
our times, I can come closer to appreciating their point of view. But if
it means, for example, using any single position, e.g., the formal aesthetic position based on Clive Bell's theorizing, to examine all manner
of objects regardless of origin, I cannot go along. Objects, particularly
art objects, are complex potential sources of expression and information, and limiting our looking to subscribe to any theoretical position
limits our human growth. "A picture will lose its essential quality as a
work of art if we look at it as the instigator of an activity that goes
beyond the picture itself; but the opposite view, that we should be cold
to the subject in order to appreciate a picture, is nonsense and would
turn us into aloof Epicurean eunuchs."[33] In my fear that aesthetic education may sap the virile energies from the act of engaging life I may
have overstated my doubts. But I cannot overstate my conviction that
the broadest possible lens must be brought to bear on the world if we
are to help youngsters achieve a sense of individualism and worth. A
limitation of education to a narrow range of exemplars seems to me an
attempt to maintain a sentimental attachment to values which, for the
mass of students, are not necessarily desirable. General education has
come to the realization that what is good for any specific subculture, the
upper middle-class Caucasian, for example, is not necessarily good for
all, and it can no longer use its institutional mandates to make any single
standard universal. The exemplars derive from an elite Western tradition and represent peaks of achievement whose values do not necessarily coincide with other traditions. They may well have qualities
which some students will come to understand and appreciate, but if
aesthetic activity is the goal, other means must be found to achieve
them. You cannot cram "greatness" down an unwilling spirit. "To enroll
in the current equivalent of the Nature Theater it is necessary only to
purge oneself of reverence for masterpieces and to respond to paintings
and sculptures as though they were phenomena belonging to the order
of rows of windows in a high-riser or snowflakes melting on the hood
of a parked car."[34] Perhaps there are other ways of getting to the top
of a mountain than by being thrown out of an airplane onto it.

There is another order of doubt that goes well beyond aesthetic education but which is vital to its life in the schools. Forgetting our aforementioned objections for the moment, a question about dealing with exemplars must be answered. Pretend that there are some 500 monuments that are suitable for study. Where are they? With rare exceptions the teacher will be expected to involve his class in an aesthetic analysis based upon some form of reproduced art. Elsewhere[35] I have dealt at length with this problem. Here, perhaps, it may suffice to point out the complexity of using a substitute for an original. What choice does a teacher have if one of the exemplars he wanted to use was Michelangelo's *Last Judgment?* The obvious field trip to the Vatican becomes less than obvious when the typical budget is understood. Assuming a liberal budget for teaching aids there might be several choices: a printed reproduction in some size from a postal card to, perhaps, 2 x 3 feet, probably in color but maybe in black and white; a 2 x 2 inch slide or maybe several showing details as well as the overall painting; overhead transparencies if he can make them himself or, most unlikely, find a commercial source, a motion picture with or without sound. The range of clarity and color fidelity in commercial printing is enormous. Even where technology and human craftsmanship are at their best, as in some Swiss and Japanese examples, translating oil or fresco pigments to printing ink is an interpretive, creative task. Any printed reproduction is an approximation of the original colors, at times a barely recognizable distant cousin. Reduction or enlargement in scale is another act of distortion; reducing a very large fresco to page size completely alters color relationships to say nothing of the artist's original total expressive intent.

But even assuming the availability of high-quality reproductions— those checked against the originals in order to reduce falsification— classroom use presents another fundamental concern. The printed reproduction may be passed around, stuck on a bulletin board, held in front of the class or projected by means of an opaque projector; or any or all means may be combined. Each has merits and drawbacks, but all present the image in different ways and for different lengths of time. Projection, in particular of any opaque or transparent image, is prone to extreme variation. Consider these factors: the darkness of the room; the nature of the surface projected on; the power of the illuminating source; the angle of the projection; the length of the throw; the quality and condition of the lens; the location of the viewer. Even a fine slide can be radically distorted by typical classroom conditions. Nor may we forget that the illuminated image is about 100 times brighter than the same image seen in print.

I have taken some pains to point out important problems if one is serious about making the study of exemplars the basis of aesthetic education. A good reproduction can provide certain kinds of information if it is large and clear: identity of the iconography (subject matter); gross understanding of style including organization and use of line; some sense of the range of colors but nothing about their subtleties; very little if anything of the texture or of the nuances of transparency and shading; perhaps some clues about the artist's techniques. It is hard for me to understand how one can be expected to evaluate a work of art for its "(a) unity, (b) complexity, and (c) intensity"[36] when all we are confronted with is an image of the original in some other medium. "The medium of diffusion tends to take precedence over the direct experience of the object. . . . We are given the shadow for the thing, and in the end we live among shadows."[37] Can aesthetic education be significantly promulgated in a world of shadows? Can sculpture and architecture even be approached in this world?[38]

But even granting that a sound appreciation of great art works can be obtained through reproductions (something I remain quite skeptical about) at best we are providing for the museum experience of art, i.e., the experience of art in isolation from its social contextual meaning. Anyone seeing Michelangelo's *Pieta* in the Vatican pavilion at the New York World's Fair was, essentially, not seeing the same statue as those who saw it before and after in its chapel setting in St. Peter's, Rome. Moving along a mechanical sidewalk in a suffusion of blue light and mood music structures the aesthetic response in a way radically different from the perceptual set evoked by the dusky hush of an unhurried chapel visit. Approaching the shadows of reality as classroom images isolates them from the possibility of the peak experiences of being surrounded by the Giotto frescoes on the walls of the Arena Chapel, or circling the Bernini fountain in the Piazza Navona, or coming upon the Aztec pyramid of the Sun at Teotihuacan as it rises from the Mexican plain, or walking the snail shell gallery of New York's Guggenheim Museum. No amount of slide showing or picture book looking can provide the experiential base for such aesthetic involvement beyond the most fundamental pleasure of simple recognition. Reproduction used to simulate examples can induce a form of masturbatory experience, providing a kind of pleasure and momentary release; but the projected or printed art image is no closer to reality than is the sexual surrogate to a flesh and blood sexual partner. By offering up such substitutes as a steady diet we may be addicting our students to a life of vicarious aesthetic joys.

I have started my critiques of current directions in art education with the aesthetic movement and been so pushy because I believe it has the most going for it and is gaining the greatest support. Indeed what "creativity" was for the 1950's, "aesthetic" will probably be for the next decade—the banner leading the reforming masses. Hopefully, the important new insights inherent in the position will not be too watered down by the inevitable misunderstandings which accompany any popular reform nor will they be killed by the rigid theoreticians who insist on purity of dogma. Hints of both dangers are already appearing in print. But there can be no denying that there is a quality of human existence, a distinguishing human characteristic, which has been called aesthetic—a response to an event or object based upon the immediate or presented values without necessary recourse to past causation or future consequence. It seems redundant to say again that I believe this human quality ought to be much more broadly supported, encouraged, and developed in schools and that limiting or narrowing its teaching to the study of specific fine art objects is inadequate to do the job. Let me try to give an example from the study of history. I would suppose that a battle would be taught in terms of its economic, political, and social effects on the opposing sides. But suppose it were looked at for its aesthetic qualities, without regard for the winner or loser, its effect on subsequent history, its cost in dollars, its making or breaking of generals or political leaders, even its moral rightness? Suppose we look at the battle in terms of its "battleness"—i.e., what can we identify about the objects or events that add up to the expressed feeling of war? There are certain explosive sounds and shouting; men and machines move fitfully against one another; uniforms and flags identify the combatants; violent death with spattering blood converts some men to grotesque still puppets; machines become smoking junk; orders are given and relayed. Through analysis of the events we can understand the logistics of both sides, see the shifting plans of battle modified as the battle progresses, get a sense of the structure of the event. We can, as in a drama, respond emotionally to the energy outputs, the clash of colors, the kinesthetic reaction to charges—we can become totally enmeshed in the presented qualities and forget the per soldier cost of uniforms, the rate of deaths due to disease, the medals won by General M for his ultimate victory. The historical painter and contemporary film-maker used and use battles as springboards for their art. Battle scenes from *Alexander Nevsky, Henry V,* and the current Russian version of *War and Peace* are examples of such aesthetic individual responses to war. The people making these films were capable of abstracting qualities of "battleness" which epitomized a specific conflict and so arranged the movement of masses, the cutting from scene to scene, the angle of viewing, the pace of the movement, that the viewer came to understand and appreciate the meaning of battle. He felt the pulse of fear, the glory of victory, the depression of futility by means of the visual structure created by the film-maker. To me, any study of history which includes man's eternal conflicts would be a more significant humanistic adventure if these aesthetic qualities were attended to, through films, photographs, paintings, or whatever can be obtained. And I doubt whether a study of the exemplars could help much in this endeavor. As one way of responding to experience, aesthetic concerns cannot be made captive to art schedules and art teachers and expect to be recognized and understood by all.

Perhaps the arts have been prevented in our time from fulfilling their most important function by being honored too much. They have been lifted out of the context of daily life, exiled by exaltation, imprisoned in awe-inspiring treasure houses. . . . But works of art are not the whole world of art; they are only its rare peaks. In order to regain the indispensable benefits of art, we need to think of those works as the most evident results of a more universal effort to give visual form to all aspects of life. It is no longer possible to view the hierarchy of art as dominated by the fine arts, the aristocracy of painting and sculpture, while the so-called applied arts . . . are relegated to the base of the pyramid as impure compromises with utility. The artists of our time have gone a long way in making the old categories inapplicable by replacing the traditional works of the brush and the chisel with objects and arrangements that must merge in the environment of daily life if they are to have any place at all. One more step, and the shaped setting of all human existence becomes the primary concern of art.[39]

But the problem of restructuring the art world and art education to face up to this primary concern is a tough one, particularly if we look over our shoulders for new directions or are kept too tightly shut up in our little empires. Getting art more into the mainstream of human existence means more than simply getting works of art out of galleries into the streets. The language of the studio and the streets are quite different.[40] "We have all seen, in many cities the world over, public monuments which can scarcely claim a minimal interest as pure sculpture but which function with an undeniable grace, elegance, and environmental benevolence. There may be an aesthetic injustice in the fact, but a fact it is." Much of contemporary public sculpture "violates rather than adorns the urban environment in which it has been placed. To most of these sculptors, the language of the street is as alien as Sanskrit. They are simply—all too simply—speaking the language of the studio. . . ."[41]

The difficulty encountered by studio artists in making their art a viable public art is parallel to the difficulty which students face in school when their art education is exclusively studio-based. Self-expression and/or creativity are the underlying forces which maintain these programs, programs "now out-dated and not in keeping with the many changes which have occurred in our society and our schools during the past few years"[42] but maintained by an education establishment heavily invested in the artist-teacher model. Without taking exception to its origins, its growth or its legitimacy as a *facet* of a more comprehensive visual education, I insist that the current focus on the individual and his studio production is an educational dead end. It is inward seeking at a time when social consciousness is needed for survival; it stresses the individual amorality of the maker when what is required is a sense of responsibility for the group environment. Of course the studio workshop should be part of all schools—a considerably improved and expanded part. It should be there for those who want to take the time to shape or reorganize materials to satisfy some curiosity, some aesthetic tensions, in an effort to help themselves define themselves as specific human beings. In other words, for those students who want to get deeply involved with media, time and place must be provided. But that should not be the only route for everybody.

The workshop also is a place where any kind of aesthetic problem which requires stuff rather than words for solution may be worked out. Such problems could include an animated tabletop film expressing some idea about the meaning of poverty in the Great Depression; it could be developing a presentation to combine simultaneously an explanation of specific gravity in liquids and an evocation of sensuous delight in transparent and translucent colors; or perhaps a series of slides are needed to act as projections for a student-created opera. The studio, like the audio-visual center or library, is a resource, a place to go to get specific help, and a place to work out visual ideas. It is a place to do visual research, an arena when students confront objects in a struggle to retrieve information and to pluck emotional strings. As many aesthetic educators point out, one of the routes to aesthetic understanding is through the manipulation of media. In the attempted creation the student can become more aware of the limitations of a medium as well as its nuances, can become more appreciative of the manner in which design elements and principles take on varying expressive meaning and force as they change in emphasis and as technical mastery increases. The frustrations and glories of creation can provide for a kind of psychological empathy with artists and so add another dimension to the aesthetic appreciative act. The apparently easy facility of the artist is then known as the product of a high order of intelligent craftsmanship and one can, without being told, begin to *discover* some of the greatness inherent in some of the artifacts of the past and present. We might, in passing, speculate about the reasons for the dismissal of some of the contemporary art. Where "paintings" by chimps win awards and school children produce structures that look very much like pieces seen in galleries and machine shops fabricate sculpture from telephoned instructions—the respect for excellence derived from personal experience in the studio is dissipated. That dimension of appreciation associated with the rest of the objects from art's total history is lost and, as has been pointed out, we must look to the concept rather than the objectification of it for special qualities. To repeat the chorus of my song: rather than a single aesthetic, we must seek out whatever aesthetic position for each thing or event will evoke the most profound emotional response and/or extract the most information.

Perhaps in response to the continuing and increasingly unpopular war, certainly in reaction to the accelerating recognition of the technological cultural take-over "man is thus losing his hold on any life that can be called his own; he is being turned into a 'thing' destined to be collectively processed and reconstructed by the methods that have produced the atomic pile and the computer."[43] The thrust of education toward science spurred on by the post-Sputnik competitive spirit has dulled and there has been a growing interest in humanistic studies. The humanities, as an organizing principle, is riding the crest of a new educational wave. The arts are the visual embodiment of humane thought and tend to become an essential ingredient of a course of study which must deal with the history of man as a person.

Art ... is primarily the domain of the person; and the purpose of art, apart from various incidental technical functions that may be associated with it, is to widen the province of personality so that feelings, emotions, attitudes, and values, in the special individualized form in which they happen in one particular person, in one particular culture, can be transmitted with all their force and meaning to other persons or to other cultures. ... The work of art is the visible, potable spring from which men share the deep underground sources of their experience. Art arises out of man's need to create for himself, beyond any requirement for mere animal survival, a meaningful and valuable world."[44]

The arts become visual documents in courses purporting to help students better understand the past. Sir Kenneth Clark's film series "Civilisation" epitomizes the chronological approach to the study of Western man. Using exemplars from literature, music, philosophy, architecture, and the fine arts he attempts to show how the character of an age is captured in specific ideas or objects. The Gothic period becomes the great cathedrals, the 18th century is the music of Mozart and Beethoven and so forth. A similar insistence on studying man through his masterpieces is characteristic of those courses which use the thematic rather than historical approach. "Man and God," "Man the Symbol Maker," "Man the Warrior," are some of the themes which are used to get at those qualities of experience which define man.

While obviously delighted by the new enthusiasm for a proper study of man, I must express some reservations about the method and the use to which works of art are put. By hitting the peaks of human creativity there is apt to be a neglect of the vast reaches of human activity which lie between those peaks. The geniuses of any age can give us some clues about the supreme spiritual and intellectual achievements shared by a few members of their society but they cannot give us a full appreciation of what it meant to be alive at the time. There never was an age of total homogeneity, a period of total group commitment to a single idea, or life-style. As we drink in the lofty expressive qualities of the Parthenon high on its acropolis in the incredibly blue Athenian air we must surely wonder about the life of the slaves down in the city. What role did Phidias' dreams have in their daily existence? If the humanities are a means of helping us better understand man in order that we better know ourselves, can we be satisfied in dealing with so select a picture of history? How will it help a student in 2171 know *us* if he gets only the Seagram Building, *Guernica,* Warhol's soup cans and the Statue of Liberty? What about tract housing, the slums, *Play-*

boy, Norman Rockwell and department store bric-a-brac? I am reminded of a film seen at Colonial Williamsburg which dealt with the
music of that city in the mid-18th century. In the course of a day we
heard sailors' work songs, Couperin, spirituals, minuets, and folk dance.
Which musical form captured the spirit of that age? In our efforts to
package learning in neat bundles we seem to lose our essential purposes. It is a great deal easier and tidier to pick and choose items which
form a consistent pattern and which can be labeled Classical or Gothic
or Renaissance than to gather all the facts in a messy, unwieldy bunch
which defies clear categorization. But human life is much more the
latter than the former and we do our students a disservice to pretend
otherwise. To my way of thinking, humanistic study ought to include
a look at the hovel as well as the castle, an involvement with the popular
as well as the elite culture of any period. We may not "cover" as much
ground but we ought to get a much clearer idea of what makes for a
"meaningful and valuable world" for people.

I have reservations about the method, but I also am concerned by
the treatment that objects too often receive in courses in the humanities. Perhaps criticism is an inevitable consequence of inadequate
teacher training because such courses are most often initiated by converted history or English teachers whose aesthetic experience is rather
limited. Whatever the causes, however, the tendency has been to treat
objects almost exclusively as historical documents without attending to
their expressive content. The record of man's activities is provided in
Egyptian tomb paintings, Mayan codexes, illuminated medieval manu-
scripts, Greek vases, Dutch genre paintings, Brueghel's country scenes,
and on and on. They tell direct stories of specific events or conditions
which can be read without strain by even an untutored high school eye.
Teaching objectives which focus on such information retrieval treat
aesthetically charged artifacts the same way that we treat the annual
book of news photographs. Of course we can and should get all we can
from what we use, but there is considerably more to these fragments
of the past than is apparent in a simple reading of their representational
content; and even such reading can be complex when symbols are
incorporated that provide a meaning beyond the presented image such
as in much medieval and Renaissance work. Those inherent qualities
which are the sum and substance of aesthetic education, which provide
for emotive reactions, which help personalize a work, which help students become more visually discriminating, cannot be neglected if the

humanities are to be more than a kind of nonpolitical history course. How did the ancient Egyptian sculptor organize his forms? What is the effect of this organization as compared with the Hellenic Greek method of organization? How do we feel when looking at one compared with the other? Is one more intellectually stimulating? Does our kinesthetic response become activated by one more than the other? Why? The process of looking in these ways, *guided* looking toward a goal of personal discovery, can be an avenue of learning about Egyptians and Greeks which mere identification or explication cannot offer. For the humanities to deal adequately with the full range of man's achievements, it must include a good measure of aesthetic inquiry.

Like the humanities "movement" but purposefully separated from it, the Related Arts grow out of a reaction to the isolationism of traditional arts education. Theirs has been a search to discover the common bases of all the arts, and they are trying to integrate learning so that students may sense a central core in man's efforts to create. In some instances, particularly at the high school level, a rather strange amalgam of subject matters is grouped under the name of Unified or Related arts: home economics, music, industrial shop, crafts, fine arts, theater, and, in one case I know of, typing. In other instances just two areas combine or perhaps three; the spirit is present to seek change but no pattern has yet emerged. In one suburban Chicago school a music teacher has framed, very poor quality, small art reproductions on his wall, shows cartoony film strips while he accompanies students on the electric organ, and feels that in this way he is relating art and music. In another school weekly departmental meetings—talkfests—represent the act of unification or relatedness. In others, teams of teachers have organized rather complex courses of study showing stylistic parallels between the music and art of a range of periods in Western culture.

Much as there is merit in the notion that the arts taught in isolation from one another miss out on the broader humanistic implications of aesthetic creativity, there is a present danger that the press for simpleminded unification will force similarities where they do not exist and will neutralize the particular powers of the various arts. The temptation to level the arts is great because verbal labels for aesthetic qualities are frequently misleading in their similarity. Take the term "texture" for example. In sculpture it refers to the actual tactile sensation one gets when touching the surface of a piece. In two-dimensional work it may mean this, but because paintings, drawings, and graphics are generally meant to be "touched" by the eyes alone, texture refers to the *implied* variations in surface treatment, to the visible brushstrokes or engraved scratches. In film, texture is not as important a quality, but it is used to differentiate the busyness of backgrounds, i.e., how cluttered or uncluttered the area is behind the central action. Theater and dance do not seem to use it at all, while in music it most often occurs as descriptive of the kinds of instrumentation used to produce a certain sound, e.g., a combination of woodwinds or a mixed grouping of brasses and strings. With this range of meaning and nonmeaning, how appropriate is it to attempt to show the commonality of texture across the arts? Similarly such terms as color, rhythm, movement, phrasing, and so forth occur in many of the arts, but often the concepts to which they refer are peculiar to each individual art form. Forcing correlations because of linguistic similarities seems questionable at best.

Yet there are learnings inherent in the combined arts approach which are essential. One stems from the dangers cited above. Students should be helped to understand that verbal labels have specific meanings in each subject. Therefore they should seek to understand the terms an art uses to explicate itself within the context of that art. Of course, where there are clear parallels such as climax in a musical composition and a play, a richer appreciation can be achieved in coordinated study. What musical devices are used to achieve the climax: rhythm? crescendo? key? How does the playwright manipulate the actors' movements, the meaning of words, the phrasing, the pitch of sounds, and length of silences? Are there parallels in ordinary human life which can be seen as the bases for climax, e.g., sports, family arguments, sexual activity? What does a climax mean emotionally, kinesthetically? Artists, although using specific media, do function in broadly similar ways. They all organize and shape experience within a defined, generally self-defined, frame. Their ideas may cover the whole range of human concerns from simple decoration to lofty religious preaching, but they all set themselves a task, a medium, and a way of working. Craftsmanship and technique, the skills necessary to successfully carry out the task,are also common ingredients; but the skills are as varied as the art forms. Equally varied are the sensitivity of perceptions. Painters are not necessarily sensitive to the inherent values in dance nor even to those in sculpture. In fact, the necessary concentration, training and work within any given medium may be a dulling factor to the full appreciation of other arts. The strength, therefore, of related arts study is that it can point out the more general qualities of aesthetic experience, those dealing with choice and organization of media for specific expressive ends, while maintaining the rich sensory and emotional particulars of each art. This kind of study can much better provide for the vagaries of individual human choice than can more intensified work in a single area as it demonstrates the extensive range of the human mind and spirit in their coordinated efforts to give special meaning to life experiences.

Three major but relatively unorganized movements, which have come to dominate the present art education scene and promise to increase in importance in the future, have been identified as aesthetic education, humanities, and related arts. What they have in common is a reaction to the almost monolithic position maintained by studio art in the secondary schools. What they want to do is to provide alternatives based upon some kinds of analytical or appreciative approach. There have been others in the field who have been equally restive but who have not joined any of the crusading factions but have, nevertheless, made themselves heard. One increasingly important reformation grows out of the belated recognition that ethnic and economic variables may be extremely important considerations in curriculum building. Because of the rather sudden, if inadequate, attempts to deal with the broad problems of the poor in this country, it is no surprise that education should begin its own enlightenment in tending to their needs. Vincent Lanier summarizes the current situation well.

To say that there are no culturally disadvantaged is not to say that there are no poor in America, or that poverty has no negative aspects. To live in sub-standard housing, attend inferior schools, eat inadequate foods, lack appropriate medical care—these kinds of deprivations, particularly in the midst of plenty, are unfortunate and unnecessary. These experiences, however, do not inevitably produce ignorance, the inability to think critically, or an absence of responsiveness to one's verbal, visual, and musical surroundings. On the contrary, poor people respond to and produce their own culture, which, while it may be "simple" and unsophisticated, frequently embodies the same power and richness of image or phrase as middle-class art.[45]

Visual education, to be humanly effective, will have to work within the parameters of that, or perhaps those, value structure(s). Traditional middle-class methodology, time allotments, and content can no longer be utilized, unexamined, as the single, educational system. Lanier suggests many different approaches be tried in order to find out which ones can effectively help poor children "explore their own life problems and develop alternatives to alienation, frustration, and irrational violence." What is said about the poor ought to be the signal flags for responding to all the cultural diversity existing in our schools. For the most part what Lanier says about poor schools might be said to apply to most of art education, that it is "sometimes shabby, often inept, and always inadequate."[46]

Another flurry of activity being made to improve art education has roots in the mid-1960's and marches under the banner emblazoned with the words "Visual Literacy." Although stimulated by the writings of people like Trottenberg[47] who were distressed by the lopsidedness of liberal and scientific education, its ultimate, and current, promoters are those deep into photography and films.

Visual literacy refers to a group of vision competencies a human being can develop by seeing and at the same time having and integrating other sensory experiences. The development of these competencies is fundamental to normal human learning. When developed, they enable a visually literate person to discriminate and interpret the visible actions, objects, and/or symbols, natural or man-made, that he encounters in his environment. Through the creative use of these competencies, he is able to communicate with others. Through the appreciative use of these competencies, he is able to comprehend and enjoy the masterworks of visual communication.[48]

While it would be unfair to characterize the newly hatched Visual Literacy Conference as a vehicle for selling Kodak products, strong support by that company at least suggests that seeing the world through a lens is the approved way to gain visual literacy. The organization is too young to be anything but an indication of a direction, but its existence does recognize the very real place that camera technology has gained in schools. Some projects reported on in the past five years, particularly with poor children, make it clear that the brush and chisel are no longer totally adequate tools for visual expression. Cameras generate an excitement and provide a ready extension of self that apparently the young, raised on movies and television, find universally grabbing. And, judging from the numbers of professional artists who have recently turned to film-making for aesthetic release, it is not just the student who finds significant values in the various forms of photography. So, while the concept of visual literacy may well be too tightly boxed in by film technology at present, it has at least opened the door to a rich resource for visual education, a resource which few art teachers currently are tapping.[49]

Technology is also providing the stimulus for another kind of education—mixed- or multimedia. Growing out of what has been called the Rock Culture, the simultaneous presentation of sound, body movement, light and projected images has become a kind of standard event in some schools. Multiple slide projectors throw patterns and images on flat and billowing surfaces; several audio tapes at peak volume emit sound effects and music from strategically placed stereophonic speakers; and the audience-participants dance, mill around, sit or stand surrounded by this melange of sensory stimulation. Quite the opposite in intent from visual literacy which aims at developing discriminatory responses of a cognitive-intellectual nature, these experiences are used to spark emotions, to get the senses to awaken to "pure" experience without cognitive meaning, to make the appreciative and creative act more of a unity, to overcome inhibition. How effective they are as learning experiences is yet to be proved. That they are at least partially associated with a generation which finds drugs another way to shock ordinary sensibilities and provide new levels of psychic experience may help explain their appeal to the young. These mixed media events, in any case, do demand a range of involvements in aesthetic matters from the framing structure, the manufacture or choice of visuals and sounds, the arrangement of projectors and lights and speakers, and the relationships of the various components within the chosen space. The directions that such experience take will depend on the emerging of new kinds of aesthetic criteria and their usefulness in helping students find more than momentary pleasure in the event.

Similarly in another kind of mixed media art form, the Happening, the original stimulus provided by some members of the professional art scene has dissipated. Yet the concept of theater which has no audience, no classical script, which seeks to create new meanings by means of juxtaposed irrationalities can have lingering values if sufficient attention is given to the educational implications. Group improvisation involving the flotsam and jetsam of our materialist society can help point out the changing visual meaning of things in varying contexts. Absurdity is a real quality of human life just as rationality and sublimity are. The Dadaists helped show us how to free ourselves from the bounds of an academic straightjacket. The plays of Beckett and Ionesco force us to see ourselves as less than supreme rationalists. Becoming involved with events which somewhat depend upon their spontaneous expression can help students provide balance for a life more typically dominated by programmed expectations and scheduled segments of experience.

The acceptance of technology, the adoption of multimedia and happenings are healthy signs that education is responding to the changing milieu in which it exists. Of course, there is as much danger that these new devices will become gimmicks and the new structures clichés as the more traditional tools, methods, and content will become superficial exercises. No device or idea is free from the dangers of misuse. But, having recognized the changing nature of our lives and the diversity of human needs, it would seem foolhardy to place the emphasis of instruction on any specific subject content. "The emphasis, therefore, should be *on the student,* on helping him to understand himself, the reason for his being, and his place in the universe. The arts are merely the vehicle by which he is helped to arrive at knowing—knowing himself as human, and knowing what humanity entails."[50] In seeking better ways of helping students become more humane persons through the arts, the energies of reformers have been spent in a piecemeal attempt to find the Holy Grail. Even my overview of current trends should be sufficient to indicate the confused tug of war that characterizes the times. Certainly part of the problem has been the isolation of art education from total educational reform.

An important result of the reformers' failure to consider the curriculum as a whole is the fact that they left one of the most critical areas of the curriculum almost completely untouched: namely, the arts. . . . The Office of Education's Art and Humanities Program, established in 1964, has financed a number of curriculum projects and experiments. But the effort has been small and sporadic and . . . those concerned have made the mistake of the rest of the curriculum reform movement in attacking the problem piecemeal, as if what were needed were simply new courses and course materials.[51]

As long as the art education fraternity remains somewhat paranoid[52] about its future and uses its energies to maintain its pitifully small piece of the action by reworking its isolated course structure there seems little hope for significant change. "Most schools give their students a powerful and effective aesthetic education: they teach them that interest in the arts is effeminate or effete, the study of the arts is a frill, and that music, art, beauty, and sensitivity are specialized phenomena that bear no relation to any other aspect of the curricula or of life."[53]

Silberman's indictment is a harsh one, but one that is essentially true. In the past art teachers have helped art maintain a marginal position because of their insistence on keeping it "pure." But "by moving into the margin art does not lose its quality as art, it only loses its direct relevance to our existence: it becomes a splendid superfluity."[54] The indictment is also frustrating because "if art is again to play a more central part in our lives, it means that our lives will have to change, and this is a process which does not depend on artists and art critics alone."[55] Nor does the solution to art's peripheral status, if indeed there is a solution, lie with the art educators alone but with the total educational enterprise. Yet I remain optimistic in the face of this enormous challenge because of the effect which the social conditions, noted at the beginning of this chapter, are beginning to have on educational reform. Humanistic and aesthetic concerns appear in political pronouncements and in fundamental objectives of the various movements supporting ecological and/or environmental action. For the moment, at least, and probably for the near future social conditions seem to favor some kind of extension of visual education.

I have tried to make clear that what is *not* needed at this time is an elaboration of the studio-centered "self-expression" art program. It has been made abundantly clear that the future for artists who insist on self-expression is bleak. Such indulgence will continue as psychological therapy, but as a communicator—relating to art's social function—the artist will have to lift his eyes from his own bellybutton and look hard out into the world. "Idiosyncratic or intensely personal art has reached its ultimate state and its condition is injurious both to society and to the arts. . . . The arts are being thrust back where they did belong at one time and where they should still belong—related primarily to the 'social condition' and only secondarily to the individual condition."[56] A dramatic example of this shift from extreme introspection to a concern for the social condition was seen late in 1970 when Philip Guston, an established, highly successful "action" painter[57] had an exhibition of paintings that were images of Klan activities in the South. " I got sick and tired of all that purity! I wanted to tell stories !"[58] In a crisp review of the show Harold Rosenberg uses Guston's aesthetic transformation as a springboard for his current critical ideas.

In the last analysis, Guston's exhibition is political by way of art and does more for art than for politics. It comes at the beginning of a decade in which a pressing need has arisen for a new outlook on art—one that will end its isolation from the crises of the time. The recent influential formalist conception of High Art, pledged on the principle to refuse to take note of the destruction of the planet, seems thoroughly played out, and with it the dialectics of an increasingly self-purifying abstraction. On the other hand, the anti-form earth and raw-materials projects that were presented as the antithesis to color fields and minimal sculptures have reduced themselves to an endless lecture on counter-aesthetics. . . . The separation of art from social realities threatens the survival of painting as a serious activity. . . . Painting needs to purge itself of all systems that place so-called interests of art above the interests of the artist's mind.[59]

I would paraphrase the last remark to say that visual education needs to purge itself of all dogmas that place the so-called interests of art (all art or any single art) above the interests of the student's mind and spirit.

It should be noted that Rosenberg says that the paintings were more effective as bellwethers for art than as effective political statements. The *Time* review goes a step further. "The trouble is that painting has become a clumsy way of reporting a society as turbulent and rocked as this. Its clashes cannot be accounted for in single, painted images. . . . The task has been assumed, and done better, by film-makers. In three minutes of film the flat dispassionate eye of the movie camera can disclose more about the kind of reality that appalls Guston than his whole exhibition has done."[60] This report must not be taken as a put down for the *potential* of single images to convey significant social comment. Goya, Grosz, Hopper, Levine, Shahn, and many others have proven otherwise. What it does do is to put us all on guard that there are other art forms, like film, which have the power to move us and that visual education will have to look to new ways for traditional forms as well as for the new forms themselves. High Art is no longer the Mecca toward which we all kneel in prayer.

"The future, like the present, will hold both a spectrum of styles and a plurality of audiences in each of the arts. There will be no convergence, no stylistic consensus. Nor will there be a single unified audience."[61] I believe that any functioning citizen must, by now, be aware of the divergent if not polar values held by groups or subcultures in our society.[62] "There are only strata, groups, and individuals within a particular society, which in each case constitute more or less numerous, differentiated, localized, articulated, active, or passive, and important segments of the public interested in various fields of art."[63] Chronology, morality, economics, ethnicity, and idiosyncrasy are all factors operating in rather complex ways to mediate against any reasonable attempt to standardize aesthetic values. "Expectations based on the premise that art is, or should be, egalitarian are not only doomed to disappointment but misleading because they create false aims for education. . . . Democracy does not entail that everyone should like the same art, but that each person should have the opportunity to enjoy the art he likes."[64]

The implications for education from the simple, if revolutionary, notion that everyone should have the chance to decide what he will enjoy are profound. The lack of an agreed upon single aesthetic or functional definition of art means that there is no fixed, objective goal for all to reach. Teachers cannot be mediators of Truth, standing between students and authority as priests in a temple to tell it like it is. Rather it must become the responsibility of the teacher to help each individual develop his own aesthetic sense, his own rationale for response, his own criteria for valuing experience, his own ability to create a way of looking that will permit and encourage a continuing and increasingly discriminating visual perception, his own definition of what art is. Perhaps it is a truism to say that "the only kind of learning which significantly influences behavior is self-discovery or self-appropriated learning—truth that has been personally appropriated and assimilated in experience,"[65] but the saying acts as a reminder that the teacher's essential business is that of providing for such experiences. In order to meet the unknown but obvious range of student needs the visual experiences will have to be broad in content, complexity, duration, and setting. As I have tried to point out earlier, aesthetic qualities exist in all things and events not just in those which someone or some group has labeled "art." In the school setting the only way that these qualities can be discovered and appropriated is through examination, comparison, and verbal discourse. For students to have the opportunity to enjoy they must first have a chance to know.

Visual education is predicated on the assumption that knowledge precedes enjoyment. Elsewhere[66] I have tried to explain some of the problems surrounding the process of knowledge building. Essentially it is a process of involvement *not* exposure, a process dependent more upon personal idiosyncrasies than on extrinsic motivation, a process tied to the interrelatedness of experiences. We learn by making association.

The importance of the associative uses of school learnings is that it constitutes an important matrix of meaning for the appreciation of the arts. . . . Much of the effectiveness of figures of speech rests on comparisons once noted, now forgotten, yet still amenable to partial recall. . . . Associative uses of schooling do not all originate in the interpersonal relationships of pupils and teachers. Content, if rightly chosen, also teaches more than meets the eye on the test.[67]

Rightly chosen content, if it is to be effective in teasing students to look and learn, must include: the illustrations in textbooks; peacock feathers; a bicycle's sprocket wheel; photographs of 73 different faces; a reproduction of a Bambara mask; some stones; wood scraps from the local lumberyard; color slides of the streets of Florence, Italy; travel posters from 17 different countries; back issues of *Life, National Geographic, Natural History Magazine, Craft Horizons;* a stuffed owl; reproductions of a Dürer engraving and a Rembrandt etching. Content must also include: building blocks; clay; wires; papers; paints, crayons, and pencils; cameras; balsa wood; felt; adhesives; and colored cellophane. Content, too, must include trips to the local industry; many walks around the school community, at different times of the year and in all kinds of weather; reorganizing an empty lot; or close inspection of the local lockup and other governmental institutions. Knowledge means involvement with life experiences, manipulation of sensory inputs, confrontation with governing agencies in an effort to build the reservoir of associations that provide "the matrix of meaning" for art and life itself.

"An almost endless number of rationales for selecting content can be devised, each with a logic of its own. The element of choice depends upon what one takes to be the essential purpose of education, not upon the comparative worth of one system or another, or the respective advantages of different content."[68] I have already tried to describe my educational posture; school learning ought to help students develop humane understandings and behavior. This is a moralistic stance based upon the need for individual self-realization and freedom *and* for a responsibility toward others. Almost everything said about art and visual education, up to this point, has revolved around the first need, a response to the hedonistic drives in all of us. And this is where the bulk of current art education practice and theory presently leaves us. But I share Philip Wylie's discontent that this is insufficient and that learning exists, in good measure, for the maintenance and increase of some kinds of morals.[69] Herbert Read declares "A work of art is removed from mundane strife; it is an object of disinterested contemplation."[70] If this is true then involvement in art education must lead to an increase in disinterestedness, to a kind of human alienation and a form of moral behavior. Selfishly I want to have my cake and eat it too. "A major aim of education must be for as many poets in the factory as in the pulpit and the concert hall."[71] And I want schools to make the time and facilities available "to afford students the opportunity to explore their capacities for feeling and to experience intentions of quality in the presence of significant works of art."[72] But I also want schools to design curricula that foster what I have called visual responsibility.[73] Man cannot avoid the ugliness of his own collective making; he can adapt to it and absorb the disorder and nondescript character of his mass-produced environment into his spiritual being. Or he could try to shut his eyes, cut off all his senses, and play it cool and so gradually vitiate his passions and become an aesthetic automaton—seeing little and caring less. Both of these antihumanistic practices are operative in the contemporary way of things and can be seen in the pathetic sameness of the hamburger stands, motels, car dumps, and gasoline stations that line the approaches to any American town; in the casual acceptance of garbage-strewn streets and public transportation; in the "I don't want to get involved" attitude of city dwellers. "Education is supposed to develop minds sensitive enough to perceive, to feel the shock of tragedies taking place thousands of miles away and somehow communicate a feeling to the heart."[74] There is a scene from the film *Catch 22* that epitomizes the horror of the ineffectiveness of art to touch daily life. Our "hero" is walking through the streets at night and the only sound heard is a tenor singing a lyrical opera aria. Unnoticed, he passes a drunken sailor being rolled by a pack of street urchins; a man brutally beating an emaciated horse which could no longer pull his wagon; a gaudily made-up male prostitute offering himself; a kneeling girl providing oral sex for a standing soldier; and a group of people standing unmoved around the broken body of a young woman. How futile the beauty of the singing! How can I give myself selfishly to the pleasures of aesthetic enjoyment when confronted by such horror?

Visual education, of course, cannot deal with the totality of man's problems. But it can and must concern itself with the role that the visual environment plays in determining the kind of lives we can lead. Ecological studies have brought to everyone's attention the interrelatedness of all life systems. Visual education, as part of the very new environmental education thrust, can be effective in showing the interrelatedness of the communities of man.

The highest expression of civilization is not its art but the supreme tenderness that people are strong enough to feel and show toward one another. Art proceeds out of an exquisite awareness of life. The creative spirit and the compassionate spirit are not things apart but kindred manifestations of response to life. If our civilization is breaking down, as it appears to be, it is not because we lack the brain power to meet its demands but because our feelings are being dulled. What our society needs is a massive and pervasive experience in re-sensitization. The first aim of education should not be to prepare young people for careers but to develop respect for life. Related lessons would be concerned with the reality of human sensitivity and the need to make it ever finer and more responsive; the naturalness of loving and the circumstances that enhance it or enfeeble it; the right to privacy as an essential condition of life; and the need to avoid the callousness that leads to brutalization.[75]

In order for such lessons to become realized in schools the responsibility for the teaching will have to be shared by the total school community. Visual education, an effort to make humans more responsive to the qualities of the visual world, cannot remain the province of art teachers. All teachers must become sensitive to the ways in which the design of their rooms affects learning and to the roles that students can play in participating in that design. The entire school and its setting, in like fashion, must be examined as a place where humans meet to seek intellectual and emotional growth. Dehumanized halls, broken windows, immobile furniture, dirty and peeling walls, poor lighting, insufficient noise eliminators, carelessly decorated or barren display areas, muddy and littered playgrounds play their part well in creating environments which desensitize the senses and enfeeble the spirit. The media for learning—books, laboratory equipment, pictures, models, maps, and specimens—as has been suggested earlier have inherent aesthetic qualities that can add significantly to visual learning if adequately attended to. Specialists in their sealed compartments, separated by periodic signal bells and isolated subject matter, must come to a realization of a much fuller potential for human learning that derives from a multifaceted handling of their ideas. Students do not learn as fragmented pieces of a machine according to some arbitrary schedule. They learn as whole people and therefore should be encouraged to respond to stimuli in diverse ways. Feelings should matter in all classes, not just the arts. *How* something is presented is often more important than the specificity of *what* is being presented. Visual education is concerned with the "how" in every aspect of school life, irrespective of labels.

It is not good strategy . . . to label perceptual sensitivity as artistic or aesthetic, because this means removing it to a privileged domain reserved for the talents and aspirations of the specialist. Visual thinking calls, more broadly, for the ability to see visual shapes as images of the patterns of forces that underlie our existence—the functioning of minds, of bodies, or machines, the structure of societies or ideas. Art works best when it remains unacknowledged. It observes that shapes and objects and events, by displaying their own nature, can evoke those deeper and simpler powers in which man recognizes himself. It is one of the rewards we earn for thinking by what we see.[76]

If visual thinking, the *modus operandi* of visual education, is to become a force in the schools it must become manifest throughout the schools. The visual world, the only one we have got, is rapidly being destroyed by the competing materialistic powers of the technological society. The quality of our lives cannot be left to chance nor to any single aspect of education. "The improvement of our visual world is clearly too important to be left to the formal machinery of government or the institutionalized response of architects, planners, and artists. It remains one of the prime concerns of an enlightened citizenry, and this in turn makes it a responsibility of the educational community."[77]

NOTES

1. J. Robert Oppenheimer, *The Open Mind* (New York: Simon & Schuster, 1955), © 1955 by J. Robert Oppenheimer. Reprinted by permission of Simon and Schuster, Inc.

2. Vance Bourjaily, "Middle Age Meets the Kid Ghetto," *New York Times Magazine* (November 29, 1970), 46; 49-64.

3. Charles A. Reich, "The Greening of America," *New Yorker* (September 26, 1970), 42-111.

4. Wallace Roberts, "The Young Protestants," *Saturday Review* (December 27, 1969), 22-3.

5. René Dubos, *So Human an Animal* (New York: Scribner's Sons, 1968).

6. A. W. Eipper; C. A. Carlson; and L. S. Hamilton, "Impacts of Nuclear Power Plants on the Environment," *The Living Wilderness* (Autumn, 1970), 5.

7. Archibald MacLeish, "Trustee of the Culture," *Saturday Review* (December 19, 1970), 18-9.

8. Philip H. Rhinelander, "Education and Society," *The Key Reporter* (Autumn, 1968), 2-4.

9. Harold Taylor, "Inside Buckminster Fuller's Universe," *Saturday Review* (May 2, 1970), 56-7; 69-70.

10. Herbert Thelen, "The Humane Person Defined," *Humanizing the Secondary School.* ASCD, 1969, 18.

11. T. B. Monez, and N. L. Bussiere, "The High School in Human Terms," *Humanizing the Secondary School,* ASCD, 1969, 7-16.

12. Jonathan Spence, "Speaking of Books," *New York Times Book Review* (October 18, 1970), 2.

13. Joseph Fletcher, *Situation Ethics* (Westminster Press: Philadelphia, 1966).

14. *On the Future of Art,* Essays by Arnold J. Toynbee, Louis I. Kahn, Annette Michelson, B. F. Skinner, James Seawright, J. W. Burnham, and Herbert Marcuse (New York: Viking Press, 1970), 1-134.

15. *Ibid.*

16. John Canady, "Travel Notes from Guatemala," *New York Times* (January 10, 1971), D21.

17. *See* Note 1.

18. Michael Kustow, "Is It the Role of the Artist to Change Society?", *New York Times* (August 2, 1970), D1:05.

19. Abraham S. Maslow, "The Creative Attitude," *The Ethical Forum* (New York: Ethical Culture Publications, 1966), 2-9.

20. Located in Louvre, Paris.

21. Peter Schjeldahl, "Don't Just Stand There—Read!", *New York Times* (August 9, 1970), D17.

22. Hanna Deinhard, *Meaning and Expression: Toward a Sociology of Art.* (Boston, Mass.: Beacon Press, 1970), p. 112.

23. Edgar Wind, *Art and Anarchy* (New York: Vintage, 1969), pp. 12, 79.

24. James Ackerman, and Rhys Carpenter, *Art and Archaeology* (Englewood Cliffs, N.J.: Prentice-Hall, 1963), p. 145.

25. Stephen Pepper, *Principles of Art Appreciation* (Westport, Conn.: Greenwood Press, 1949).

26. R. A. Smith, and C. M. Smith, "Justifying Aesthetic Education," *Journal of Aesthetic Education* (April, 1970), 37-51.

27. H. S. Broudy; B. O. Smith; J. R. Burnett, *Democracy and Excellence in American Secondary Education* (Chicago, Ill.: Rand McNally, 1964), pp. 21, 22.

28. *Ibid.*

29. *See* Note 26.

30. Arturo B. Fallico, *Art and Existentialism* (Englewood Cliffs, N.J.: Prentice-Hall, 1962).

31. Ernst Fischer, *The Necessity of Art: A Marxist Approach* (Baltimore, Md.: Penguin Books, 1963).

32. Harold Rosenberg, "The Art World," *New Yorker* (January 2, 1971), 44-7.

33. Derek Clifford, *Art and Understanding* (Greenwich, Conn.: New York Graphic Society, 1968), p. 120.

34. *See* Note 32.

35. Kenneth Marantz, "The Work of Art and the Object of Appreciation," *Improving the Teaching of Art Appreciation,* David Ecker, Project Director, U.S.O.E., Cooperative Research Project, No. V-006, 1966, Washington, D.C.

36. Reid Hastie, "A Primer for Aesthetic Education," *Art Education* (January, 1971), 13-20.

37. *See* Note 23.

38. The situation is made even more complex if we include the function of replicas, copies, and forgeries. Some media like etchings and watercolors can be reproduced with great fidelity as can small sculptures. Others cannot. Do we limit our aesthetic studies to what is best among what is available? What becomes our basis of selection? I look forward to seeing the "resource packages" now being field tested by the Central Midwestern Regional Educational Laboratories in order to learn how the massive research efforts expended have solved this problem.

39. Rudolph Arnheim, *Visual Thinking* (Berkeley, Calif.: University of California Press, 1969), p. 295.

40. Hilton Kramer is an art critic in a prestigious newspaper. He writes about modern art for a very select public, a public he just assumes travels internationally. Does the art he talks about necessarily have any value for other publics?

41. Hilton Kramer, "The Studio vs the Street," *New York Times* (October 15, 1967), D23.

42. Leon Frankston, "Toward Aesthetic Education," *Art Education* (November, 1970), 18-9.

43. Lewis Mumford, "The Megamachine," *New Yorker* (October 24, 1970), 55-127.

44. *See* Note 43.

45. Vincent Lanier, "Art and the Disadvantaged," *Art Education* (December, 1970), 7-12.

46. *See* Note 45.

47. A. D. Trottenberg, "Colleges Graduate Visual Illiterates," *Saturday Review* (February 19, 1966), 73-5, 103-4.

48. *See* Note 47.

49. The first two Visual Literacy Conferences had only a small proportion of art teachers in attendance compared with psychologists, English teachers, and industrial people. In the many film education conferences I have attended, again, art teachers tended to make up a very small fraction of the participants.

50. J. A. Christensen, "Humanities: A Force to Trouble the Waters," *Media & Methods* (November, 1970), 22-3; 56.

51. Charles E. Silberman, *Crisis in the Classroom* (New York: Random House, 1970).

52. There is a genuine history to support this harassed feeling. Notoriously it is the arts which are last to be incorporated and the first to be pushed out of schools. Even when accepted, art teachers frequently must teach more classes per day and larger classes than teachers of other subjects. Very recent events at Columbia University (when the theater program was dropped) and The University of Chicago (when art education was terminated) indicate that higher education shares the notion of the arts as frill.

53. *See* Note 51.

54. *See* Note 23.

55. *See* Note 23.

56. Aneurin M. Thomas, "Wales: The Arts and Technology," *The Journal of the Royal Society for the Encouragement of Arts Manufacturers and Commerce* (October, 1970), 712-18.

57. "In action painting, the experience on the canvas is *the* experience. The work is not a means of communication; it is the event itself, a piece of history, a rival of social action," Rosenberg, Harold, "The Art World," *New Yorker* (November 7, 1970), 136-41.

58. "Art." *Time* (November 9, 1970), 62.

59. *See* Note 57.

60. *See* Note 58.

61. Leonard Meyer, *Music, the Arts and Ideas* (Chicago: University of Chicago Press, 1967).

62. Mass advertising and television producers are constantly trying to create situations that will cut across divergent values. The educational implications of mass media, however, are a can of worms I would rather not open now.

63. *See* Note 22.

64. *See* Note 61.

65. Carl Rogers, "Personal Thoughts on Teaching and Learning," *Improving College and University Teaching* (Winter, 1958), Corvallis: Graduate School of Oregon State College, pp. 4-5.

66. Kenneth Marantz, "Indecent Exposure," *Studies in Art Education* (Autumn, 1964), 20-4.

67. *See* Note 27.

68. J. C. Parker, and L. J. Rubin, *Process as Content: Design and the Application of Knowledge* (Chicago, Ill.: Rand McNally, 1966).

69. Philip Wylie, *Generation of Vipers* (New York: Pocket Books, 1942).

70. Herbert Read, "In Defense of Abstract Art," *New York Times Magazine* (April 17, 1960), 32-3; 40-8.

71. *See* Note 68.

72. Edmund B. Feldman, "Projections: Hopes and Fears," *Art in American Higher Education* (Washington, D.C.: National Art Education Association, 1970), 104-10.

73. Kenneth Marantz, "New Dimension for Citizenship: Visual Responsibility," *Art Education* (October, 1966), 15-9.

74. Joseph P. Lyford, "In My Neighborhood, An Adult is a Dead Child," *The Center Magazine,* III, No. 6 (November/December, 1970), 49-55.

75. Norman Cousins, "See Everything, Do Everything, Feel Nothing," *Saturday Review* (January 23, 1971), 31.

76. *See* Note 39.

77. *See* Note 47.

LEOPOLD E. KLOPFER
University of Pittsburgh

III

DIALOGUE CONCERNING TWO RIVAL SYSTEMS OF SCIENCE EDUCATION

Once again sagacious Sagredo has thrown open the gates of his villa to stage a timely discussion of an issue of the day. The interlocutors of former days are expected momentarily, if both can find their way. Since they last met here in an earlier time, the villa has been transported from the canal-crossed city of Venice to a slope above a stream-threaded valley harboring a large industrial city of America. Simplicio is first to arrive, just as Salviati is spied panting up the slope.[1]

SAGREDO: You are on schedule as usual, Simplicio. Welcome!

SIMPLICIO: I daresay you haven't changed much since our last meeting. Do you know that we first met in this villa nearly 440 years ago?

SAGREDO: Yes, it's a long time. And the world has changed greatly since then.

SALVIATI: I'll say it has. I could barely find my way up here through the smog. But, I made it. Hello, Sagredo. Hi, Simplicio.

85

SIMPLICIO: It is a pleasure to see you again, Salviati.

SAGREDO: Welcome, Salviati! You must be exhausted from your hard journey. I have refreshments prepared.

SALVIATI: I hope you've brought out some of that fine Marsala you keep in your cellar. I could use a little wine to inspire our discussion this afternoon.

SAGREDO: And so you shall have it, Salviati. Simplicio, what may I get for you?

SIMPLICIO: I'll just have a glass of ice water, please.

SALVIATI: I see you've prepared a manuscript, Simplicio.

SIMPLICIO: These are merely some notes I wrote down in response to Sagredo's request. I trust that you are not unprepared to present your views.

SALVIATI: Don't worry. I'm ready.

SAGREDO: Good. Then we can begin without further delay. Our purpose is to define what the science curriculum in American schools should be in the next decade. It seems important to me to settle this question, since science affects almost everyone in today's world.

SIMPLICIO: Yes, the growth of science during the last four centuries has truly been amazing. When we first met here, natural philosophy was a subject of interest for only a small number of scholars and a leisure-time diversion for a few gentlemen of means. Today, many thousands are engaged in pursuing the study of science in its various branches.

SALVIATI: It's not only that science has grown into a vast and important enterprise. Through technological applications of scientific discoveries and ideas, people's lives have been transformed, and that's literally so. There's an entirely new quality in life today—some might say a lack of quality—and the changes in society engendered by science and its technological applications are largely responsible for it.

SAGREDO: To be sure, science now plays a central role on the world's stage, and it will continue to fill that part in the years to come. That is why, I believe, it is just as essential today for young people to become literate in science as it is for them to learn how to read and write. This means that the schools must provide them with a proper education in science in the 1970's. The question is: What is a proper education in science?

SIMPLICIO: We cannot begin to answer that question until we have taken certain realities into account. One of these realities is society's continuing need for large numbers of competent research scientists to man the many posts in the vast and still-expanding scientific enterprise.

Concomitant with this need for talented, well-trained men and women to push forward our understanding of the natural world, there is an equally important need for many able, imaginative people who will fashion the means of design, development, and production that make possible the application of scientific advances for the benefit of man. I am referring, of course, to the real need for applied scientists and engineers, who serve as the vital articulating backbone of technological progress throughout the world. And there is still another great need of society for persons whose work is closely allied with science. This is the need for physicians who, through their utilization of the scientific understanding of living processes in their practice of medicine, are exemplary implementers in applying the advances of science to the benefit of man. There is and will continue to be a large demand for these three types of professions—scientists, engineers, and physicians—all of whom make decisive contributions in the dynamic 20th-century society of today and the coming decades.

SAGREDO: I think I see the point you're going to make, Simplicio. One way to approach the question of what constitutes a proper education in science is to look at the goal which the student's learning of science seeks to attain.

SIMPLICIO: Exactly. And I suggest that for prospective scientists, physicians, and engineers, the primary goal of their school science studies is to obtain the basic preparation for their professional courses and experiences, in which a sound understanding of science is crucial. For this reason, the competencies of these students in science must be developed as broadly and as deeply as possible in their secondary school years.

SALVIATI: Now, just a moment, Simplicio. I can see that the goal of preprofessional preparation in science may be appropriate for students planning to become scientists, physicians, or engineers, but only a very small part of the population works in these professions. The vast majority of students will not become professionals and will not do work related to science.

SIMPLICIO: That's true, of course. Statistically speaking, well in excess of 90 percent of all working people in the United States are engaged in occupations that are not directly related to science.

SALVIATI: And that 90 percent doesn't include the millions of so-called "unemployed" women who are housewives and mothers.

SAGREDO: Clearly, almost all adults are not personally engaged in science or in work directly allied to science. Nor will almost all students be who are now in school. You aren't suggesting that the goal of science education for all these students is the same as for the prospective scientist, physician, or engineer, are you, Simplicio?

SIMPLICIO: Certainly not. The goal of science education for these students is the development of their scientific literacy. I would be the last to propose that the goal of preprofessional science preparation is appropriate for this group of students. I do say, however, that the existence of these two student groups is a reality we must take into account in planning the science curriculum. One group is headed toward science or science-related professions; the other group is not.

SALVIATI: I think I would be happier if we were talking about individuals, instead of typing students into two groups.

SIMPLICIO: There are individual students in each group, of course, Salviati. I cannot comprehend your comment.

SALVIATI: That's probably so.

SIMPLICIO: The goals of both groups for their science education are worthy, but long experience has shown that it is very difficult to accommodate both groups simultaneously in the secondary school. Therefore, I believe it is necessary to devise a well-organized plan to assure the attainment of each group's goals, preprofessional preparation in science and development of scientific literacy.

SAGREDO: From the way you are shuffling your papers, Simplicio, I judge that you have such a plan to present to us. Please proceed.

SIMPLICIO: The key feature in the plan I envision for science education is a clear distinction of two curricular streams through the secondary schools for two groups of students. One curricular stream is designed for the group planning to enter careers as scientists, physicians, and engineers. I call this the Prospective Scientists stream, or PS stream. The other curricular stream is designed for the group of students who will constitute the bulk of the nation's citizenry in all strata of society, that is, people who will be occupied as housewives, service workers, salesmen, business managers, nurses, artists, accountants, government officials, history professors, clergymen, etc. I call this the Scientific Literacy stream, or SL stream. Differentiation of students into the PS stream or the SL stream will occur at about age 13 or 14 when they choose the high school they will attend. At that time, objective information for making this decision will be provided by means of a Career Prediction Test Battery, which is administered to every student during his final year in middle school or junior high. With the results of the student's performance on this prediction test battery and in consultation with career guidance counselors, the student and his parents will be able to choose either a high school in the PS stream or a high school in the SL stream.

It can be anticipated that somewhere between 10 and 15 percent of all students will be in the group that attends the high schools in the PS stream. Since the curriculum of the PS stream high schools will be highly specialized and demanding, attendance at these special schools will be determined by a student's strong interests and high predicted probability for a career in science, medicine, or engineering, not by the prestige of the school's selectivity. The high schools in the PS stream will be associated with, and may be located near, a college, university, or industrial organization which has a direct interest in the careers of the students who attend these schools. Appropriate cooperative arrangements will be established between each school in the PS stream and its associated collegiate or industrial institution. These arrangements will be particularly significant for the students in their last year in the PS stream high school when they have numerous options available for taking college-level science courses and carrying out independent research.

Before the students arrive at this point, however, they will have experienced a sequence of science studies which represents a significant improvement over the high school science courses commonly offered today. The science sequence is very carefully structured, and its content is based on the structure of the science disciplines. Clearly stated behavioral objectives inform the students about exactly what is expected of them at each step along the learning continuum. At the outset of their science learning experiences in the PS stream high school, the students study the Science Alpha sequence. The purpose and scope of this initial science sequence as it might be described in the school's curriculum guide would read like this:

Science Alpha is an exploration of fundamental ideas in science. The student reexamines what he has learned about these ideas in his previous study of science, and he is confronted with questions concerning what knowledge is and what can be known. Ideas explored in Science Alpha include: length, mass, force, time, growth, life, mind, man. Science Alpha raises many questions, but does not provide final answers.[2]

Following the completion of the Science Alpha sequence, the students move into the comprehensive core program in physical science and life science. Here the stated objectives for each learning step specify the understandings of concepts, the competencies in investigative procedures, and the interdisciplinary syntheses that every student is expected to master. In addition to the statements of the objectives, the standards of proficiency for each objective are also specified. Thus, there can be little doubt about what the students have achieved in science as they proceed through successive steps of the learning continuum. Moreover, with the proficiency standards clearly defined, it becomes possible for students to proceed at different rates along the learning continuum, and individualization is provided for in the comprehensive core program in physical science and life science. In the curriculum guide of a PS stream high school, an overview of this program might read as follows:

The core program consists of the sequential study of the disciplines in physical science and in life science. Students study in both areas in parallel, and several alternative learning experiences are always provided. The study of each discipline emphasizes the structure of that discipline and its relationships to other disciplines in physical science and life science. (The study of the structure of a science discipline includes the delineation of its subject matter, the principles of inquiry appropriate to the subject matter, and the development of the key concepts used to organize the subject matter.) In the main, the several disciplines are introduced in the approximate order of their historical appearance in modern science. This order helps each student to develop some notion of the evolution of scientific thought. Once a discipline is introduced into the sequence and its historical development is reviewed, the treatment of the subject matter is in the terms of the present-day structure of the discipline. In physical science, the sequence of disciplines studied begins with astronomy; in life science, the sequence begins with human biology. The subject matter of each of these disciplines early engaged man's attention for investigation by processes of observation and reasoning. In the initial study of astronomy and human biology, however, only the data and the problems of each discipline are developed, since the present-day structure of both these disciplines incorporates much of the structure of all the other disciplines in physical science and in life science, respectively. For this reason, the sequence of studies in physical science returns in the end to the discipline of astronomy, and the sequence in life science culminates with a return to the discipline of human biology. These disciplines are now thoroughly treated, completing the sequence of studies in physical science and in life science.[3]

It is no doubt obvious from what I have related that the content of the high school science program I propose has been well organized and brought into accord with the best current thinking. The careful organization of the program makes learning more efficient and makes individualization possible. Efficiency and progress at individual rates are facilitated also by the fact that the major part of the students' learning is on an autoinstructional basis. The learning centers of the PS stream high schools have ample facilities to give the students ready access to numerous autoinstructional media, including books, films and filmstrips, programmed lessons, audiotapes and videotapes, and, in some instances, computer-assisted instruction. In every learning center, at least one science teacher is always available to confer with students, to organize discussion groups, to guide students in their laboratory investigations, and to help students evaluate their individual progress along the science learning continuum.

SALVIATI: May I break in a moment, Simplicio, to ask a question?

SIMPLICIO: Well, all right, if you insist.

SALVIATI: What does "individualization" mean?

SIMPLICIO: That's a simple question. Individualization means to make provisions in a school program for individual students to progress along a learning sequence at different rates according to their backgrounds, abilities, learning styles, and other individual variables.

SALVIATI: Is that all?

SAGREDO: Excuse me for interrupting, Salviati. I think we should defer this discussion until Simplicio has finished his presentation. We have so far heard only about the science curriculum of the PS stream high schools. I am most curious to know what the science curriculum is to be for the 85 to 90 percent of the students who go into high schools in the SL stream.

SIMPLICIO: Thank you, Sagredo. It won't take me long to explain the part of the plan for the high school student group for whom the goal is development of scientific literacy. To accomplish this, it is necessary that students in the SL stream high schools obtain an accurate and comprehensive view of science. Many high schools today offer so-called "nonacademic" science courses, such as general science and general biology, for this purpose, but these courses are clearly not adequate to accomplish it. They are not structured well, and they rarely follow a carefully planned sequence. As a result, these kinds of courses cannot efficiently accommodate the diversity of students that we can expect to find in a SL stream high school.

It is fortunate that we already possess a model for the kind of learning sequence which is needed to give the students a comprehensive view of science. This is the sequence for Science Alpha and the core program in physical science and life science that is used in the PS stream high schools. This sequence embodies the best current thinking regarding the structuring of a science curriculum, and there is no valid reason why this up-to-date, comprehensive view of science should not be made accessible to the students in the SL stream high schools. Accordingly, the science curriculum in these schools follows the same basic philosophy and makes use of the same learning continuum as the science sequence in the PS stream schools. There are differences, to be sure. The science sequence in the SL stream high schools does not go into nearly so much detail as the PS stream sequence, and the quantitative treatment of the various topics is greatly reduced. Since some key areas of physical science are treated only qualitatively and descriptively, certain of the interdisciplinary syntheses are more explicitly presented, rather than being developed inductively; and there are numerous additional illustrations of the practical applications of science in technology and everyday life.

The science learning sequence has been carefully structured, of course, and the proficiency standards for each step have been specified, so that different students can progress at their own individual rates. Individualization becomes particularly important in a SL stream high school since the students here represent a broad range of scholastic ability and vary greatly in their capability in science. Regarding instructional facilities, the SL stream high school offers the same kinds of learning centers, autoinstructional media, laboratories, and other resources as the PS stream high school. In summary, the organization and management of the science sequence, as well as the underlying philosophy, are quite similar in the two schools. One feature which the science curriculum of the SL stream high school does not offer, of course, is the options for college-level science courses and independent research during the last year. There is no need for these options, because the students in a SL stream high school generally do not elect more science since they are not going into a science or science-related profession.

SAGREDO: As I understand your plan, Simplicio, you have identified and structured a sequence of essential science learnings for students in PS stream high schools and another similar sequence for students in SL stream high schools. Could you tell me why the two sequences cannot be operated simultaneously in the same school?

SIMPLICIO: There are three basic reasons for having separate schools. First, to meet the continuing need, which I discussed before, for people in the science and science-related professions, special provisions must be made to direct students into these careers and to assure that they move along in their training swiftly and effectively. The PS stream high schools are an excellent means of making these special provisions, and I believe you will agree that science is sufficiently important in today's world to justify their expense. Second, having separate schools allows every PS stream high school to develop a unique character and to easily arrange cooperative programs with colleges and science-based industries. This would be very difficult to do if the school were also cluttered with large numbers of SL stream students. Third, operating different curricula in separate schools is simply more efficient.

SALVIATI: You seem to think that efficiency is quite important, Simplicio.

SIMPLICIO: I certainly do. We are entering an era where we cannot afford to be wasteful. The concerns currently expressed on all sides for accountability in education testify to this. Educational planning has become a serious business.

SALVIATI: Let me come back to the meaning of individualization. You said before, Simplicio, that individualization means making provisions for allowing students to progress at different rates in a learning sequence. In your plan, you make these provisions. Your plan also suggests two science learning sequences, one for the PS stream students and the other for SL stream students, but the goal of each sequence is essentially the same: to have the students attain a comprehensive view of science. Since your plan lets PS and SL stream students progress at different rates through their respective sequence, you claim that you have individualization.

SIMPLICIO: Yes, that is correct.

SALVIATI: Then I don't think you understand what individualization is at all.

SIMPLICIO: And I presume that you think that you do. Well, if you . . .

SAGREDO: Gentlemen, gentlemen! Let's not become angry. If there's a difference of opinion about the meaning of individualization, we should explore that. Would you tell us, Salviati, what your conception is.

SALVIATI: Gladly. To me, individualization means providing a unique sequence of learning experiences for each student, a sequence that is especially selected for and by the student according to his individual capacities, interests, and goals. With regard to the study of science, a few goals are common to all students. One of these is the development of scientific literacy, which we still need to define properly. Beyond these few common goals, each student approaches his learning in science with goals of his own. To attain his goals, some of which may change as time passes and experience broadens, the student must be able to plan an individual program of science study and activities, to carry through his plans, and to revise them when necessary. The result of these arrangements is that we no longer have a single science learning sequence which supposedly serves everyone. Instead, there are about as many individualized sequences as there are students.

SIMPLICIO: I don't see how such a program of individualized science can possibly be operated efficiently.

SALVIATI: Well, maybe it can't be, but maybe it can. I'm not ready to say right now.

SAGREDO: There is another aspect of Simplicio's plan that troubles me a little. Before the student completes middle school or junior high, he must decide to go into either a PS stream high school or an SL stream high school. To make this decision, he obtains information about his performance on a Career Prediction Test Battery. The question which troubles me is whether or not this battery of tests provides an adequate basis for making such an important decision. Further, I am not sure if it is wise to channel a person into a career path for a whole lifetime when he is only about 13 years old.

SIMPLICIO: I am quite certain that we can have confidence in the Career Prediction Test Battery, which measures all the relevant aspects of the student's aptitudes, interests, personality, and knowledge in various school subjects. As a whole, the test battery is a sophisticated instrument for making career decisions, and it is vastly more reliable than the crude vocational preference tests which were used in the past. The battery has evolved from the significant progress recently made in creating successful career guidance systems through the application of computer technology.

As to channeling youngsters of age 13 into a lifetime career path, I believe that the concern you express is exaggerated, Sagredo. Does this not, in fact, occur in most instances today when the student makes a choice in high school between an academic program and a general program? Moreover, the Career Prediction Test Battery does not seek to make a pinpoint career prediction for everyone; rather, it identifies two groups of students: a group likely to be successful in the science and science-related professions, and a group not likely to fare well in these careers. For its quite restricted and intended use in deciding whether or not to specialize in science in high school, the test battery is eminently fair to all the students. Prior to taking this battery, all students have engaged in common experiences in elementary school science.

SAGREDO: I take this to mean that you also have a plan for elementary school science. Please tell us about it.

SIMPLICIO: The plan which I propose for the elementary school has some resemblances to the core science program of high schools in the SL stream. Indeed, building the students' scientific literacy is the main aim of elementary school science. To do so, students deal with some of the fundamental content of physical science and life science. You will notice that I said "deal with," and that was intentional, because the students do more than simply study science in the elementary school. They learn the scientific concepts they need to know and understand in becoming scientifically literate through direct experiences in solving problems and carrying out investigations. This approach and these experiences provide the students with an appreciation of the processes of science. Another important resemblance of the high school and elementary school science programs is that the science concepts are arranged and presented in a carefully structured sequence. In elementary school science, however, the structure of the science disciplines is not the only consideration for determining the sequence.

In recent years, studies by various psychologists have thrown considerable light on the processes by which young children acquire science concepts. Although the picture is still far from complete and a number of unresolved dilemmas remain, it would be foolhardy to ignore the insights already attained when designing a sequence of science learning for elementary school children. Probably the best general guide for structuring a science program in accordance with children's cognitive development comes from the work of Piaget. The several stages in the growth of children's cognitive structures which Piaget elucidated and other researchers have generally confirmed frequently suggest an optimal order for presenting certain science concepts. These suggestions and other findings from psychological research are taken into account in establishing the sequence of physical science and life science content in the elementary school science curriculum.

If you are acquainted with the developments in elementary school science during the past decade, you will recognize that the principal features of the plan I am proposing have already been implemented in one of the new programs, the program developed by the Science Cur-

riculum Improvement Study. In this program, there is a sequence of
physical science units dealing with material objects, interaction and
systems, subsystems and variables, relative position and motion, energy
sources, and models of electrical and magnetic interaction. Running in
parallel with the physical science sequence, there is a sequence of life
science units on organisms, life cycles, populations, environments, communities, and ecosystems. The units in both of these sequences have
been ordered by considering both the cognitive development of the
student and the logic of the science they contain. The lessons and
activities within the units have also been sequenced with these considerations in mind. To perfect the structure of the Science Curriculum
Improvement Study program, it would be necessary to clearly specify
behavioral objectives for each step in the sequence and to specify the
proficiency standards for mastery of each step. This would make it
possible for individual students to progress through the program's
learning sequence at different rates. Furthermore, it would help to
assure that every student completing the sequence has mastered the
fundamental science content of the program.

SAGREDO: Thank you, Simplicio. I can see how the elementary
school science program you've described will contribute to the students' scientific literacy.

SIMPLICIO: Yes, the students will have a strong base of scientific
literacy by the time they finish elementary school. They will know and
understand the most fundamental concepts of physical science and life
science.

SALVIATI: Is that all?

SIMPLICIO: No, of course not, Salviati. As I indicated before, most
of the time the students learn the science concepts through solving
problems and doing investigations. This gives them a good appreciation
of the processes of science.

SALVIATI: And is that what scientific literacy is—understanding of
what you call fundamental science concepts and appreciation of scientific processes?

SIMPLICIO: There have been debates about the definition of scientific literacy, but that's what it is essentially.

SAGREDO: Would you add something to Simplicio's definition of
scientific literacy, Salviati?

SALVIATI: Let me put it this way. I cannot go along with assuming
a sacred set of fundamental science concepts that everyone must learn.
You hold that certain concepts are fundamental because they occupy

key places in the structure of the science disciplines. But, cite almost any of your fundamental science concepts, and I can point to myriad individuals who would be very little wiser, or any happier, if they learned that concept. Is there much value in learning about these key pieces of the structure of science? For most people, not much. So, I can't believe that learning those science concepts dubbed "fundamental" is a necessary part of everyone's scientific literacy.

Now, I'm not claiming that a person doesn't need to understand any science concepts to be scientifically literate. On the contrary, there certainly are some concepts which are a part of scientific literacy. They can be identified, not by looking to the structure of the science disciplines, but by asking what an individual has to know and understand to stay alive, remain healthy, and live happily in today's world. I'm thinking of concepts that are relevant to the individual's sheer physical survival and to his mental well-being. Concepts concerning the physiological functions of the human body are examples, as are concepts concerning phenomena which a person encounters daily, such as combustion and electricity. And, I'm thinking of science concepts that are relevant to contemporary social problems, like the air pollution that is plaguing that city in the valley below us.

Would I add something to Simplicio's definition of scientific literacy? Yes, definitely. I agree with Simplicio that a part of scientific literacy is an appreciation of the processes of science, but that doesn't go far enough. I think that a most important component of scientific literacy is an understanding of the nature of scientific inquiry. Through any educational program designed to promote scientific literacy, the student should come to fully comprehend how scientific ideas are formulated, tested, and revised. This is of value for two main reasons. If a person doesn't understand the nature of scientific inquiry, his confidence in science and scientists may well be shaken when he learns of newly proposed scientific concepts and ideas that seem to contradict concepts he previously studied. On the other hand, someone who understands the nature of scientific inquiry can accept such reformulations of scientific ideas and remains unperturbed. Moreover, the student who has comprehended the nature of scientific inquiry has obtained access to a significant mode of thought. Scientific inquiry has been abundantly successful in helping man gain understanding of the natural world, and adaptations of scientific inquiry have been applied profitably to many of man's other endeavors where there were questions to be answered. Knowing the nature of scientific inquiry, the scientifically literate person possesses a model of a way to conduct one's thinking, and when he confronts a problem or a question to be answered, he may choose to use that model to guide his own thinking.

Another important component of scientific literacy I want to add to Simplicio's definition is an understanding of the social aspects of science. Is there any real substance in the understanding of science concepts and of the nature of scientific inquiry if a person is unaware of the impact of science and related technologies on contemporary society? I hardly have to remind you that the two principal characteristics of civilized life in this century have been the progress made possible by technology in reducing man's labor, in communication, in transportation, in increasing material comforts; and the transformations engendered by science in man's thinking and beliefs. A scientifically literate person recognizes the multiple interactions between science and the society at large, and incorporates what he understands about these social aspects of science into his personal planning, into his political decisions, and into his view of the world.

All this is what scientific literacy means when it is properly defined. I have been patient, but I haven't seen scientific literacy fully taken into account in anything which Simplicio has proposed to us today.

SIMPLICIO: I must say, Salviati, that your definition of scientific literacy is quite comprehensive. Up to now, I had not considered all of its ramifications. On the other hand, I don't see how all these things about scientific literacy can be incorporated into a science program. There is only a limited amount of time available for teaching science at any school level. Even if you use your time efficiently but devote a great deal of that time to building up the student's scientific literacy, you may not be able to preserve the integrity of the science in the program.

SAGREDO: I was wondering about that also. I agree that scientific literacy is very important, probably the most important emphasis for science education in these times. I wonder if it is also important, then, to display the structure of science to the student by the way the science curriculum is structured.

SIMPLICIO: The structure is necessary. After all, what good is a science program if it isn't good science?

SALVIATI: What good is a science program if it isn't relevant to the individual?

SAGREDO: I see the point of your question, Salviati. One can devise the most neatly structured curriculum in the world, but if the student isn't attracted to it and isn't motivated to learn, you've accomplished very little.

SALVIATI: Right you are. And for this reason, relevance is a primary consideration in designing a program of science education. In fact, I suspect that considering the relevance of learning experiences to the student ought to be at the heart of all educational planning.

SAGREDO: I don't think I would be mistaken if I thought that you were ready to tell us about a plan for science education that is based on relevance. I shall be most interested to hear about it, and I'm sure Simplicio feels the same way.

SALVIATI: Thank you, Sagredo. I'll do my best to fulfill your expectations.

If we pause for a moment to consider what relevance of a school program means, two aspects become apparent. First, there is the relevance of the proffered learning experiences to the individual student's needs and interests. Second, there is the relevance of the content and operation of a program to the social circumstances of today and in the foreseeable future. A science program that truly is relevant encompasses both these aspects.

I think it's worth reminding ourselves that the education of children takes place throughout their whole world, not only in school. This has always been true. Children learn in their homes, on the street, in the woods, and they learn from many people and many sources. On the contemporary scene, television and other mass media have greatly expanded the range and opportunities for learning. Without doubt, the opportunities for a child to learn outside formal schools will continue to grow and will become even more significant in the future. In a culture which offers these many opportunities, the main contribution which the school can make is to focus the learning of the child and to give him a better basis for learning from the world around him.

Another social circumstance we should remind ourselves of is the alteration brought about by new technologies in the traditional pattern of occupations and careers. No longer will a person choose a career specialty as a youth, be trained for it in school, and pursue it throughout his life. Rather, the career of a young man or woman starting to work in the 1980's is likely to include several major occupational shifts, as specific occupations are made obsolescent by technological change. Even within a line of work, there will be few jobs that are not periodically affected by innovations. These characteristics of occupations and careers will require that the individual often learn new skills and tasks and acquire new knowledge. He will be a learner for much of his life, not only during the years of formal schooling. For this situation, the best preparation the school can offer is to help the child become an effective independent learner.

Well then, what implications for planning a science program are there in these reminders about two social circumstances of the 1970's? Quite clearly, they tell us that a science program which is relevant to contemporary social circumstances must make provisions for the student to become an effective and competent independent learner. This can be done by including in the program's goals, not only the customary objectives which pertain to achievement in science subject-matter content and in scientific inquiry, but also objectives for developing the student's skills in self-direction and self-evaluation. Of course, setting up goals for student self-direction and self-evaluation is not in itself sufficient to guarantee that the goals will be attained. The organization and operation of the science program must also be consciously and conscientiously planned to assure that each student will attain these goals. Now, I am not claiming that the shaping of student self-direction and self-evaluation is solely the responsibility of a science program. This should, in fact, be a commitment of all school programs in these times. Nevertheless, it is altogether fitting to stress self-direction and self-evaluation in a school science program. In science itself, the investigator is obliged to direct his own work and to judge its worth. Self-direction and self-evaluation are indeed a part of the nature of scientific inquiry. By stressing these same qualities in a science program, we are doing no less than emulating the scientific enterprise, and thereby providing the student with an additional perspective of the nature of scientific inquiry.

I believe that the ideal way to assure that the student will learn to direct and evaluate his own learning is through a program of individualized science. As you no doubt remember from our earlier discussion, individualization means much more than allowing a student to progress at his own rate through a single sequence of science learnings. In an individualized science program, each student essentially has his own unique program of learning experiences, which he selects according to his needs, interests, goals, and capacities. Since the student constantly makes choices in an individualized program, he becomes increasingly sophisticated about making sound decisions. Feeding into his decision making are judgments the student makes about the worth of his accomplishments, and resulting from it are self-prescribed directives for his subsequent learning activities. In a sense, the very operation of an individualized program requires the student to learn to direct and evaluate his own learning. Naturally, the requirements of the child to select his own learning activities and to evaluate his own work are minimal in the early stages of an individualized program. Here he may choose to take a particular science lesson, do a science activity, or play a science learning game that occupies him for only a day or two. As the student progresses in the individualized program, he becomes able to specify and follow a fairly long-term learning plan, covering several weeks or even months, that will lead him toward desired knowledge, insight, or satisfaction.

A program of individualized science, as I conceive it, begins in the elementary school, when the child is in kindergarten or first grade, and carries right through high school. I can see no really valid reason for advocating any different form of program for the high school years. After all, the child's development is a gradual, continuous process, and he does not suddenly change into something different at the moment when he enters the hallowed halls of a high school. An individualized science program is best for the student in the elementary school because it provides for and is relevant to his needs and interests; an individualized science program is best for the high school student for the same reason. Perhaps it is even better for the high school student because of his greater maturity, which enables him to make wiser decisions about choosing his own learning experiences, makes him more thorough in evaluating his accomplishments, and gives him more perseverance in following through on extended investigations he has elected to pursue. Because of the high school student's greater maturity, also, and because of his greater range of interests and greater knowledge, individualized science in the high school will be able to give the student considerably more freedom to explore and investigate a broader spectrum of topics and areas. He will have acquired the necessary skills and sense of responsibility to make the most of this freedom through his prior experiences in the individualized science program.

It must be rather obvious, I suppose, that an individualized science program demands the availability of a considerable array of diverse learning resources to meet all or most of the needs and interests of individual students. There must be units of study representing a broad range of science, units which should be largely self-instructional. There must be suggestions for experiments and laboratory exercises which develop skills in the processes of scientific inquiry, and there must be write-ups of intriguing problems which challenge the student to investigate them. There must be science articles and science books, audiotapes and films, filmstrips and pictures, programmed instructional materials, and science learning games, all of these available for the student who may wish to use them. In addition, it is both wise and necessary to make it possible for the student to have easy access to the many learning resources outside the school. Yes, an individualized science program must seek to offer the student such a rich and captivating environment that he will never be at a loss for something to do.

Now, even when a rich environment is offered, I'm not so naïve as to believe that every student is ready to make maximum use of it at the outset of an individualized science program. Many, perhaps most, students entering this program will be more confused than comfortable, and too much confusion is not a good route to encourage learning. The student's capability to direct his own learning doesn't develop all at once, and if he is to become an effective independent learner, he needs to have opportunities for practice in the process over a period of time. These opportunities to practice self-direction are provided in the early stages of an individualized program through a core of common learning experiences. We might call this common core, "the mainstream." The units of study on the mainstream offer the student opportunities to make choices, relatively few in the first few units but increasingly more as he progresses. Not too far along on the mainstream, the student can make decisions about whether or not he wants to study certain alternative units. And, by the time the student has progressed in his individualized science program to the middle school years, the mainstream has faded entirely; all of his science study is now in alternative units and other science learning activities which he chooses. So, the mainstream provides the students with continually expanding experiences in directing his own learning and with much practice in doing it. Having experienced and practiced self-direction in his learning on the mainstream of the individualized science program, the student may well become confident about directing his own learning in many other situations.

I must confess that developing the student's capability in self-direction is not the sole reason for having a mainstream in the individualized science program. The mainstream units also serve to provide the basis for developing scientific literacy. You know that I'm very concerned about this, and in my speech a little while back, I identified three components of scientific literacy, viz, understanding of certain science concepts, understanding of the nature of scientific inquiry, understanding of the social aspects of science. The content and instructional materials of mainstream units are selected so that they will contribute to the student's attainment of understanding in all three of these components. Admittedly, the mainstream units don't and can't do the whole job of developing scientific literacy through the individualized science program, but they provide a minimal basis for it. Let me also say that another equally important purpose of the mainstream units is to introduce the student to the processes of scientific inquiry and to sharpen his skills in using them. In lessons, exercises, little investigations, and games of mainstream units, the student learns and practices such skills as observing, measuring, interpreting data, formulating hypotheses. These skills are important in themselves, but they also help the student to acquire a better grasp of the nature of scientific inquiry, and they equip him to carry out the small and large investigations which permeate the entire individualized science program and which are the backbone of its upper stages.

I want to tell you more about the student's investigations and the place of inquiry in the program, but first I feel obliged to say something about what the science subject-matter content is. That obligation is easily dispatched. Recall that earlier I said that the science content of the program should have relevance to the social circumstances of today and the foreseeable future. I've prepared a little chart which identifies that content. In the left-hand column of the chart I've listed five groups of current and imminent social problems. In the right-hand column is a list of the science content relevant to each problem. This list represents the subject-matter pool from which the science content in the mainstream and alternative units of the program is drawn. The units are organized around the science content, not around the social problems. (The content of a few mainstream units doesn't appear on this list. These are the units in the early part of the program which deal with the process skills of observing and measuring.) There's something quite interesting about the science content list. At least half of the topics listed are related to topics which the child most frequently asks questions about. For example, the child is invariably interested in how his body performs its various functions, how he grows and develops, and how man is related to the world of other living things. This suggests that most of the science content selected for inclusion in the program has relevance both to the social circumstances of today and to the interests of the individual child.

CHART III–1

Current and Imminent Social Problems with a Sizable Science Component

Problem	*Relevant Science Content*
A. Overpopulation and Its Consequences:	Human Reproductive System
	Birth, Growth, Development, Death
1. Air Pollution	Reproduction, Contraception
a) Industrial	Atmosphere: Composition, Movement,
b) Private	Weather and Climate
c) Chemical pollutants	Conversion of Energy in Living Things
2. Water Pollution	Oxidation: Respiration and Combustion
a) Industrial	Sun as Energy Source
b) Private	Photosynthesis
c) Chemical pollutants	Chemistry and Physics of Certain Industrial
d) Radioactive pollutants	Processes
3. Strain on Ecological Balance	Water and Solutions
	Physiological Effects of Chemicals and Radioactivity on Plants, Animals and Man
4. Strain on Resources	
a) Water	Microorganisms: Decomposers of Wastes,
b) Clean air	Carriers of Disease
c) Food	Transmittal of Disease
d) Space	The Ecosystem
5. Quality of Life in Cities	Ecological Niches
a) Overcrowding and aggression	Diversity of Species
	Natural Selection
b) Noise	Water, Carbon Dioxide-Oxygen and Nitrogen Cycles
c) Sanitation	
	Food Chains
	Predator-Prey Relationships
	Man's Requirements for Good Health
	Nutrition: Essential Nutrients, Sources, Substitutions
	Growth, Nurture and Selective Breeding of Food Animals
	Conservation of Natural Resources: Water, Mineral, Plant and Animal
	Psychological and Physiological Effects of Noise
	Social Behavior of Animals, Aggression

CHART III–1 (Continued)

Problem	*Relevant Science Content*
B. Everyday Hazards of Technological Life:	Physics Principles: Momentum, Expansion, Moments, Levers
1. Automobiles	Electric Circuits
2. Electrical Gadgets and Tools	Electrical Units
	Physiological Effects of Chemical Agents
3. Household Chemicals	Acids and Bases, Neutralization
4. Household Gadgets	
	Human Anatomy and Physiology: including
C. Biological Engineering:	Circulatory, Digestive, Nervous, Reproductive, Endocrine, and Immunological Systems
1. Transplants	
2. Eugenics and Genetic Manipulation	
	Cell Physiology
3. Drugs	Genetics, Genetic Code
D. Extraterrestrial Exploration:	Newtonian Physics
1. Feasibility and Extent	Propulsion of Space Vehicles; Chemical Fuels, Nuclear Energy
2. Necessity and Costs	Geography of Solar System
	Biological Needs of Man in Space
E. War and Disarmament:	
1. Massive Nuclear Assaults	Nuclear Physics
2. Detection and Surveillance	Physiological Effects of Radiation and Radioactive Isotopes
3. Chemical and Biological Weapons	Electronics Systems
	Effects of Chemical and Biological Agents on Physiology of Plants, Animals, Man

SAGREDO: I have been studying your interesting chart, Salviati. It certainly seems to be a good plan to build a program around science content that is relevant to social problems. Don't you agree, Simplicio?

SIMPLICIO: Yes, the content that is listed is good science. However, I think the organization of the content list is somewhat faulty. I don't see the logical connections between the different science content areas on the list.

SALVIATI: Oh, rubbish! Showing logical connections between content areas isn't a purpose of this chart. It simply shows the science content the student deals with in the various mainstream and alternative units of the program. The units on the mainstream are logically sequenced, of course, but there's no need to make a fetish of that. The important point is that the program's science content is relevant and appealing to the student and that it stimulates inquiry.

SIMPLICIO: Do you mean to take the position that it doesn't matter what the science content of the program is? I can't agree with that.

SAGREDO: Nor can I. You can't avoid being concerned about the science content. If you neglect the science content, you run the risk of no longer having a science program.

SALVIATI: The science content *is* important, of course, gentlemen. If I didn't think so, would there have been any sense in going to the trouble of identifying the content that is relevant? What I am trying to emphasize, however, is that the selection and logical organization of content should not be used as the sole basis for building a science program, particularly an individualized program. It must be built on a broader base. I've already spoken about developing self-direction and scientific literacy, and I still want to say some things about developing the student's ability to inquire.

SIMPLICIO: You cannot promote inquiry unless the student has some science content he can inquire into.

SALVIATI: How right you are, Simplicio! And that is probably the chief function served by the program's science content. It provides the subject matter for inquiry. If we want to engage the student in inquiry, I don't think that there's a better strategy than to provide subject matter that interests him. That's why content which is relevant has been selected for the units of the individualized science program.

SAGREDO: I gather from what you've just told us, Salviati, that you place great emphasis on inquiry.

SALVIATI: I certainly do. Frankly, I think the goal we hope the most to achieve in science teaching is to have the student become an active inquirer. The individualized science program holds this goal in common with the best of the science curricula extant today. While no one claims that inquiry occurs only in science, the student's ability to engage in inquiry and the development of his inquiry skills are most readily facilitated in the context of science. That is why the spirit of inquiry pervades the individualized science program.

I want to be sure that we are clear about what I am talking about when I refer to inquiry. There is often considerable confusion about this, and many people fail to make the necessary distinction between inquiry and scientific inquiry. When the creative scientist pursues his quest for increased understanding of the phenomena of the natural world, he is engaging in scientific inquiry. It is an activity which is carried on at the frontiers of man's knowledge. Scientific inquiry requires its successful practitioners to have a firm base of broad generalizable knowledge, and it characteristically employs certain general operating modes, which I've called the "processes of scientific inquiry." While these processes can be emulated and practiced meaningfully by students in a science program, instances where school-age children can engage in scientific inquiry are very rare. It's obvious, then, that attaining proficiency in scientific inquiry can hardly be justified as a goal of any school science program designed for general education. At the same time, I am sure that developing the ability to engage in inquiry is a worthy goal for every student.

What I mean when I say "inquiry" is a general process of learning. Inquiry can be seen operating at all age levels and in virtually any human situation. In fact, it is a uniquely human learning process, which results in the building of new personal knowledge and insight. Inquiry begins with asking questions and proceeds in the individual's seeking of answers to the questions posed. The question may be merely a curious "why?" or "how?", or it may be a personal puzzlement, a constructed problem, an observed discrepancy, an incongruous life situation. Whatever the starting point, the process of resolving the question results in "accommodation," as Piaget would say, or the modification of internal mental schemas to fit experience. There is change in the mind of the individual; he has learned. An inquiry methodology in science teaching or anywhere else provides the child with

opportunities to experiment, and I mean experimenting in its broadest
sense. The child is encouraged to try things out to see what happens,
to manipulate objects, to manipulate symbols, to seek his own answers
to questions, to reconcile what he finds out at one time with what he
found out at another, to compare his findings with those of other children. All these are attributes of the process of learning through engaging in inquiry. Inquiry enables the individual to use his experiences in
adapting to life situations. Developing this ability is of real value to
everyone.

The individual's ability to inquire is developed in the individualized science program, not only by virtue of the spirit of inquiry which
pervades the program and its learning resources, but by means of various specific features and practices. I've already mentioned the mainstream units in the early levels of the program that are designed to
introduce and develop the student's skills in using the processes of
scientific inquiry. These processes, as I've explained, are general operating modes that characterize the inquiry of scientists. Since the processes
of scientific inquiry are all represented among the attributes of the
process of learning by inquiry, the student's ability to use them with
skill and confidence is an important part of his ability to inquire. I have
alluded also to the many opportunities the program offers the student
to carry out investigations, either by himself or together with several
other students. Each investigation is an opportunity to practice inquiry.
Early in the program, the student is offered several series of little investigations (called "Mini-Explorations"), through which he can integrate
his skills and knowledge gained from other learning resources into
elementary inquiry experiences. Each series of investigations focuses
on the science subject-matter content of a particular mainstream unit,
where some of the topics dealt with are human respiration, human
nutrition, the process of digestion, burning, systems and interaction,
chemical change, water in natural systems, and the circulation of the
blood in man. As the student progresses in the program, the little
investigations in the series associated with particular mainstream units
become longer and more sophisticated. They now call on the student
to integrate a broader range of skills, knowledge, and previous experience, and to bring these to bear on his inquiries.

At about this stage in the program, the student also begins to make
choices from among numerous alternative units which are offered for
investigation. Each alternative unit makes it possible for the student to

inquire at some length in a science content area which interests him. You might guess, and you would be right, that the content areas covered by the alternative units of the program are those included in the list I previously showed you of science content relevant to current and imminent social problems [see Chart III–1]. In the program's succeeding levels, the number and variety of alternative units offered continually expands, giving the student ever-increasing opportunities to engage in inquiry related to program-presented science topics. At the same time, the student may choose to inquire in topics the program doesn't present by opting to work alone or with others in self-initiated independent investigations. By the time the student is in the individualized science program in his high school years, such self-initiated investigations will probably take up his entire time. Here the topics for inquiry may no longer be limited to science content alone. As inquiry proceeds along its natural course, the student could very easily find himself investigating contemporary social problems related to science, as well as spanning into areas of logic, philosophy, history, sociology, economics, literature, and the arts. I do not say that this will happen for every student, but the opportunity for the individual to let his inquiry range freely will be there.

Well then, I have tried to show you how the individualized science program provides many opportunities to practice inquiry, so that the student may develop his ability to inquire. But, the most crucial factor, I must confess, still resides within the individual student. An individual will carry out inquiries only insofar as they are relevant to him and only as long as he derives satisfaction from pursuing them. A science program whose goal is the development of inquirers must offer a broad range of relevant experiences from which many different individuals can gain satisfaction. I suggest that this requirement is best fulfilled by the individualized science program I have described to you.

SAGREDO: Yes, Salviati, I do see how the development of the student's ability to inquire has been made an integral part of the individualized science program. And the development of this ability is also tied in with the program's emphasis on self-direction, is it not?

SALVIATI: Of course, it is. The seeds for developing the student into an active inquirer are sown at the beginning of the science program in elementary school. Simultaneously, we plant the seeds that initiate the student into the process of directing his own learning. From these beginnings, the student's growth as an inquirer and his growth as a self-directing learner are nurtured in the program's middle years. Both come to full fruition in the individualized science program's later stage, where the student engages in inquiry in many areas to which his interests and his individual plans have directed him.

SIMPLICIO: It is really quite inconceivable to me that a program which is so loosely structured could be operated effectively. It is almost frightening to contemplate that, in the later stage of the program, the students are free to do almost anything. There is hardly any structure at all in evidence.

SALVIATI: You are wrong, Simplicio. There's much more structure here than you can possibly impose on the student from the outside. Excuse me, I should have said that there are many more structures, for each individual student builds his own structure for learning according to where his inquiries and his goals and his individuality are leading him.

SIMPLICIO: It is rather doubtful that we shall be able to come to an agreement on this issue.

SALVIATI: I don't think it would be hard if you gave up your fixations about designing structured sequences for groups of students, placing students on an almost inviolable learning continuum, and planning primarily for efficiency.

SIMPLICIO: These are not my fixations, my dear Salviati. They are the fundamental basis upon which the science curriculum of the next decade must stand.

SALVIATI: I suggest a much better basis. It is simply to place the individual student at the focus of the planning of the science program. If we do this, we shall produce a program that is relevant, meaningful, and of greatest benefit to the individual. We shall have science learning experiences which involve the student because they interest him and because he can enjoy them. We shall see the student developing positive feelings about science and about himself through his involvement in self-directed, self-fulfilling, satisfying science learning.

SAGREDO: Gentlemen, we must conclude our discussion. When I invited you here, I thought we would be able to settle on what the science curriculum in American schools should be during the next decade. Each of you has argued well for your respective system of science education. Simplicio's plan has the merits of structure, and Salviati's plan has the merits of openness. I suspect that both systems will be with us in the school science curriculum in the 1970's. Don't you think so, too?

NOTES

1. As the historically minded reader probably recognizes by now, the participants in this dialogue first appeared in Galileo Galilei's *Dialogue Concerning the Two Chief World Systems (Dialogo sopra i due Massimi Sistemi del Mondo; Tolemaico, e Copernicano),* published in 1632. They met again in Galileo's last work, *Discourses Concerning Two New Sciences (Discorsi e dimostrazioni matematiche intorno a due nuove scienze),* published in 1638. In both the *Dialogo* and the *Discorsi,* Galileo presented his own opinions through the words of Salviati. Save for the contribution of the participants' names and for inspiration to use a dialogue form, Galileo cannot be held responsible, nor can anyone else except the author, for the dialogue presented here.

2. This description is taken from Leopold E. Klopfer, "Science Education in 1991," *The School Review,* Vol. 77 (1969), pp. 199-217. Copyright 1969 by The University of Chicago, page 211.

3. *Ibid.*

ROGER PILLET
The University of Chicago

IV FOREIGN LANGUAGE IN THE SEVENTIES

The two decades leading up to the 1970's were productive and exciting in the foreign language field. They were characterized by innovations, increased enrollment, growth of professional solidarity and confidence in the future. Stimulated by a positive national attitude and supported generously by federal funds, foreign language teachers took giant strides in terms of organization, methodology and evaluation and recorded their ideology and practices, their successes and deception in an exhaustive literature.

Projections into the future are expected to convey overtones of the intuitive, the optimistic, even the visionary. As we look into the future of foreign languages in the United States in the seventies, we shall not hesitate to take the kinds of risks inherent in making predictions. We feel, however, that a systematic analysis of observable trends, of such hard data as is available to date, is a prerequisite to speculation. Consequently, we shall devote serious attention to the main directions apparent in foreign language education in the hope that our estimate will reflect more accurately the vitality which assures the continuation of certain trends, the problems which call for the modification of others and the lack of momentum which suggests that yet others must be discarded.

Aware that some of our readers will be interested primarily in the broad lines of our discussion while others may wish to investigate in greater depth some of the major points to which we allude, we have attempted to keep the text relatively free of references and have relegated the supporting documentation to footnotes. Our references will usually be to publications which are comprehensive and which provide bibliographical entries appropriate for further investigation.

The limitations of space will make it necessary at times to oversimplify or overgeneralize. The overall presentation, however, ought to be accurate and instructive.

TRANSITION TO THE "NEW KEY"

Prior to World War II, the study of foreign languages was considered an academic pursuit little related to social conditions and world politics. With few exceptions, American citizens were seldom intent on maintaining the language skills which would strengthen cultural ties with the European countries of their forefathers, and even less interested in developing conversational skills with a view of participating in communication with countries outside the United States.[1] Foreign language study was primarily the domain of higher education and intended as a preparation for the "professions." Latin and Greek were, at most, thought essential in preparing for the ministry, and to some extent, for the law and for medicine. Eventually, modern languages began to be more generally included in the curriculum on the still persistent rationale that German was a valuable asset to those entering the field of science and that French was the language essential to those interested in a diplomatic career.

The interest in developing conversational skills prevailing in special ethnic or religious institutions (German schools, French convent schools) was soon reduced by forces outside the foreign language sphere. The national attitude during and after World War I was a serious threat to the study of German. For many years, the prevailing tenor of isolationism made the study of any foreign language appear frivolous if not wasteful.

But as time went on, the study of foreign languages was increasingly considered as a tool prerequisite to humanistic studies in the colleges and universities. To know a foreign language, ancient and modern, was to possess the key necessary for unlocking the treasures of rich literary heritages. Concurrently the increasingly varied demands made on the total curriculum, led to a search for economy and specificity in terms of the most appropriate foreign language preparation. The Coleman Report, responsive to these pressures, prescribed concentration on reading as the skill most realistically achievable and most appropriate for successful pursuit of literary studies.[2] A large sector of the profession resisted this position vehemently, but its protest, unsupported by such documentation as would justify a multiple skill approach, failed to reverse the political and pedagogical trends.

Although, in retrospect, the turning point in the reorientation of foreign language studies is generally attributed to the launching of Sputnik, the latter event merely served to dramatize concrete, significant changes which had been gestating during the previous 10 years, particularly in connection with the Army Specialized Training Program.[3]

These were crash programs instituted to meet a very real national need: personnel in the Armed Forces who found themselves abroad in their line of duty were incapable of coping, even at a minimal linguistic level, with situations involving their own safety and the successful conduct of military operations.

The design of these programs (as subcontracted to educational institutions for implementation) had a number of features distinct from those characterizing "traditional" programs:

1. The program was to be functional, that is, it focused entirely on the communication skills (understanding and speaking) as its primary if not sole objective.
2. The program parameters were situational. The topics of conversation were narrowly circumscribed to enable the student to cope with real and projected needs in the field.
3. The program was to be intensive. Both national urgency and pedagogical theory suggested some 600 contact hours compressed in some 12-15 weeks of instruction.

4. The method was predicated on the theory of overlearning to the point where stimulus-response was "automatic."

5. The method implied intensive drill on vocabulary embedded in structures, usually modeled by a native informant with provision for additional practice facilitated by technology (records, wire recordings.)

6. The program addressed itself not only to the foreign languages "traditional" in our schools but to more "exotic" languages as well (Japanese, Chinese, or whatever language was spoken in areas in which our Armed Forces were located.).

It is to be noted that the Army programs, in addition to redirecting the goals of foreign languages study, represent a convergence of resources instrumental in meeting these goals. On one hand, the objectives and teaching techniques were consistent with and supported by the science of linguistics. On the other hand, electronic technology, yet in a crude state of development, was seen as an instrument of high potential in facilitating the instructional process.

The "new look" in foreign language teaching was not discarded at the end of military activities. The fact that universities had been involved as subcontractors for the Armed Forces during the war facilitated the transition to the peacetime classroom.

An Investigation of Second Language Teaching conducted by Agard and Dunkel (1948)[4] focuses on the period of ferment in the postwar years, particularly on some 48 institutions committed to continuing the type of foreign language instruction consistent with the objectives of the Army Specialized Training Program (ASTP).

The *Investigation* not only served to evaluate the positive and negative features of these programs but also to caution on the "transferability" of the military programs concept to general education. By extension, it called for more rigor in setting goals and evaluating results in the area of foreign language instruction. A companion book, *Second Language Learning* by Harold B. Dunkel, is a penetrating study of the complex factors interacting in the foreign language class.[5] Subsequently, we shall have occasion to refer to these studies as a measuring stick of progress in the foreign language field during the intervening years.

The Chicago Language Conference held at the University of Chicago in August of 1948 addressed itself to translating the above research into practice.[6] A committee on resolution chosen from distinguished foreign language educators suggested the formation of two working committees.

The first committee was charged to direct its attention to "the most urgent specific projects suitable for immediate experimentation and early implementation in actual teaching practice" by considering the following:

a. Preparation of materials which careful descriptive linguistic analysis would show to be useful in the teaching of the more common foreign languages to the American students, such materials to be made available in terminology and form suitable for use by the average secondary school teacher.

b. Preparation of more satisfactory auditory materials and tests.

c. Preparation of materials for an oral-aural approach which will narrow the gap between them and the usual reading materials, and offer a solution to the problems of transition to and the achievement in reading.

d. Controlled experimentation on the results obtained from large amounts of contact hours in an intensive program, and problem of satiety and the rate of forgetting.

e. Controlled experimentation on the relationship of oral-aural instruction to reading efficiency.

f. Compiling of frequency lists of spontaneous, colloquial speech, in respect to syntax and idioms as well as vocabulary.

g. Well-organized pilot and experimental courses should be planted in institutions able and willing to cooperate fully. The work of existing experiments, in which the latter stages may show even more significant results, should also be followed up.

h. Such pilot courses might include the following projects:

    1. Determination of the difference between ear-minded and eye-minded students and the proper teaching techniques for each.

    2. Developing of instruction at the secondary school level leading to actual tool use of the language in content subjects in following years.

A second committee, concerned with long-range supervision, would "undertake to plan a whole comprehensive survey of the psychological and practical factors in language study, and eventually assign them to various agencies as it may become feasible." Among the more essential topics to be included in such a survey were:

a. The appropriate and attainable objectives in language study at various levels both for the individual and for society.

b. Criteria for the selection of students.

c. The nature of language, including a clearer definition of the skills expected.

d. Effective articulation between primary schools, secondary schools, and college courses in language.

e. The organization of pupil activity in the language, for better motivation and more effective practice, since pupil use of the language in some form is the basic justification of language learning.

f. The possibilities of transfer in language learning, and the integration of language learning with pupil activity in other disciplines.

g. The conditions necessary for effective language learning— time, equipment, size of classes, etc.

h. Complete and adequate testing techniques and materials for all objectives.

i. Development of audio-visual aids, especially the sound film, for more effective teaching at the elementary level.

j. Teacher training in all its phases.

k. A move toward better relations with other disciplines, through cooperative effort.

l. The role of language in general education.

m. Cooperation with UNESCO in a program of activities in the field of language and language teaching.

n. Investigation of the possibility of establishing a service for the collection and distribution of information on language teaching projects, materials, and work in progress.

A cursory look at the above suggests a blueprint for the "New Key" and an inventory of concerns to which the profession has addressed itself in varying degrees during the intervening years.

COMMITMENT TO THE "NEW KEY"

The conference referred to above is representative of the commitment to foreign language instruction which the Modern Language Association had expressed in previous years. William Riley Parker's tenure as secretary of the association marked a period dedicated to the systematic planning for more extensive and improved foreign language instruction.[7] Supported by Rockefeller grants (1952–55; 1955–58), the Foreign Language Program of the Modern Language Association vigorously pressed for analysis and reversal of the trends which had contributed to the low status of foreign language instruction both in the eye of the public and in the educational domain.

Significant (though perhaps unexpected) support for the foreign language cause came from officialdom: in 1952 Earl J. McGrath, then Commissioner of Education, endorsed foreign language study as important to general education; in 1953 Oliver J. Caldwell, then assistant commissioner in the Office of Education, subscribed to the importance of teaching foreign languages at as early an age as practical.

The launching of Sputnik in 1957 served to crystalize public opinion and ensure support for the positions taken by McGrath and Caldwell. It was in this climate, supportive of increasing the competence of Americans in foreign languages as well as in other areas in order to satisfy a national need, that the National Defense Education Act was passed and signed in 1958. Particularly under Title IV and Title III, the Office of Education committed itself to the vigorous support of such research as would lead to improved instruction in the foreign language area.[8]

By and large, USOE support not only implemented plans developed by MLA but multiplied dramatically the impact intended. Table IV–1 illustrates the scope of NDEA programs as contrasted to the relatively humble aspirations of MLA.

The impressive commitment of the Office of Education to research resulted in massive support for a number of related areas. Statistical surveys and studies of enrollment, trends, and needs were subcontracted to appropriate individuals and/or institutions.[9] Evaluative studies concentrating primarily on self-evaluation by the USOE of the proposals being implemented or submitted as related to the efficiency of the total effort were carefully planned. Research in Method of Instruction was not limited to the study of the place of foreign languages in the overall curriculum. It extended to the application of psychological and linguistic research to foreign language learning equipment, primarily audio-visual devices. Research resulting in the development of prototypical materials providing models for audio-lingual instruction in several languages was initiated. This eventually resulted in making

TABLE IV-1

MLA Plan	*NDEA Five-Year Achievement*
Expenditure: $5,425,000	$135,000,000
Institutes: 15 for 900 teachers	300 for 15,000 teachers
Fellowships for secondary teachers: 500 ..	0
Fellowships for potential college teachers: 0	
....	3,450 (Title VI)
Grants for foreign travel for in-service teachers: 250	0
Contract teaching materials for uncommon languages: "several"	120
Language and area centers established: 0	55
Tests: 7 areas for 6 languages	7 areas for 5 languages
State supervisory services, 3 states for 2 years, 47 states for 1 year	38 states
Demonstration centers: 15	0

available audio-lingual packages for teaching common languages (French, German, Italian, Spanish, and Russian) as illustrated by the production and the dissemination of the Glastonbury Materials.

These eventually appeared on the commercial market under the rubric of A-LM materials, (Harcourt Brace and World, Inc.), and were the first to provide for a four-year audio-lingual sequence and to set the pattern for subsequent competitive packages. At the same time, substantial support was allocated to research on so-called "exotic" languages, almost completely neglected in this country in spite of their importance in various sections of the globe. Textbooks, grammars, readers, and dictionaries provided the tools necessary for instruction in this area.

Money was also provided for the development of standardized tests, intended to measure not only student proficiency in several foreign languages but to assess teacher competence in language skills, in linguistics, and in pedagogical background.[10]

As important as was the thrust of NDEA in the developmental phase of language programs, the support provided for implementation was even more impressive. Fellowships and institutional support were made available to encourage the study of foreign languages at the undergraduate level. The preparation of better qualified teachers was a major concern. Preservice programs were handsomely supported. The "institute" pattern, both at home and abroad, had immense impact on in-service training, particularly for those teachers with low linguistic ability, but, more generally, for all teachers needing to adjust their teaching strategies to become effective in the audio-lingual method. Money was made available to state departments of instruction to monitor and improve, through foreign language supervisors, the quality and scope of foreign language teaching and learning in most of the States.

In addition, the policy of the Office of Education to effect a change in the foreign language field is obvious in the massive financial support it provided for the purchase of new materials and equipment, the most important investment going for the purchase of language laboratories.[11]

More subtly significant was the effort to popularize the cause of foreign language study through a number of publications addressed to students, counselors, and teachers setting forth the need for knowing a foreign language and specifying the desired outlets for foreign language competence.[12]

THE "NEW KEY" IN ACTION

The stimulation provided by federal funding had profound effect on the foreign language profession. Supportive public opinion, new prospects for achieving functional goals through a new methodology, and financial resources available for constructive action converged to contribute to a climate of optimism and innovation. Greatly encouraged, foreign language educators not only participated within the government programs but engaged in activities beyond the scope and design of funded programs. The 1960's leave us with an impressive record of achievements in the foreign language field.

We shall consider a number of the characteristics of the past decade with a view of assessing, on the basis of available data, the impact of foreign language teaching on the American scene. At the same time, we shall discuss (in a necessarily more subjective vein) the *degree* to which the respective trends have contributed to the position of foreign languages today in the curriculum at all levels of instruction. We shall try to determine in what area and to what extent success promises a continuing thrust, where internally generated deficiencies suggest questionable prospects and in what measure debilitating, external factors have retarded the evolution of this massive movement.

PROFESSIONALISM

Perhaps the most impressive achievements of the sixties are related to professional solidarity. Committed to the audio-lingual method (perhaps exaggeratedly so), language teachers developed a new "identity" in terms of pedagogical aspirations. Involvement in existing professional organizations and attendance at regularly scheduled meetings increased. A number of serious regional conferences were initiated and ACTFL[13] emerged as a viable new association dedicated to serving professional needs at many levels.

The product of organizational cohesiveness and aggressiveness was the publication of increasingly sophisticated pedagogical articles in existing and new journals, and the circulation of a number of substantive Conference Reports and Compendia[14] invaluable for their scope and scholarship. These publications contributed substantially to the dissemination of information through periodic bibliographies. The establishment of an ERIC Center for foreign languages marks a culminating point in this direction.[15]

On the basis of the achievements listed above we are confident that the momentum developed in the sixties will be difficult to brake and that the profession is "ready" to cope in a constructive way with any problems facing the new decade.

FOREIGN LANGUAGES IN THE ELEMENTARY SCHOOL

In contrast, there is strong indication, in spite of the optimism which had been generated in the late fifties, that the introduction to foreign language in the early grades (FLES) stands little chance of becoming universally accepted as an essential feature of the elementary school curriculum. Although many fine and long-established programs prosper, few new ones are being initiated and many "experimental" ones have been moved up to the middle school (7–8 grades), an extension of foreign language learning downward rather than a distinctive attempt to initiate foreign language study in the early years. This, in spite of the evidence that third or fourth grade is the latest point at which the child is best equipped, psychologically and linguistically, to make maximum progress in the understanding and speaking skills.[16]

It is of little comfort to emphasize that the movement "never had a real chance," that it was sabotaged by administrators' indifference (speaking euphemistically), by a shortage of qualified teachers, by the lack of unanimous support by foreign language teachers at the secondary and college levels, by the insular attitude of FLES teachers to the rest of the elementary curriculum. The hard facts are that, in a period of budget crisis in the schools, the movement is at a point where "holding its own" is about the best it can expect in view of still apparently insurmountable obstacles of "articulation" and, more importantly, because no hard data is available to point to dramatic and lasting progress in foreign language competence attributable to FLES on a wide enough population to make its justification incontestable.[17]

THE "NEW KEY" IN THE SIXTIES

Professional commitment to an audio-lingual methodology based on the conviction that understanding and speaking a foreign language is the first priority in terms of national needs is perhaps the most significant and complex factor which characterized the last decade. It looms all the more important since, in our opinion, it has serious implications for many subelements related to the method: materials, media, culture, etc.

We are not questioning the plausibility of initiating foreign language instruction through the hearing-speaking skills. Nor are we unsympathetic to the excessive zeal that initially resulted in somewhat doctrinaire prescriptions and *caveats* attending the implementation of the "new key." With no intent to minimize the importance of the lessons learned and the results achieved with the audio-lingual method, that is, without succumbing to the current tendency to "throw out the baby with the bath water," we shall try to outline the erosion of the movement's unidirectional thrust as affected by a number of related areas.

The development and use of appropriate classroom materials, for instance, were influenced to a great extent by linguistic theory. Emphasis on the primacy of speech, on the priority of mastering structures rather than accumulating vocabulary, on the insistence of authentic, conversational speech (primarily "dialogues") as the vehicle of instruction were readily accepted as consonant with the aims of the audio-lingual method.

Linguists, however, once they had provided a theoretical framework, soon (and advisedly) disassociated themselves from the problems of implementation. Fortunately, applied linguists emerged to bridge the gap between theory and practice.[18] One might argue that the insistence on contrastive features may have focused too narrowly on so-called "areas of interference" and that concern for the spoken word resulted in a rich documentation related to phonemics with relatively too little attention given to linguistic problems inherent in the transfer of oral skills to the areas of reading and writing. This would in no way detract from the invaluable contribution of this group.

There is little evidence that linguistics will fill this lacuna or, for that matter, that even applied linguists are particularly concerned with dealing with classroom problems through improved channels of communication with teachers. Any issue of *The Linguistic Reporter* reveals the Center for Applied Linguistics' concern for "language sciences," for research. Its interest in implementation is reflected primarily in development of textbooks for the teaching of "exotic" languages.[19]

A reversal in trend is also evident in the degree of commitment to and utilization of media as instrumental to achieving audio-lingual competence. Pilot programs in TV instruction were spectacular but short lived. Although the modest tape recorder is still very much in evidence in the foreign language classroom, the complex language laboratories, once heralded as indispensable to the process of mastering language utterances and drilling structures to the point of "automaticity," have either been much simplified or, in many cases, discarded altogether.[20]

A combination of factors rather than any single one may explain the gradual diminishment of enthusiasm for the language laboratory. Operant conditioning may not be sufficiently motivating to the majority of the pupils scheduled. Mechanical complications, maintenance and scheduling problems are oft-cited as reasons for bypassing the lab. Perhaps more serious is the still prevailing attitude of many teachers for whom apprehension of mechanical problems, reaction to "depersonalization" and sensitivity to students' lack of response combine to form a negative set.

Perhaps the most serious handicap yet to be overcome consists of sequencing appropriate materials into the obedient machine, materials which are not only stimulating and effective but which, at the same time, are tightly integrated with the learning activities prescribed in the teacher's total course.

The burden of transforming audio-lingual theory into effective classroom practices inevitably fell on the shoulders of the teachers. The massive measures provided to achieve the transformation for both pre-service and in-service teachers (institutes, in-service training, literature, etc.) have been alluded to in previous paragraphs. In spite of this concerted effort, conversion to the "new key" was less than universal. Many teachers, because of personal commitment to "traditional" objectives, because of apprehension for new procedures (particularly those involving use of electronic devices), because of resenting the imposition of a new approach which, unintentionally, was demeaning to their training and experience, rejected the doctrine of audio-lingualism outright. Others accepted the new orientation in principle but began to "adjust" the new method in terms of practices and materials more congenial to their own teaching style and to the "needs" of their students. Beset with the demanding task of instruction, the best intentioned teachers found themselves unable to invest sufficient time and energy in developing the expertise they thought necessary for effective implementation of the "new key." Increasingly, as audio-lingual practices proved no panacea for sustaining student motivation and as research findings failed to attest dramatically to the effectiveness of the new method, malaise was followed by disenchantment. In some cases, this resulted in confirming hostility. In most cases, teachers settled for an individual, eclectic approach which incorporated the "best" features of traditional and audio-lingual methods.[21]

This trend away from "pure" audio-lingual practices found partial support in the position of psychologists interested in language learning problems. Most often deplored was the tedium inevitable during the relentless drilling inherent in the new method. Concern was also expressed for heavy emphasis on rote learning to the exclusion of properly exploiting the students' capacity for intellectualization.[22]

CULTURE AND THE "NEW KEY"

Our previous references to the audio-lingual orientation have focused primarily on methodologies appropriate to the teaching of language skills. However, "new key" exponents suscribe to a conviction that language is a significant cultural feature, inseparable from the setting in which it is used. A broader definition of culture was adopted by proponents of the new school: without denigrating art, literature, music, etc., as the highest forms of cultural expression of a people, a new emphasis on "deep culture" was posited as a means of providing a stimulating context for language study and as a frontal assault on the typical American monocultural syndrome.

Looking to anthropology rather than humanities for a framework, exponents of this position turned their attention to characteristics (not stereotypes) of the social institutions prevailing in the countries whose language was being studied. Visuals are, of course, ideal for presenting "authentic" models and much effort was made in this direction. More difficult is the integration of significant cultural features into the syllabus of the language course: illuminating intellectually sophisticated concepts through rudimentary language tools proved a most vexing problem. The gap between commitment to theory and functioning classroom plans in this area is far from being bridged.[23]

The concern for cultural values has had an important side effect. The new interpretation of culture as associated with the languages popular in the schools was accomplished by an assessment of what other cultures were important to and/or visible on the American scene. This, in time provided impetus for the study of the languages appropriate to that culture. Hence the spurt of interest in Russian, the nascent demand for Swahili and the heavy trend to Spanish and bilingual education.

Endorsement of foreign language study by popular opinion and the promise of "new key" theorists that foreign language instruction could be more productive, that foreign language learning could be converted into a more participatory academic experience had a substantial effect on foreign language enrollment. As a result of the expansion of foreign language instruction across levels and of an increase in student population at each level enrollment figures were indeed gratifying to the profession.

For the first time, the foreign language field was sharing in the "universalism" characteristic of education in a democratic society. The flood of new students, particularly at the secondary level, included many who were not among the very able and very motivated elite which had previously graced the foreign language class.

The situation called for adjustments in setting goals appropriate to various elements of this heterogeneous population, for adopting a flexible attitude toward students of different capacities, for exploring, perhaps for the first time, the educative impact of the foreign language sequence on each individual as contrasted to measuring the language competence of a selected few.

Sharing the curricular limelight with other disciplines and dealing with increasingly complex instructional problems attending increased enrollment at all levels and across a wider range of levels served to challenge the previous "insular" posture consistent with teaching a highly selected student body for a relatively short span of contact hours. The literature of the 1960's records the intent to integrate foreign language study as part of the total curriculum.[24] More specifically, the profession is aware of the usefulness of microteaching and interaction analysis with respect to teacher training.[25] A number of language programs have been fitted into modular schedules, the structuring of performance objectives has been promoted as a means of responding to the need for accountability, serious consideration has been given to systems analysis, differentiated staffing and other innovative practices.

Of these important trends, the concept of individualized instruction has perhaps the most serious implication for foreign language teaching. In a broader sense, this concern speaks to determining the readiness of individual students to different language skills at different times and through different modes of instruction. The concept seriously challenges the notion that while a traditional approach was *bad* for all students of one generation a new approach must be *good* for all students of a subsequent generation.[26]

Furthermore, whereas preselection might have preserved the foreign language profession from the turbulence of the sixties, the commitment to the proposition that *all* students could benefit from exposure to foreign language study sensitized the foreign language teacher to the unrest, the critical attitude, the experiential orientation characteristic of a large portion of the school population. No longer set apart by his own definition from the English teacher, the social studies teacher, and others, the foreign language instructor was forced to deal with problems of curricular trends, with the conflict between rote learning and inquiry, and, more generally, with the dominant fixation on relevance.

RESEARCH

The foreign language profession was in no way remiss to measure the massive efforts of the 1960's. Several impressive research projects were mounted and scores of less pretentious evaluations have been recorded. These efforts are disappointing on several scores.

Given the complexity of action research we tend to overlook the inadequacies in research designs which failed to weigh sufficiently the infinite variables contaminating the available data. Perhaps more important to the impact of research findings is the fact that much of it focused on "proving" the effectiveness of television, the laboratory, or the overall effectiveness of audio-lingual approach.[27] It is unfortunate that concentration in this area served as a deterrent to more basic (and open-ended) research aimed more specifically at measurement of the relationship of teaching to learning in all of the language skills, particularly with a view of exploring the interdependence of the skills and subskills to each other. There is little research evidence, for instance, that one order of sequencing skills is superior to another. Practically no attempt was made to research the problem of memorization and retention as one of the conditions most important to the heavy stress on mimicry-memorization inherent in the audio-lingual approach.

It is doubly unfortunate that the emphasis on the kind of measurement that would validate the "new key" did not produce dramatic evidence as to its effectiveness. Audio-lingual methods have not been proved to double or triple, in a given period of time, the command of even the oral skills to which the method addressed itself.[28] Research findings have been more valuable for the negative conclusions implicit than for their incontestable proof of efficiency: FLES did *not* retard children's progress in other curricular areas;[29] television was *not* effective unless used under ideal conditions; audio-lingual training did *not* shorten the prospects of a long sequence but pointed instead to a prerequisite number of years as necessary to achieve even minimum command of the language.

FINANCIAL SUPPORT AND ENROLLMENT

Two radical reversals of trends which prevailed in the sixties must be noted for the probable effect they will have on the future direction of foreign language instruction. The first of these is the withering of federal (and foundation) support in the area of foreign languages. The second involves a decrease in the proportion of foreign language enrollment to the total school population.

Curtailment of funds whether attributable to a shift in the national perception, or to the resetting of priorities by the Office of Education, or to a general depression in the national economy, or to all of these in combination, raises the basic question: Will professional momentum generated by financial aid during the preceding generation be sufficiently self-sustained to maintain a high operational level, to consolidate gains, to fill lacunae and to turn to unexplored ways of perpetuating, maintaining, and possibly increasing the status of foreign language instruction?

The second condition, inseparably related to and dependent on the first, constitutes a challenge vital to the profession. Given the decreasing dependence on "requirements" to provide a captive audience, can foreign language instruction be so structured as to provide a viable educational experience which, because it is meaningful and productive, will increase the number of students participating on a voluntary basis?

The situation is not as desperate at this time as many prophets of doom within and outside the profession would have us believe. On one hand, from the point of view of current commitment, of available cumulated information now available, of increased flexibility and objectivity in adjusting, on the basis of past experiences, to meet current challenges, the foreign language profession has never before been in a better position. On the other hand, the enrollment picture, while alarming from the point of view of apparent trends, leaves room for optimism in terms of total enrollment. There is still an impressive number of students in foreign language classes and, in spite of a "tight" market for teaching positions, explained in part by an overkill in the number of teachers trained in the past, a high level of employment still prevails for foreign language instructors.[30] In short, we are not talking about a major salvage operation requiring a complete reversal of trends. We are suggesting that identification of problem areas, analysis of alternate ways of attacking the problems, of setting priorities that are likely to provide more effective programs might indeed be the major task for the seventies.

It may well be that the current period of stress will have a salutary effect as it reduces the tensions between traditionalists and "innovators," between humanists and educationists, between the colleges, secondary schools, and the grades. The instinct for survival may well serve to mitigate contentions as the profession concentrates on a common effort to solve problems which, regardless of ideological stance, affect all levels of instruction.

PROJECTIONS FOR THE SEVENTIES

In defense of our projections which may appear too pedestrian, too pedagogically oriented, let us indicate that we are aware that today's pen pals may become the phone pals of the seventies, indulging in Telstar communications across the world. We also project increasingly sophisticated, prototypical self-instructional carrels in which the student will have access, through television, tapes, and the computer, to a selection of self-instructional programs. We are also aware of changing practices through which the students' creative propensities will be exploited in more "open" dialogues, structured as impromptu, relevant conversations by the participating students.

We are reasonably sure that all of these space fiction practices will bear fruit in the next few years. We are less confident that they will be available to the majority of students, that the tools can be perfected in so short a span of time. In our opinion, the seventies may be more ready for consolidation in a period of transition than for implementation of visionary techniques.

Because of this conviction, we are striving to direct attention to a narrow area where implementation seems more feasible, where there is greater opportunity to exploit the gains of the previous generation, where immediate attention is needed since it involves *all* students and eventually serves to determine the path and degree of language exposure for these students.

We have chosen to focus our projections on the initial phase of foreign language instruction as needing radical revision, as central to the modification of all subsequent instruction, as providing the linguistic base line for continuing programs.[31]

Our projections in this area will perhaps give the impression of having an exaggerated pedagogical orientation. This, in a sense, is inevitable since the reorganization of the learning climate is principally a professional responsibility. We hope that the implications for more responsive student behavior, for modifications in the curriculum, for administrative decisions will be apparent as product is related to instructional input.

During the 1970's increasing attention will be given to student responses as an index of the appropriateness of goals, teaching strategies, and course content. We do not see this trend as an irresponsible transfer of responsibility leading, at best to chaos and, at worst, to sterile activities resulting from the teacher's abrogating his responsibilities as expert in the subject and the way it is taught. Rather, we project a systematic and continuing inquiry leading to improved learning (and teaching) in which students (through their reactions and suggestions) and teachers (through their observations and individual innovations) provide a vast corpus of data. Available for analysis, this information will result in subsequent recommendations by research agencies at the national level. Needless to say, we anticipate student responses to vary in sophistication, to reflect the needs of students at various levels from elementary through graduate school. Whereas the third grader will throw light on what activities are "enjoyable," the graduate student will emphasize what is essential to his career objectives.

There is already evidence that a thoughtful portion of the foreign language profession is sensitive to student opinion.[32] It must equally be prepared to incorporate student reactions into its future plans and procedures. There is growing recognition that students bring to the foreign language task different expectations based on differences in age, social milieu, and career orientation, and that, furthermore, they see foreign language instruction from different attitudinal perspectives depending on individual academic orientations. In addition, each student brings to the subject widely divergent aptitudes for coping with some of the peculiar demands made by the nature of foreign language learning. It is imperative that the profession consider the problem of *individualized* instruction as the *sine qua non* of maintaining foreign languages in the schools.

We interpret individualization in a much broader sense than providing different tapes for individual students as a means of enabling them to reach the same level of proficiency roughly within the same time constraints. We prefer to think of individualization as the opportunity for students to explore, during initial exposure, their capacities for handling the several skills, to exploit their preferences, to exercise the prerogative of studying at a particular time, for an appropriate period what seems productive and rewarding.

We are suggesting a flexible language program which is the antithesis of one based on "requirements" or justified in terms of vocational or abstract academic goals, the type of program which constrains all students to demonstrate proficiency "on schedule" in terms of narrowly defined linguistic objectives.

The new program must provide opportunity for success in at least one language skill as a means of eliciting, maintaining and increasing interest in the total foreign language process. It is imperative that the full resources of the profession be devoted to structuring an initial experience which, while permitting proper diagnosis, will ensure maximum opportunity for linguistic achievement.

We project the initial component of such a program to have several characteristics. The lexical and structural parameters must be clearly defined and must be accepted and adopted as the core of instruction in all schools and at all levels of instruction. The topical content must be "relevant" to the current scene and appropriate to utilization beyond the confines of the classroom. Within this rigid framework, provisions must be made for individual concentration on any single skill or on a combination of all skills without prescription as to a predetermined sequence. A mastery learning approach, based on achievement rather than time exposure, must constitute the basis of instruction and evaluation. Each student's total potential will be brought to bear on the learning task: his gift for mimicking, for memorizing, for intellectualizing, will be nurtured according to the individual's aptitudes. In short, each student will have the opportunity to succeed while working at his own pace in at least one section of the component. The measure of his success in the respective language skills will determine in what way and toward what subsequent goals he should proceed.

The prescriptive aspects we propose will undoubtedly be resisted as threatening to teacher autonomy and demeaning to the "art" of teaching. We suggest, that with a more specific content parameter, more inventive strategies can be encouraged and exercised to meet the multiple goals possible within the common framework.

We are convinced that a situation can no longer be tolerated in which a multitude of texts reflecting personal "inspiration" or commitment to disparate content and methods lead to conditions where articulation is impossible, where evaluation is arbitrary and where neither teachers nor students know where they are or where they are going in terms of normative standards.

It is time that the long-standing recommendation as to control of lexicon and structures (see p. 117) be implemented, that the work accomplished in the intervening years particularly in connection with frequency lists for the "popular" Western European languages be translated into coherent and uniform materials.[33] The criterion of "currency" must be superimposed on the frequency lists already available. The latter presupposes research into what students say to each other in situations outside of the classroom in the hope that incorporation of this type of lexicon into the materials will stimulate substitution of the foreign language for English in informal situations. This task is not insurmountable and well within the purview of existing professional resources.

Control over the *content* of instruction rather than over the *method* of instruction suggests the possibility of achieving extreme flexibility without resultant chaos. Any clearly delineated corpus of material can be viewed from different perspectives depending on what language skill is being taught and what subskills are seen as essential to mastery of that particular skill. Clear understanding of the relationship of each subskill to the total process increases the prospects of structuring exercises and using teaching modalities which will lead to more efficient learning (or remediation) by ensuring mastery of the subparts essential to achievement of the final linguistic task.[34] Furthermore, mastery of any discrete amount of material (rather than exposure to a vaguely defined continuum) will also serve to convince the student of the immediate functionality of the foreign language and tend to neutralize the disenchantment which gradually develops as continuing investment of effort is justified only in terms of ever-receding rewards.

A more systematic approach to the foreign language learning process may well renew interest in existing electronic audio-visual aids and stimulate the design and application of new devices. The language laboratory, for instance, may again become an important tool if it can be respecified for whom, to what end, and under what consideration it can be most effective. The renascent interest in the reading skill calls for adaptation of existing electronic devices for the purpose of developing correct oral reading habits in the foreign language. The possibilities and limitations of programmed instruction need be reviewed to assess the extent of their effectiveness with respect to the respective subskills. Eventually, specific ways in which the computer can assist foreign language instruction must be determined.

Specificity will also provide a better focus for utilizing available drill materials and techniques, for identifying areas in which little is available, for development of presentational and remedial techniques in areas yet unexplored.

The central thrust on a common instructional problem will have inevitable implications for teaching (and teacher training). Assuming that the best teachers will be involved in the initial phase of instruction, we project that, even among these, no single person will be equipped to deal with all the aspects of differentiated teaching suggested in the above. We see this as leading to specialization, to differentiated staffing, to a situation in which teaching as well as learning is individualized.

Working with materials as a constant, removing what, to date, has been a built-in variable will facilitate the task of researchers and permit a more direct application of research findings to improved learning conditions. Research, in addition to measuring the effectiveness of various instructional strategies aimed at very specific objectives, may turn its attention to the interrelationship of these objectives and to problems of improved sequencing as appropriate to pupils of different aptitudes. More basic studies will use this vast laboratory to isolate such important factors in the basic languages learning process as memorization and retention. Lastly, continued attention will be paid to the complicated phenomenon of motivation as it relates to success and participation, to basic attitudes toward school in general and toward the foreign language in particular.

Implementation of a common "preparation" course will, in many cases, lead to experimentation in the distribution of contact time. The modular schedule approach is ideal for attacking specific language skills and subskills in a given module and provides an ideal pattern for differentiated programs based on recognized need for remediation in some areas and/or pursuit of skill goals determined by individual predilection. Where modular scheduling is not in effect it will be instituted to accommodate the new approach to foreign language learning.

There will be a new interest in the saturation approach, that is, in concentrating initial foreign language exposure to one quarter or one semester in blocks of three or four hours a day, during which time extensive use will be made of individualized programs and audio-visual devices. Saturation will permit testing the effectiveness of the "total immersion" principle. By shortening the time between initiation and reaching functional competence, students will be able to enjoy subsequent foreign language courses sooner, will be prepared earlier for double credit courses in other subject areas conducted in the foreign language, or simply for nonacademic use of the language. Early mastery of a basic repertoire will also make study abroad more rewarding.

Where the school, because of size, lack of financial resources, or conflicting policies, cannot support a sustained program, subcontractors will be called upon to supply the necessary instruction. Small communities, unable to support major language programs in individual buildings, will either turn to consolidated foreign language centers capable of handling students from several feeder schools or, again, rely on commercial agencies to provide the service. Centers and outside resources will become the standard way of providing instruction in those foreign languages which, because of limited enrollment, cannot be economically justified in the school's curriculum (Russian, Chinese, Japanese, etc.).

A realistic clarification of the relationship of culture to language skills from a pedagogical point of view will result in several modifications of the present *modus operandi.*

The integration of culture and language has led to some observable difficulties. The student struggling with language learning seldom tends to reflect on the degree to which his labor is contributing to the breakdown of monocultural tendencies. The teacher, pressed for time and competent in various degrees to "teach" the cultural dimension, often pays only lip service to this area. Discrepancy between the degree of language competence of the student and his intellectual capacity to be interested in and deal with sophisticated aspects of the foreign culture constitutes an even more serious impediment.

Recognizing these serious limitations in achieving acculturation points to a revision of current practices. Culture units will be available *in English* and offered by people competent in the methods of the Social Sciences. It is not inconceivable that some foreign language teachers might be or may become the best qualified persons to teach such units. (Here again the principle of specialization and staff differentiation applies.)

Accepting this point of view suggests that exposure to culture can become immediately relevant to students. Visuals (films in particular) can play an important role regardless of the language of the commentary. Pending the time when it can be done in the foreign language, sophisticated discussion appropriate to the interest and maturation of students can take place based on books, or periodicals written in English. In short, the study of a foreign culture can be validated for its own sake and exploited as a motivating force *before* and *independently* of achieving language competence.

Less emphasis will be placed on studying the "great" Western European cultures. Greater attention will be paid to the empathy which various groups of Americans have for cultural values which they deem part of their heritage. The pattern has already been set with respect to

Spanish-speaking Americans and will be extended to meet the needs of other groups. The interest of American Blacks in emerging African nations is a case in point.

In some cases, cultural interest will stimulate interest in the language of the geographical areas in question. Fascination for Israel is certainly responsible for the institution of an increasing number of offerings in modern Hebrew. The study of Swahili, as indigenous to much of Africa, is considered by some as "legitimate" as the study of French, official language of many African countries.

In addition more latitude will be provided as to the range of cultural studies. The prevailing equations French: France, Spanish: Spain will be reinterpreted to include respectively *all* francophone countries (even long-neglected Canada) and all Spanish-speaking countries, regardless of the geographical distribution or the relative importance of their respective literary heritage.

Lastly, the direction of cultural interaction will be radically modified. Whereas current texts and syllabi concentrate on bringing Mecca to the American scene, a new, important dimension will be added: the impact of American culture and of the American language on the world at large will be seriously considered. This new emphasis will more realistically address itself to the concept of one-worldness and will be provocative to American students observing that their language, their experiences and their concerns are reflected in the press, in the customs, and in the quest of youth the world over.

SUMMARY

We have deliberately concentrated our projections to a very limited part of the foreign language continuum. We have felt impelled to do this out of a conviction that unless some dramatic improvement occurs at the national level in terms of the introductory phase of foreign language teaching, the total sequence, in terms of academic justification, continued enrollment and functional terminal goal, is in great jeopardy. We are less concerned with a reduction in total enrollment than with a disgraceful dropout rate attributable to nebulous goals, incoherent instruction, and questionable results.

We have focused on a discrete area of instruction as the best way of exploiting the gains achieved in the last 20 years, of bringing positive strength to bear on those areas of legitimate concern which have been neglected or which have been obscured by an overenthusiastic commitment to the apparent panacea of exclusive and narrowly defined audio-lingualism.

The incontestable achievements of the period, professional solidarity, impressive instruments for the collection and dissemination of information and data, a more enlightened and effective teaching corps, available tests and testing procedures, establishment of lexical and structural base lines can, it seems to us, best serve the cause of foreign language study if efforts are concentrated in a collective endeavor with common focus rather than diffused to meet a number of legitimate but disparate goals. We feel that progress is more certain where the criteria of need and feasibility are convergent.

The concepts outlined above point to the possibility of investigating in depth a number of problems neglected since 1948. Our projections suggest a systematic review of appropriate societal and individual objectives within a more flexible and sensitive instructional context. We have also alluded to the possibility of rigorous research to determine the effect of instruction as it relates to aptitudes, attitudes, and learning rate. We maintain that there is a need to determine the relationship of various skills, particularly reading, to each other for purposes of sequencing. We submit that a renewed exploration of saturation techniques can lead to more extensive use of the foreign language in other content areas.

We are indeed proposing a total research program in lieu of fragmentary research aimed principally at validating narrow hypotheses. We are proposing a methodology which will exploit linguistic findings to date while encouraging linguists and psychologists to assist in resolving newly identified and defined complexities. We are suggesting that classroom performance, systematically measured, can supplement prognostic tests as an accurate index not only as to *who* should study foreign languages but also as to *what* skill these students should pursue and as to *how* the sequence can be structured to reduce the possibility of failure and discouragement. We submit that this concentrated effort will facilitate articulation, improve student motivation and provide a basis for more efficient use of time and equipment.

We are confident that the profession's concentration on a narrow area will in no way stifle innovations and imaginative individual efforts. Excellent instruction will continue for such advanced students as have managed to survive the elementary maze. Some will learn to express themselves in the foreign language and many will learn to appreciate literature. An increasing number will "complete their education" through residence abroad.

We are aware that unpredictable factors may affect foreign language instruction in the next decade. Isolationism may increase. Financial support may become even more restricted. Student perceptions may lead them increasingly to curricular areas which meet political and experiential needs. Prevailing educational philosophies may proscribe skill development activities more convincingly than in the past. But, while these discernible trends may continue, it is not impossible that the decade of the seventies will witness a degree of reaction which will contribute to the reversal of some or all of them. It is highly possible that the student population will split into a politically oriented, existentially motivated sector while another opts for such "traditional" academic activities as will meet its rediscovered goals. For many, we hope, a compulsion to pursue knowledge as a delectable, personal activity, uncontaminated by utilitarian considerations, may replace the current fixation on "relevance."

It is this group that the foreign language profession must be prepared to serve. If it succeeds in structuring an initial experience which is meaningful and productive, which serves either as a terminal course or as preparation for continued success, it will have accomplished an impressive task: sufficient reward for the labor of a single decade.

NOTES

1. For an elaboration of this phenomenon, see Joshua A. Fishman (ed.) in *Readings in the Sociology of Language* (The Hague: Mouton, 1968).

2. Algernon Coleman, *The Teaching of Modern Languages in the United States* (Chicago: The University of Chicago Press, 1929).

3. Paul F. Angiolillo, *Armed Forces' Foreign Language Teaching* (New York: S. F. Vanni, 1947).

4. Frederick B. Agard and Harold B. Dunkel, *An Investigation of Second Language Teaching* (Boston: Ginn and Company, 1948).

5. Harold B. Dunkel, *Second Language Learning* (Boston: Ginn and Company, 1948).

6. For the name of the participants in the conference and the complete "Resolutions" quoted in part in this section, see Harold Dunkel, *Second Language Learning,* op. cit., Appendix B, pp. 191-96.

7. William Riley Parker, *The National Interest and Foreign Languages,* Department of State Publication No. 7324 (3d ed.; Washington, D.C., U.S. Government Printing Office, 1962).

8. For these and subsequent remarks dealing with federal commitment to improved foreign language instruction we are indebted to John S. Diekhoff, *NDEA and Modern Foreign Languages* (New York: Modern Language Association, 1965), Chart, p. 127.

9. One of the first such surveys is the *Reports of Surveys and Studies in the Teaching of Modern Foreign Languages* (New York: Modern Language Association, 1961). The 21 studies cover a wide range of topics (enrollment, curriculum evaluation, etc.). We call attention to "The Teaching of German in the United States from Colonial Times to the Present" by Edwin H. Zeidel and "The Teaching of Spanish in the United States" by Sturgess E. Leavitt, "The Teaching of French in the United States: A History" by George B. Watts which appeared in the *French Review,* Vol. XXXVII, No. 1 (October, 1963). See also Albert Parry, *America Learns Russian* (Syracuse, N.Y.: Syracuse University Press, 1967).

10. We refer to the Modern Language Association Foreign Language Proficiency Tests for Teachers and Advanced Students and to the Modern Language Cooperative Tests. For a list of other commercial tests, see Rebecca M. Valette, *Modern Language Testing* (New York: Harcourt, Brace and World, Inc., 1967).

11. See Alfred S. Hayes, *Language Laboratory Facilities,* Bulletin No. 37 (Washington, D.C.: U.S. Government Printing Office, 1963).

12. See Marjorie C. Johnson and others, *Modern Foreign Languages: A Counselor's Guide,* Bulletin No. 20 (Washington, D.C.: Office of Education, 1960); and Ilo Remer, *A Handbook for Guiding Students in Modern Foreign Languages,* Bulletin No. 26 (Washington, D.C.: Office of Education, 1963).

13. Sponsored by the Modern Language Association, the American Council on the Teaching of Foreign Languages (ACTFL) was created in 1966. In the brief interim, ACTFL has demonstrated vigorous leadership in the foreign language field and through the *Foreign Language Annals* justified the existence of one additional organization to meet professional needs at a national level without overlap and undue competition with other regional or language-specific groups.

14. Emma M. Birkmaier (ed.), *Britannica Review of Foreign Language Education,* Vol. I (Chicago: Encyclopaedia Britannica, Inc., 1968); Dale L. Lange (ed.), *Britannica Review of Foreign Language Education,* Vol. II (Chicago: Encyclopaedia Britannica, Inc., 1970).

15. The Educational Resources Information Center is a nationwide information system. The Modern Language Association (62 Fifth Avenue, New York, N.Y.) conducts the ERIC clearinghouse on the Teaching of Foreign Languages. *Foreign Language Annals* the official journal of the American Council on the

Teaching of Foreign Languages, provides a regular review of ERIC developments.

16. From an instructive account of the FLES movement, see Theodore Andersson, *Foreign Languages in the Elementary School* (Austin, Tex.: University of Texas Press, 1969). Mildred Donoghue, *Foreign Languages and the Elementary School Child* (Dubuque, Ia.: William C. Brown Company, 1968), is an invaluable guide to practices and materials appropriate in the grades.

17. An evaluation of our own FLES program (Harold B. Dunkel and Roger A. Pillet, *French in the Elementary School* [Chicago: The University of Chicago Press, 1962]) confirmed our opinion that, for many children, the experience had been productive. We and others have continued FLES in that conviction. We see the current retrenchment as caused by a combination of external factors rather than by the ineffectiveness of good FLES programs. See also Roger A. Pillet's "The Impact of FLES: An Appraisal," *Modern Language Journal,* Vol. LII (December, 1968).

18. Among the major contributions of linguistics, we cite M. A. F. Holliday, Angus McIntosh, and Peter Strevens, *The Linguistic Sciences and Language Teaching* (Bloomington, Ind.: Indiana University Press, 1964); Charles A. Ferguson and others, *Linguistic Reading Lists for Teachers of Modern Languages* (Washington, D.C., 1963); also the works of Robert L. Politzer, *Teaching French* (Boston: Ginn and Company, 1960); *Teaching German* (Waltham, Mass.: Blaisdell Publishing Co., 1968); and (with C. Stanback) *Teaching Spanish* (Boston: Ginn and Company, 1961). We also call attention to Charles A. Ferguson (ed.), *Contrastive Structure* Series (Chicago: The University of Chicago Press, 1962–65) dealing with contrasts in sound and structures of English with Spanish, Russian, and German and the D. C. Heath "Series" providing insights into the phonology of French, German, Spanish, Russian and Italian.

19. *The Linguistic Reporter,* Newsletter of the Center for Applied Linguistics, 1717 Massachusetts Avenue, N.W., Washington, D.C.

20. One of the best overviews of the use of media in foreign language teaching is provided by Elton Hocking in *Language Laboratory and Language Learning* (Washington, D.C.: NEA, Department of Audio-Visual Instruction, 1964).

21. For a sympathetic analysis of the teacher's plight, see Roger A. Pillet "Demands of New Dimensions," *The School Review,* Vol. 73, No. 2 (Summer, 1965).

22. A balanced discussion of the relative merits of different methodologies can be found in Wilga M. Rivers, *Teaching Foreign Language Skills* (Chicago: The University of Chicago Press, 1968).

23. A good overview (and an extensive bibliography of this much discussed area) is available in H. Ned Seelye, "Analysis and Teaching of Cross Cultural Context," *Britannica Review,* Vol. 1, pp. 37-81, footnote 14.

24. Illustration of a modest effort in this direction is provided in the FLES Report of AATF, Roger A. Pillet (ed.), *FLES and the Objectives of the Contemporary Schools* (Philadelphia: Chilton Books, 1967).

25. For a brief discussion of this area, see Roger A. Pillet, "Teacher Education in Foreign Languages: An Overview," *Modern Language Journal,* Vol. LIV, No. 1 (January, 1970).

26. Our own views on the subject are outlined in "Individualizing Foreign Language Instruction," *Foreign Language Notes,* Department of Foreign Languages of NEA, Vol. 5, No. 2 (December, 1967).

27. We have in mind the following studies: Raymond F. Keating, *A Study of the Effectiveness of Language Laboratories* (New York: The Institute of Administrative Research, Teachers College, Columbia University, 1963); George Sherer and Michael Wertheimer, *A Psycholinguistic Experiment in Foreign Language Teaching* (New York: McGraw-Hill Book Co., 1964): The "Pennsylvania Study," Philip D. Smith, Jr. and others, *A Comparison Study of the Effectiveness of the Traditional Audio-Lingual Approach to Foreign Language Instruction Utilizing Laboratory Equipment* (Washington, D.C.: U.S. Department of Health Education and Welfare, 1969). Each of these studies caused much ink to flow. All of them were disappointing, particularly in the sense that the findings were not overwhelmingly conclusive with respect to the effectiveness of "new key" practices.

28. John B. Carrolls in "Foreign Language Proficiency Levels Attained by Language Majors Near Graduation from College," *Foreign Language Annals,* Vol. 1, No. 2 (December, 1967) concludes: "It is pointless to try to summarize an essentially statistical report like this. The study has provocative and even disturbing things to say about the attainment of foreign language majors in our colleges. The overall level of attainment of these foreign language students, particularly in the audio-lingual skills, leaves something to be desired when judged against a criterion of what could be reasonably expected of them. At the same time, the study suggests a number of ways in which the instruction and training of foreign language majors might be improved."

29. Following is a sample of this type of research: Joseph M. Vocolo, "The Effect of Foreign Language Study in the Elementary School upon Achievement in the Same Foreign Language in the High School," *The Modern Language Journal,* Vol. LI, No. 8 (December, 1967), pp. 463-69; Evelyn Brega and John M. Newell, "High School Performance of FLES and Non-FLES Students," *The Modern Language Journal,* Vol. LI, No. 7 (November, 1967), pp. 408-11; Joseph Justman and Martin L. Naas, "The High School Achievement of Pupils Who Were and Were Not Introduced to a Foreign Language in the Elementary School," *The Modern Language Journal,* Vol. XL, No. 3 (March, 1966), pp. 120-23; Mildred R. Donoghue, "Spánish in the Elementary Schools: What Research Tells Us about the Effects of FLES," *Hispania,* Vol. XLVIII, No. 3 (September, 1965).

30. For a discussion of enrollment figures, see John P. Dusel in Volume I of *Britannica Review, op. cit.* (pp. 415-38) and Richard I. Brod in Vol. II (pp. 341-62). The table below is reprinted with permission from *The Britannica Review of Foreign Language Education,* Volume II, copyright 1970 by Encyclopaedia Britannica, Inc., Chicago.

TABLE 4

Trends in Registrations in the Five Leading Modern
Languages 1960-68 (All Types of Institutions), by Language

	1960	1963	1965	1968
French . . .	228,813	302,226	371,625	388,096
German. . .	146,110	182,609	213,901	216,263
Italian. . . .	11,142	16,874	22,920	30,359
Russian. . .	30,570	33,538	33,710	40,696
Spanish. . .	178,689	246,673	310,340	364,870
Total	595,324	781,920	952,496	1,040,284

Index of growth (1960 = 100)

	1963	1965	1968	1960-63	1963-65	1965-68
French.	132.1	162.4	169.6	32.1	23.0	4.4
German	125.0	146.4	148.0	25.0	17.1	1.1
Italian	151.4	205.7	272.5	51.4	35.8	32.5
Russian	109.7	110.3	133.1	9.7	0.5	20.7
Spanish	138.0	173.7	204.2	38.0	25.8	17.6
Total.	131.3	159.9	174.7	31.3	21.8	9.2

31. We see the initial period as corresponding to the current concept of "Level 1" with emphasis on achievement of a given corpus of material rather than on a given time limit. We suggest, however, that, as a diagnostic period, "Level 1" should probably not be extended for over a year in the secondary school and one semester at the college level. We are aware that efforts are in progress to delineate the content of "Level 1." We are afraid that, to date, definition reflects local rather than national consensus and that emphasis has been placed on structures while the choice of vocabulary remains an arbitrary decision.

32. As an example, see "Foreign Languages and the 'New' Student," in Joseph E. Tursi (ed.), *Reports of the Working Committees of the Northeast Conference on the Teaching of Foreign Languages* (New York: MLA Materials Center, 1970).

33. In spite of the reservations which are legitimate in considering criteria for any kind of frequency list we suggest provisional acceptance of the lists available (Le Français Fondamental, for example) as a productive expedient until such time as a more refined lexical stock has been determined. Analysis of the vocabulary loading of classroom texts currently in use reveals that relatively few vocabulary items are common to the popular "Series."

34. The following schema of skills and subskills points to the variety of subskills which can be attained singly or in combination with each other.

I. *Aural Understanding*
   The student can
   a) discriminate among auditory cues
   b) identify signals provided by
      1. stems
      2. morphological segments
      3. syntactical features
      4. intonational features
   c) identify subcomponents
   d) conceptualize the total message in terms of the above information

II. *Speaking*
   The student can
   a) produce all necessary phonemes correctly
   b) recall appropriate
      1. stems
      2. morphological segments
      3. syntactical signals
   c) produce the total message
      1. with proper breath groups
      2. with proper stress characteristics
      3. with proper intonation
      4. with reasonable "flow"

III. *Reading**
   A. Oral Reading
   The student can
      1. Produce the phoneme corresponding to
         a) single letters
         b) letter combination
         c) anomalies
         d) diacritical modification
      2. Read aloud the total message
         a) with proper breath groups
         b) with proper stress characteristics
         c) with proper intonation
         d) without undue "stoppage"
   B. Context Reading
   The student can
      1. Identify the signals provided by
         a) stems
         b) morphological segments
         c) syntactical features

       d) diacritical signals

       e) punctuation marks

    2. Identify subcomponents of the total message

    3. Conceptualize the total message in terms of the above information

IV. *Writing**

   A. Spelling

   The student can spell correctly

    1. on the basis of oral repertoire (or recall)

       a) single letters reflecting phonemic-graphemic correspondence

       b) letter combinations reflecting phonemic graphemic correspondence

    2. on the basis of recall

       a) silent letters

       b) anomalies

       c) diacritical signs

       d) morphological segments

       e) punctuation marks

   B. Composition

   The student can

    1. recall appropriate

       a) stems

       b) morphological devices

       c) syntactical devices

    2. Organize subcomponents of total message

    3. Relate components of total message to each other

    4. Produce total message in writing at reasonable speed

   *In the case of several languages (e.g., Russian, Greek) calligraphy constitutes an additional subskill.

MAX S. BELL
The University of Chicago

V MATHEMATICS EDUCATION FOR THE NEXT DECADE—NEW EMPHASES IN THE WAKE OF THE "NEW MATH"

INTRODUCTION

In attempting yet another assessment of the prospects for changes in the school mathematics experience, one naturally reviews what others have said on this matter, both those on the contemporary scene and their predecessors. Such a review can only leave one with a profound sense of discouragement. Everything needful has been said, it seems; persuasively, repeatedly and with justified urgency for over 50 years. Yet little seems to change, and the school mathematics experience for most people is dangerously, incredibly, poor, considering the actual requirements of our actual world. On the other hand, such a review reveals that over the years many good things have happened here and there, and some things almost everywhere. These would justify optimism if only they could be extended to larger populations or developed to fulfill the promise they seem to hold out.

The several emphases of this chapter are reflected by its division into four main parts. First, the sense of urgency felt by those close to mathematics education seems to be shared by very few others. That is, there seems to be some sort of cultural lag between the actual mathematical needs imposed by the world we live in and the awareness of these needs on the part of most people. Hence, this introduction includes an orientation to those needs as seen by mathematics educators. Second, in school mathematics education the most significant event of this century has been the widespread acceptance within the decade just ended of what is popularly known as "the new mathematics." Since few people know what lies behind that phrase, the second main section gives a definition. Third, the curriculum reforms that comprise the new mathematics were soon seen to have had much less effect than the reformers assumed they would have and a painful assessment of that fact coupled with a number of new initiatives have also been a part of the decade just past. A summary of what this looks like on the current scene comprises the third main section. Fourth, realistic and likely extrapolations from this current scene over the next decade will be considered, followed by some desirable things that would also be *possible* as extrapolations from the present scene but which for a variety of reasons are relatively unlikely. The chapter will close with several "postscripts" that support points made briefly in the chapter and with a brief bibliography.

An Orientation to Mathematics Education

There can be no doubt that mathematics education over the next decade must be a prime concern of many people, and not only those who are mathematicians or mathematics educators. For better or worse in the world we have built countless fields of work and inquiry have come to depend heavily on mathematical methods. Nor is this true only of our science and technology. Social, business, political, and economic decisions increasingly depend both on understanding information given in various mathematical forms, and on use of mathematical tools to facilitate decision making. Hence, anyone with poor understanding of certain basic mathematical tools and concepts is to that extent a stranger to the actual world he lives in and to that extent unable to exercise responsible citizenship or control over events. Furthermore, for increasingly large numbers of people, poor understanding of mathematics constitutes a serious handicap in pursuing one's daily work. Unfortunately, for many years and for the majority of people, poor understanding has been the net result of school mathematics instruction, and we have grown tolerant of this fact. But now with mathematics such a dominant factor in everyman's life, this can no longer be accepted.

Since most of the intended audience for this book will not be mathematics educators, a brief introduction to mathematics education may be helpful. To begin with, everyone knows that 'Rithmetic—the third R—has long been a major part of elementary school instruction. The x's of algebra and theorems of geometry have long been hurdles to be jumped (or scaled) by high school students with college aspirations. Each year beyond the elementary grades some of the survivors of the previous year took the next course in line. By mid century it was clear that there were too few survivors, and even those were poorly trained. Consequently, widespread alarms were sounded, from which there ensued the following sequence of events.

The "new mathematics" reform decade (starting about 1958) showed that substantial change in school mathematics can be accomplished in a relatively brief period, and that there can be effective cooperation among mathematical scholars, school teachers, mathematics educators, and others. There was rapid progress in changing the content of textbooks over the whole K–12 school range and use of these textbooks is now the rule in nearly all "good" schools serving relatively privileged youngsters; less so otherwise. There was much progress with education and reeducation of teachers of pretty much the same relatively privileged groups; again less so otherwise. There was an enormous amount of "research" done during the decade, most of it inconclusive and of little direct use, but with many intriguing results to follow up on. Finally, the reform decade produced considerable agreement on *what* should be taught, if not on how or when.

Beginning about mid-decade, and in full flower by now, widespread disillusionment set in because the substantial accomplishments just outlined were having little basic effect. Larger numbers of students were taking more and better mathematics (hence the initial reform aims were met) but for most people the school mathematics experience was still very poor. This served to dispel much of the optimism about rapid achievement of basic and thorough changes that had permeated the reform movement. It also began to reveal the extent of our ignorance and call into question a number of our basic assumptions. In particular, what was thought to be the basic problem (content of text-books) turned out to be only the easiest problem.

Most distressing to many was the failure to remove the disparity between the results of "everyman's" mathematical education and the obvious needs of the times. The chief problems in this area seem to be these:

a) The early school experience of a child is probably a crucial factor in his later learning, but we haven't begun to implement a really effective early school mathematics experience.

b) At least until we get the early school experience in hand and effective for most children, we need effective remedial procedures for salvage (by the middle school years at latest) of as many youngsters as possible. We do not have such procedures, though encouraging work has been done in a few places.

c) Everyone acknowledges the need to "teach mathematics so as to be useful"[1] but no such emphasis appears in any current school curricula.

d) Teachers adequately trained for tasks *(a–c)* just above were seen very early in the reform years as a crucial missing link, and this is still the case.

The reform decade persuaded most of us that a substantial research and theory building effort is a clear necessity, grounded first of all in gathering and assimilating clinical and empirical data. Though it seems surprising, we have only begun to realize the extent to which we have relied on unsupported assumptions (now shown to be in fact questionable). There are very few empirically supported theories to guide and inform our efforts.[2]

Mathematics educators became increasingly conscious of the need to consider the general school situation beyond the mathematics class-rooms and with many others now see many barriers there to the basic reforms that seem essential.

Some Assumptions of Mathematics Educators

The reform efforts have brought us to a new awareness of the magnitude of the tasks still to be accomplished. As a further orientation for those unfamiliar with mathematics education consider some of the assumptions shared by many of us as we now tackle these tasks.

The root intuition for many mathematics concepts and skills is best, and sometimes perhaps only, implanted early. The early mathematics experience is as crucial to later learning of mathematics (and fields that use mathematics) as is ability to read is to later studies in English, social studies, etc.

Mathematics learning is to some extent sequential. We aren't as sure as we once seemed to be that we know what the optimal sequence is, but we do insist that a random order of presentation is unlikely to be effective, and that one cannot arbitrarily skip certain learnings without causing later difficulties.

For most people a well-organized and well-taught experience is essential to learning mathematics. It is not easy to learn mathematics on one's own initiative, in part because of its sequential nature as just discussed and in part because unlike humanities, science, and much social science, few books exist from which a student can learn by reading on his own. Environment or everyday experiences are unlikely by themselves to teach much mathematics, though they can be utilized to make learning more interesting or lively.

For several of the foregoing reasons, mathematics learning is very much dependent on good teaching. For most people, interest in mathematics dies at the point they take a poorly taught course, or one for which they are unprepared. Indeed, the successful survivor of mathematics instruction has usually either been quite lucky in his teachers, or is one of those rare people who doesn't need a teacher.

The teacher of mathematics at any school level should have mathematics training sufficient to illuminate the foundations of the subjects he teaches. This training should have resulted in a thorough, gut level understanding of basic mathematical concepts and a broad view of what mathematics consists of and how it is used.

It is widely assumed by those outside mathematics education that school mathematics is *the* prime example of a field with clear-cut, uncomplicated objectives (usually seen as a set of definite arithmetic skills) that can be easily evaluated by "objective" tests. On the contrary, though certain arithmetic and symbol manipulation skills are a *necessary* part of mathematics learning, they are no more the whole story than is alphabet learning or spelling for the language arts; or memorizing names, dates, and places for history. What everyman needs is far more complicated and fundamental than a set of arithmetic reflexes.

Some of these assumptions may in the long run turn out to be untenable, but they do shape much current thinking in mathematics education. With this brief introduction to mathematics education let us turn to consideration of the widely publicized but little understood "new mathematics" that is the most prominent mathematics education event of the decade just completed.

THE NEW MATHEMATICS

Mathematics education since 1900 has been characterized by alarms at about 20-year intervals, resulting in published reform recommendations from prestigious groups and individuals. These have usually been followed by varying amounts of reform activity, then by decades where such reforms are partially absorbed and become clichés. Previous reform decades can be identified by the work of Perry and Moore about 1900;[3] a landmark joint commission report in the early 1920's;[4] and a later joint commission report whose effect was largely vitiated by World War II.[5] Each of these reports coincided with indications of concern from a number of sources.

In the meantime, the mathematical sciences themselves were experiencing extraordinary growth, presenting by 1950 a completely different landscape than, say, 50 years earlier.[6] Mathematics has long been important in such fields as the physical sciences but an astonishing range of new applications have been discovered in the past 30 years, especially since the development of practical electronic computers about 1950. But little of the phenomenal growth of mathematics and its uses was reflected in undergraduate college curricula (hence in the training of teachers) and there was no effect whatever on school mathematics. Elementary school aimed only to inculcate a set of arithmetic procedures; junior high school merely reviewed these. (See postscript 1.) High school college preparatory mathematics was dominated by "cookbook" algebra in the 9th and 11th grades; a pale imitation of plane and solid Euclidean geometry in the 10th and 12th grades; and a trigonometry course at least 100 years out of date. (As a beginning teacher in the late 1950's in an excellent suburban high school, I was given a set of textbooks first published about 1890 for use with my senior level trigonometry class—surveying and ship navigation dominated the problem sections.)

By 1956 the disparity between the rich growth of mathematics and its uses as opposed to the stagnant quality of school mathematics could be characterized as a "national weakness" and was generating widespread alarm.[7] Excellent work to correct the situation was already begun by such groups as the influential but seldom acknowledged College Mathematics Staff of the University of Chicago, the University of Illinois Committee on School Mathematics, and the University of Maryland Mathematics Project. In 1955 the College Entrance Examination Board set up its Commission on Mathematics, which by 1958 had circulated a draft report that became virtually a handbook for what was later dubbed by journalists "The New Mathematics."[8] Things happened very quickly thereafter: A joint commission of mathematics professional organizations met and formed the School Mathematics Study Group (SMSG) with E. G. Begle as director, and obtained substantial financial backing from the National Science Foundation (NSF). (SMSG was by no means the only organization active in the reform, but it was the largest and is sufficiently representative to characterize "the new mathematics" reform.) Within weeks outlining and writing teams were at work and that same autumn some units were tried in schools. On the basis of these preliminary soundings, a massive writing effort took place in the summer of 1959, and the entire range of new courses for "college capable" students in grades 7 through 12 was available for trial by the end of that same summer. Several groups of high school teachers used the materials that school year, meeting regularly with university mathematician consultants, and submitting evaluations based on actual student use. On the basis of these trials, writing teams produced completely revised versions of the secondary school textbooks, as well as voluminous teacher commentaries, during the summer of 1960. Thus within two years sample materials for a complete and substantially revised secondary school curriculum were at hand; surely an extraordinary performance by any standards. Throughout, all the outlining and writing teams were composed both of university specialists and of high school teachers, with this combination working better than anyone had imagined it would.[9]

With the spectacular example of a secondary school series at hand, SMSG extended its efforts to the elementary school curriculum and to various alternatives to the secondary school books. Again the pattern was production by school-university writing teams in a single summer, trial in schools with university consultation for a single school year, revision in a second summer, then publication in paper covers of the revised version. During the same period, SMSG writing teams and panels produced a large number of volumes for teacher training and supplementary materials for youngsters. At the same time several other groups and a number of individuals were making numerous contributions in the reform spirit.

It will be remarked that these exemplar books were produced in haste, and SMSG resisted urging to revise and polish them. They were intended solely as demonstrations that good mathematics can be put into school books and learned by children. It was presumed that with such a demonstration, authors and publishers would produce better and even more experimental textbooks for the school market. As these became widely used, the SMSG books would be withdrawn from circulation, and SMSG itself would quietly fade away.

By 1963 the whole range of exemplar books was available and in 1966 the SMSG director reported that: "Since its beginning in 1958, SMSG has prepared 20 textbooks covering the sequence from grade 1 to grade 12 and already over 5 million child years have been devoted to study from these textbooks."[10] More important, these books (and those produced concurrently by other reformers) had so influenced commercially published textbooks that the content of school mathematics for college capable students, and to some extent for all students, was permanently changed; at least to the considerable extent that school content is dictated by textbooks. (Contrary to SMSG hopes, however, the reform examples were nearly always echoed rather than surpassed.) Surely one could not ask for a better proof that some part of school practice can be dramatically changed with just a few years of well-directed (and well-financed) effort.

"The New Mathematics" is best defined as the content of the reform produced textbooks. For college capable high school students, the changes are summarized by the nine point Commission on Mathematics recommendations. (See Postscript 2) For grades 1–6, formerly devoted almost exclusively to developing arithmetic reflexes, the effect was to superimpose a genuinely mathematical structure and flavor on the work in arithmetic, and to add work in sets, geometry, simple algebra, probability, patterns, and structures.

Formulating new textbook content was certainly necessary, and it is amazing that it was accomplished within five years. The optimistic spirit that pervaded the early reform movement assumed not only that this was *necessary*, but that it would be *sufficient* to bring about a drastic and salutary change in the school mathematics experience of children. But the years since 1963 have demonstrated conclusively that textbook reform is *not* sufficient. The disillusionment, puzzlement, and new initiatives that thus accumulated in the second half of the reform decade will be the subject of the next section, which discusses the current mathematics education scene.

THE CURRENT SCENE

The new mathematics was hardly launched before such alarms as these were sounded: The reforms were much too conservative. Even though conservative, they were too much for most teachers to handle without retraining; and this was especially true for those (including elementary school teachers) who had the least opportunity for such retraining. Not merely new textbooks were needed, but new approaches to methodology and creation of materials in media other than books. There was still virtually no attention to the uses of mathematics. An adequate school mathematics experience for everyman had not been achieved. Too little was known about how children learn mathematics.

Before the reform fervor was spent such groups as SMSG launched scattered attacks on these and other problems. But long before the decade ended, the expectations of the reformers that substantial breakthroughs were just around the corner faded and gave way to new assessments of the difficulties. As the decade closed, the SMSG director summed up the situation like this:

Further improvements are essential. Our children will live in an even more complicated and quantified world than that of today. They need better mathematics programs than they are now getting. We still have many difficult problems to solve before we can make further improvements. In fact, I believe that so far we have attacked only the easier problems in mathematics education.[11]

In trying to change the school experience of youngsters, it seems that a decade (or the 13 years since 1958) is a pretty short time span.

For the next decade in mathematics education, any progress achieved will no doubt be by extrapolations of things already existent. At this point I will review the current situation, structuring this review with a model which says that "curriculum" consists of the sometimes complex interactions among *objectives, learning experiences,* and *evaluation.* The "evaluation" category includes an assessment of research in mathematics education, and the "learning experiences" category a broad look at many things which affect a youngster's actual school mathematics experience. Sections following this review will use the same structure in considering some relatively likely and relatively unlikely extrapolations over the next decade of things existent in the present scene.

Objectives

As the reform movement was cranking up in the mid-1950's, the objectives of mathematics education, as revealed by school practice, were clear and uncomplicated: Elementary instruction (K-6) aimed only to drum in the third R of the "Readin', Ritin', 'Rithmetic" triumvirate. This third R included addition, subtraction, multiplication, and division of whole numbers, fractions, and decimals. Seventh- and eighth-grade work was more of the same, with percentage thrown in along with "real life problems" in the form of consumer arithmetic. The high school objectives for that half of the students that took "general mathematics" as a terminal mathematics course was to review (or learn) material just like that in grades 7-8, which in turn was mostly a rehash of K-6. Hence up to that point there was no such thing as *mathematics* education, only *arithmetic* education. For the students who took the two years of math generally required for college, the objectives were to give them, for the first time, the technical skills needed for manipulating algebraic expressions and solving equations, many facts about geometric relationships, and the theorem-proof structure of geometry. For those few students who continued beyond algebra and geometry, the usual objective was to prepare them to begin as college freshmen the "college algebra" and "college trigonometry" courses by which the colleges in desperation tried to repair the inadequacies of the school experience. (College mathematics curricula were not in much better shape in most places than high school curricula, but reform was well under way there.)

As indicated in our discussion of the "new mathematics," the reform movement altered these objectives to make the school experience reflect the actual structure of mathematics and to exploit via spirals of experience such unifying threads as sets, functions, patterns, and structures. Elementary school 'Rithmetic, became not merely computation, but also stressed structural properties and their relation to why computation procedures work. In addition to 'Rithmetic, there were introductions to sets, geometry, algebra, probability, and other topics, so that by the eighth grade the student could have an intuitive grasp of a broad range of elementary mathematics. The high school mainstream college preparatory courses (algebra and geometry), could then assume this intuitive understanding and concentrate on mathematical structure, with proof not now reserved for the geometry course but also part of the algebra course. It became an objective to increase markedly the numbers of students continuing mathematics beyond the college entrance requirements, and for those who did continue, the junior-senior course was drastically revised in order to prepare students to begin a rigorous calculus course on entrance to college.

In the wake of the textbook reforms, concern has by now turned to additional objectives, including: a better geometry course; a satisfactory experience for everyman; effective diagnostic and remedial procedures; making the role of applications and mathematical models a viable aspect of mathematics education; some appropriate response to the computer revolution; making permanent the bonds between school mathematics and the rest of mathematics to keep the school experience genuinely relevant and not too far out of date; production and widespread use of more effective nonbookish materials; and new approaches to methodology. In addition, having learned that we know very little about how to implement these new objectives, the overriding long-range objective right now is to put together a research and theory building effort that will inform us on how to achieve a better fit between how children learn and the teaching of mathematics.

Evaluation and Research

In the objective-learning experiences-evaluation model of curriculum, "evaluation" has been for mathematics education pretty much a matter of achievement testing in schools and classrooms, either by teacher-made paper-pencil tests or by "standardized" paper-pencil tests. This is still the case, and there is virtually nothing on the present scene to indicate that new approaches to evaluation of achievement

will materialize within the next decade. It is possible that better exploitation of the data handling potential of computers will give some new
twists to the *utilization* of test results and may even make different sorts
of evaluation possible. But for the moment, supposed objectives of
mathematics education for which paper-pencil tests don't exist are not
evaluated, and testwise students draw the obvious conclusion that what
really matters is that which is tested, homilies in books and by teachers
notwithstanding.

For the main part of this section I would like to give "evaluation"
as a crucial part of curriculum a different twist from in-class testing by
discussing some more encompassing recent and current research efforts
to evaluate mathematics education itself.

Two landmark evaluations of relative achievement have been completed recently. First, the International Study of Achievement in Mathematics compared achievement in 12 countries at age 13 and at the end
of secondary school. Roughly speaking, U.S. students did as well as those
in many countries with far more selective secondary school systems, but
not nearly so well as students in the only other country (Japan) with
similarly inclusive pre-university schooling.[12] Second, SMSG's National
Long-Term Study of Mathematics Achievement (NLSMA) followed for
five years thousands of children using "the new mathematics" materials
and thousands of others using conventional materials. The reports on
this are appearing now and they, along with the raw data from the
study, will give us material to digest for several years.[13] One result
common to both studies and unsurprising in retrospect is that children
learn best that which is emphasized most.

Numerous other attempts at evaluation of some aspect or another
of mathematics education have been carried out over the past few years
under the general rubric of "research" in mathematics education. Several very useful summaries of this mass of research studies have recently
been published.[14,15] Here are some typical conclusions:

Current research in mathematics education is large in quantity, poor but improving in quality, and diverse.[16]

There are many ingenious ideas and suggestions that ought to be followed up
but in general the results are too special or incomplete to be of wide use.[17]

I doubt if many of [the often contradictory results] are completely wrong.
Rather I believe that they were usually too simplistic and that the mathematical
behaviors and accomplishments of real students are far more complex than the

answers would have us believe. . . . To improve this situation we must begin with extensive, careful, empirical observations of mathematics teaching and mathematics learning.[18]

With widespread puzzlement about why the massive reform efforts did not have more fundamentally revolutionary results, there is widespread agreement with these conclusions among thoughtful mathematics educators. It seems clear that we must start with empirical observations in actual classrooms, as Begle suggests. Excellent models for such investigations have already been provided by Soviet scholars, and a sample of these is being made available in translation.[19]

From an accumulation of such investigations, new theories of mathematics learning and teaching may be formulated and tested. Lacking those, the present scene is dominated by two more or less contending theories. One identified with Bruner and Piaget emphasizes giving the child much experience, from which he will "discover" various things depending on the developmental stage he is in. The other, identified with Gagné, seems to say that one decides what knowledge is needed, breaks this down into its parts and prerequisites, and then makes sure that child is presented the right things in the right order.[20] Each model of mathematics learning is sufficiently well formulated to provide the basis for interesting empirical work, but either by itself is probably too simplistic. Both theories make far more optimistic assumptions about everyman's ability to learn mathematics than the assumption implicit in current school practice:

There is a universally held belief that mathematical ability, like intelligence, is not shared equally among individuals . . . some have high, some low mathematical ability and others somewhere in between. We also assume that students of low mathematical ability cannot learn as much mathematics or learn it to as great a depth as those of high mathematical ability.[21]

As a matter of fact, some of the most intriguing (if inconclusive) results of recent research in mathematics education throw considerable doubt on these beliefs, indicating that mathematics learning may be mostly a matter of the experience provided and the amount of *time* devoted to learning rather than being dependent on fixed, innate, ability.[22,23] This is only one of the sacred cows of mathematics education currently being questioned. Current evaluation of mathematics education by research activity is replete with such intriguing but quite inconclusive suggestions and results.

Learning Experiences

A youngster's school mathematics learning experience is dominated these days by his books, other curriculum materials, his teachers,
and the general school context he finds himself in. In this section we will
briefly assay each of these.

Books for the High School College Preparatory Sequence. As a
direct result of the reform activity a variety of excellent books now exist
for the standard college preparatory sequence of courses and textbooks
also exist that would allow such alternatives to the standard sequence
as statistics and probability, computers, modern algebra, vectors, and
matrices. There are excellent supplementary and enrichment books
that can be read on an independent study basis by many students who
have mastered 1st-year algebra and the standard 10th-grade geometry
course. Furthermore, writing of books is the most accessible way for
mathematicians or high school teachers to contribute their ideas about
mathematics curricula, hence there is unlikely to be a diminution of
writing activity for this level student.

This is not to say that there are no problems. It is still the case that
no high school books satisfactorily deal with the uses of mathematics.
The standard geometry course has been under fire for many years and
is a lively area of controversy. Individual courses are well served by a
variety of books, but there is little unification of the mathematics experience; that is, various subject matters still stay in their own year-by-year
compartments. (A few unified mathematics textbook series have been
published, but they have generally not been adopted by schools.) Still,
on the present scene, textbooks for the college preparatory high school
sequence represent the best served aspect of mathematics education.

*Textbooks for High School Students Not in the College Preparatory
Track.* Books for "general mathematics" and other such courses have
always echoed and rehashed the material in elementary school textbooks (especially seventh and eighth grades), and these have improved
greatly. The resulting improvement in books for "general mathematics" and other noncollege preparatory courses has not, however, solved
the serious problems that have always plagued these courses: problems
of remediation, of motivation, and of relevance.

Books for the K–8 School Years. A number of excellent textbook
series are now available for the elementary school years. Unlike the
general run of their pre-reform predecessors, they are characterized by

sound mathematical underpinnings; clear exposition; a wide range of significant mathematical subject matter (not just 'Rithmetic); scope, sequence, and spiraling that are well conceived and that make good logical sense; and by excellent teacher manuals and other aids to implementation. Most of the complete K–6 or K–8 series depend heavily on verbal exposition which resembles the high school college-preparatory books, with a definitely mathematical flavor, emphases on structural properties and sound mathematical vocabulary, and unifying threads such as sets, functions, and geometry running through them. By contrast, several series of books, usually for the primary school years (K–3) have a quite different flavor to them, emphasizing "discovery" via work with concrete materials, work sheets, and laboratory activity. These materials also exhibit careful thought and sound mathematical concepts but they are not much used at present in the United States.

In spite of the generally high quality of available textbooks, however, there is every indication that relatively few youngsters have even a moderately good elementary school mathematics experience. That is, greatly improved books have had relatively little effect. The reasons for this are probably quite complicated, as may be clear in the remainder of this review. Since mathematics learning is reasonably sequential and the early years are quite crucial in the sequence, the failure of better books to improve the early mathematics learning experience is of the utmost seriousness.

Here again, the problem of making the uses of mathematics a viable concern has not been solved.

Nonbook Materials. The situation with nonbook material is much less favorable than for textbooks. Such materials have been characterized for many years by boom and bust cycles as new panaceas are proposed, exploited, and then dropped as they prove not to be panaceas, but merely useful aids to learning. At present only nonbook materials that can be published and marketed much as books are widely available. These include overhead projector transparencies, filmstrips, programmed practice materials, diagnostic and achievement tests, and, recently, audio tape cassettes. The programmed learning materials that enjoyed such a boom in the early sixties are now in the bust phase; few have been produced that do not fail either in mathematical quality or in liveliness and interest.

Enough intriguingly excellent materials in film and TV media have been produced to indicate the great potential usefulness of these media.

But production cost and distribution problems have generally made many such materials essentially unavailable for school use in the United States. Many school systems invested considerable money in TV systems early in the sixties, but backup programming never materialized and the systems remain virtually unused. Some excellent filmed material has been produced in the United States (usually with NSF financing) but remains frustratingly unused. Canada has made much more headway with actual production and school use of both TV and film, indicating that the problems are merely difficult, and not insoluble. Here, certainly, is something to work at over the next decade.

Computer-assisted instruction (CAI) (with students in actual dialogue with computers) has been the subject of much ballyhoo during the sixties, with mathematics instruction often seen as a chief beneficiary.[24] The required "hardware" certainly exists in time-sharing arrangements and in the enormous data handling capabilities of third- and fourth-generation computers. But the use of computer hardware is everywhere complicated by the shortage of suitable "software"—in this case, the learning materials that must be supplied the computer before it can supply them to the student. In this writer's opinion, the experiments with CAI to date are not persuasive of the possibility of widespread use in school mathematics instruction, not merely because of the well-known conservatism of schools but also because of this shortage of good "software" and the fact that a number of theoretical and technical difficulties have yet to be wrestled with. The main effect visible so far is a possibly regressive emphasis on those parts of mathematics education that lend themselves to teaching by memorization, drill, and practice.

Computer-*managed* instruction is another matter altogether. This involves principally better *use* of existing, conventional, materials; it will be considered later in this chapter.

Teachers. There is probably no more potent force in the actual mathematics learning experience of a youngster than his teachers. The earliest second thoughts about the reforms were prompted by supposed limitations imposed on them by teachers:

The reforms assumed that the student's capacity to learn was far beyond anything we have been accustomed to attribute to him. But . . . serious limitations are imposed on the student's ability to learn by the instructor's ability to teach. . . . Most curriculum reforms, practically enough, have chosen to limit their ambitions and create such new courses as existing teachers, after brief retraining, can competently handle. If the matter were to end there, the result might well be disastrous.[25]

The real obstacle lies not in our knowledge of mathematics or our knowledge of pedagogy but in the outmoded preparation we are still giving . . . teachers. It is high time we stopped prating about this difficulty and take counsel as to how to remove it.[26]

The reform groups produced a great quantity of materials to help teachers adapt to the reforms. In addition, the National Science Foundation provided stipends for tens of thousands of experienced high school teachers to attend university-based Summer and Academic Year Institutes to learn the "modern mathematics" that was probably not a part of their original training to become teachers. With the improvement of college mathematics curricula, beginning high school teachers were better trained than formerly. In spite of all this, there are indications that only about two out of three high school mathematics teachers meet the rather modest standards for subject-matter preparation that have been set by recommending and accrediting groups. Preparation is strongest in calculus and modern algebra. It is generally weak in probability, statistics, linear algebra, modern approaches to geometry, and weakest of all in the uses of mathematics. In other words, preparation is deficient in precisely those subjects most likely to be the focus of continuing reforms of secondary school content.[27]

Still, most students in the college preparatory high school course sequence will have some teachers expert in mathematics (which does not, of course, guarantee good teaching). This is not likely to be true of seventh- and eighth-grade students even though mathematics classes in these grades are usually taught by specialist teachers, for these "specialists" rarely have strong training in mathematics. It is very unlikely to be true for elementary school students, where the mathematical preparation of teachers is near zero. Although many dedicated elementary school teachers have done a good job with the new mathematics materials, the chances of a given youngster having a good mathematics experience under well informed teachers several years in a row are very slim. Clearly, improvement of this situation is one of our main pieces of unfinished business.

Methods and Organization of Instruction. At the high school level nearly all mathematics instruction takes place in self-contained courses meeting 40-50 minutes each day. There is usually some sort of "tracking" system, based on results of standardized achievement tests. Upper track students frequently finish a college calculus course while still in high school; middle track students take standard college preparatory courses; and lower track students take only a remedial rehash of elementary school work. The proportion of students in the remedial track ranges from perhaps 10-20 percent in some excellent (usually suburban) high schools to 80-90 percent in many "inner city" high schools. Given the crucial importance of mathematical competence, there is increasing recognition that the latter state of affairs is quite unacceptable, and this is one of the few places where the school establishment itself is actively seeking remedies. (However, the only long-range remedy—a better pre-high school experience—seems still out of reach.)

For all students, the mathematics experience is heavily book oriented, and the standard methodology consists daily in a brief exposition of new material from the teacher, discussion of homework, then assignment of the next problem set in the textbook as homework. Variations on this pattern are rare, as is the use of teaching aids other than blackboard or overhead projector. Mathematics laboratories have been much discussed and government funds have been available to equip them. Hence a room labeled as a laboratory frequently exists, but is rarely effectively used; the only exceptions to this are based on the efforts of scattered individual teachers.

In the pre-high school years, the mathematics experience is oriented to workbooks during the early years, with increasing dependence on standard textbooks each year. Many high school teachers have enough training in mathematics to throw in interesting sidelights and departures from the generally book-oriented experience and recognize interesting ideas from students. But the mathematics training of pre-high school teachers is so poor that such departures from routine are necessarily rare, and original student ideas are unlikely to be rewarded.

A recent trend for the primary school years is more use of what the British call "apparatus"—concrete materials that embody in their proper use the roots of significant mathematical ideas.[28] Teachers, after all, are generally very humane people with an excellent, if often frustrated, sense of what is good for children. Hence they have responded enthusiastically to the evidence that young children *like* to work with concrete materials and in other gamelike situations. Unfortunately, our general ignorance about how children learn mathematical concepts extends to the uses of apparatus, so much of the activity in this area is random and unfocused. Although the use of such materials is much better established in Great Britain than in the United States there is a hopeful trend here that may mature within the next decade.

The Conditions of Schooling. In my opinion the dreariness and dullness of the school mathematics experience is *not* what teachers want, but what their situations often impose on them. That is, the general conditions of schooling are very far from satisfactory. In a few city schools and in some suburbs conditions are fairly tolerable but in the majority of school settings the situation is bleak. To consider only instructional tasks, we note that most high school teachers will have five classes daily (125–150 students) with two or three different subjects to prepare for. If a teacher were to be so ambitious as to average one minute per pupil per day in checking homework, personal consultation outside of class, and other follow-up of class activity, two or three hours would be added to his five-hour teaching day. If he were to take seriously the need to devise diagnostic, remedial, and evaluation procedures and if he spent no more than one-half hour per day preparing for each of his two or three subjects, another few hours would be added. How can he also find time to keep up on new developments in mathematics, curriculum, pedagogy, and methods? The plight of the usual elementary school teacher, with up to 45 youngsters in many classrooms and with the expectation of expert teaching in at least language arts and reading, social studies, and mathematics is surely not less discouraging. Now add to this heavy teaching load a number of extra duties: supervising a so-called study hall; keeping student records for a homeroom or division; policing the halls, cafeteria, rest rooms, playgrounds, and parking lot during his nonteaching hours. What of crowded and dreary classrooms; of petty and demeaning administrative nonsense? Finally what about the fact that teachers almost everywhere must do without secretarial or clerical help of any sort? This last needs special comment since nearly every vision of the future of education includes delegating some instruction to such things as programmed materials, computers, television, film clips, and the like. But since teachers at present cannot delegate even the most trivial tasks to human helpers, how are they to learn to delegate important tasks to nonhuman helpers?

In sum, since a teacher's own training is frequently deficient and since the conditions of schooling often seem to make teaching-learning nearly impossible, it is hardly fair to make teachers scapegoats for the fact that the learning experience is so often unsatisfactory.

PROSPECTS FOR THE NEXT DECADE

Introduction

It is clear that there exists in the present scene the raw materials that could be developed to bring about an order of magnitude progress in mathematics education within the next decade. This is an event much to be desired but unfortunately it is very unlikely. One can be reasonably optimistic with respect to those things that can be put together from *outside* the school-school supplier establishments. That is, it may be possible to continue for another decade such characteristic aspects of the recent reform decade as the optimistic action-oriented spirit; the fruitful cooperation among mathematicians, mathematics educators and the best of our teachers; continued development of curriculum materials; and university efforts in training and retraining of teachers, perhaps now turned to pre-high school teachers. There will probably be improved and better focused research and theory building efforts. These outside inputs would assure substantial progress, but they would still be insufficient for the needs, and perhaps disastrously so. This is so because the most pressing problems that still remain are simply too massive to be solved from the outside of the school-school supplier establishment. The most puzzling thing about the reform decade has been the passiveness of that establishment. It has to some extent been able to absorb and accommodate materials and ideas produced outside, but has itself made few original contributions. It is as if the school establishment were merely a huge consuming organism, dumbly and patiently waiting to be fed and unable to forage for itself or move to help itself.

Two examples may illustrate the point. First, the National Science Foundation (NSF) and Office of Education (USOE) supplied several million dollars per year to various reform-oriented organizations during the past decade, and this money fueled very productive curriculum development efforts and some good research. But this amount of money is miniscule compared with total school budgets. The resources needed to adapt and implement the results to bring about genuine change in the tremendously varied school situations that make up American education cannot begin to come from outside agencies. Second, NSF Summer and Academic Year Institutes provided further training opportunities for tens of thousands of experienced high school mathematics teachers during the decade. But even leaving aside the fact that up to a third of high school teachers are still poorly prepared in mathematics, consider the fact that there are over a million public school teachers of grades K–8 in this country (to say nothing of private and parochial school teachers), nearly all of whom need varying amounts of additional training in mathematics if they are to be even minimally equipped to teach mathematics in the pre-high school years. To release them from some of their weekly labors, or provide for several summers work or a year off would cost several billions of dollars. Now, we spend billions for many things in this country, but it is fantastically unlikely that such will be supplied for this purpose from sources outside the schools themselves. Retraining could be arranged fairly cheaply *within* school systems and become a reasonable part of total school budgets, but this is unlikely to happen.

In sum, the next decade will probably be characterized by considerable activity and much progress in those areas amenable to influence from *outside* the school-school supplier establishment, and by relatively little activity generated within that establishment. Since the latter dwarfs the former, my net assessment is on the side of pessimism; the gap between needs and accomplishments in mathematics education is unlikely to be closed and may widen. Hence prediction of fundamental improvements in the mathematics education of children would be foolhardy, yet only such fundamental change will meet the needs.

With my pessimistic bias clear, let us nevertheless assess in more detail the prospects for mathematics education in the next decade. For this purpose "curriculum" will again be regarded as an interaction among objectives, evaluation (including research), and learning experiences. Under these headings I will outline what seems likely over the next decade given these two minimal assumptions:

1. At least the level of creative energy and financial support that characterized the reform decade will continue, and will be channeled into appropriate new enterprises.
2. The school establishment will be able to absorb at least that outside activity which is in its own best interests and which does not require additional effort on its part or dislocation of its accustomed ways.

Following this review of what is fairly likely to happen, an additional section will indicate some fruitful and realistic extrapolations from things for which existence proofs exist now, but which would require more sweeping assumptions for effective and large-scale implementation than the two assumptions just listed.

Objectives

There is considerable agreement that the most important objective of mathematics education for the next few years is to equip not just the college capable student but "everyman" with the mathematical concepts and skills he will need if he is to exercise responsible citizenship (in the social-political sense) and if he is to have some sense of control over a world increasingly dominated by technology, computers, information given in mathematical terms, and decisions made using mathematical tools. This is clearly a large order and it is necessary to formulate the sub-objectives with respect to mathematical intuition, skills, and theoretical knowledge (as well as teaching procedures) that will contribute to such "everyman" competence. Several groups are currently working on this; I will hazard here an illustrative and tentative specification that many might agree with.

What will probably be needed is to build into children a solid, gut level, grip on such things as the following:

1. Use of numbers for approximations and comparisons in rough and ready terms, whether the numbers are the billions of the Defense Department, the millions of local political issues and national statistics, the hundreds and thousands of personal finance, the ones and tens of counting, or the fractions, percentages, tables, graphs, and other numerical information of newspapers and other media.
2. Number and computation sense, including an understanding of computational procedures and the ability to make intelligent use of such aids to computation as slide rules, tables, calculating machines, and computers.
3. Fundamental measure concepts and the ability to use measures in their countless guises.
4. Functions and transformation.
5. Basic logic and analysis of arguments.
6. Chance, fundamental probability ideas, and statistical measures.
7. A sure intuition about geometric relationships in two or three dimensions.

8. A basic understanding of computers and how human beings exercise control in a highly automated world.
9. An understanding of how mathematics becomes useful via the process of constructing and exploiting mathematical models.

This list is not, of course, exhaustive, but is illustrative of the kinds of everyman objectives we need to try for in the next decade. Such understanding must be built deep into children via effective and humane experiences that will make children both willing and able to use them in tackling actual problems. This puts the main burden on pre-high school education, and our inability up to now to make effective the early school mathematics experience makes me pessimistic about accomplishment of what must surely be our prime objective. Nevertheless we must try.

The level of understanding just discussed should be sufficient for informed citizenship and a sense of control over the world. At the same time, it provides an excellent base for study of more technical mathematics, either in school or in response to some need encountered after leaving school. With mathematical models and mathematical methods influencing so many fields of study and work, and with the need for many teachers with good mathematical training, one of our objectives must be to have large numbers of students continue mathematics training beyond the basic, everyman, competence. For the continued health of mathematics itself (and other mostly mathematical disciplines) there needs to be a continuing supply of a few students who progress rapidly into advanced study and become professional mathematicians. This last has never been a problem, however and is unlikely to become one.

Objectives such as those just suggested for everyman should be our most important concern over the decade to come. Other objectives concern continued development of college preparatory and specialist courses. A determination to work with others to make the general school experience a more humane one must be implicit in all these objectives.

Evaluation-Research

We have already reported that the effect of much recent research has been to foster skepticism with respect to assumptions underlying much mathematics education over the years. It has become clear that our current level of ignorance is such that the main need now is for large numbers of empirical observations: carefully done in clinical situations with individuals and small groups; in classroom situations with informed, careful, observers present; and with large groups using ingenious evaluation instruments and sophisticated statistical tools. It is also clear that the sort of empirical observation that must be done can only come from close cooperation with at least a few schools.

This sort of research presents an attractive challenge to many astute university people, including some mathematicians, many mathematics educators, and many trained in nonmathematics disciplines related to education (psychology, for example). The work of the past decade or so has cleared away a lot of the underbrush and the several recent summaries of mathematics education research have also been fairly lucid indicators of what should be done next. In academia, we have great faith in the usefulness of accumulating research results. Investigations such as are now needed require cooperation of a few schools, but not much investment of school money and not much dislocation of established patterns. It may be possible to channel a number of Ph.D. studies in ways that contribute usefully to the total picture. Funding should not be a problem: small-scale empirical studies and clinical investigations are not so very expensive, and well-conceived, large-scale efforts should readily find sponsorship.

Hence, in this area one can project with some optimism that by the end of the decade, a number of the questions raised by recent reviews of the current scene will have tentative answers; answers, furthermore, that point the way to actual practice in schools. Many proposals for improved school practice based on a sound body of research results will have tangible existence in one or a few school settings. But it can be just as confidently predicted that general school practice will have been little affected within the decade by research results. For one thing, it will take at least half the decade, starting from our present level of "informed ignorance" to have enough empirical results to form the basis for hypotheses and theories. It will take time beyond that to test these and examine their implications for school practice. These factors along with the well-known difficulty of moving schools to make fundamental dislocations in their current practice, make wide-scale implementation of anything requiring more than minor adjustment extremely unlikely over a 10-year period. But, by the end of the decade, clear indications for improved practice may be at hand.

It is also safe to predict progress in course and student evaluation on a smaller scale as opposed to the sort of evaluation-development that comes under the "research" rubric. Here the amount of progress may be a function of the extent to which school systems subscribe to computer services for management of the school generally, and for pupil accounting and management of instruction in particular. The simplistic nature of evaluation in the past has been in part a function of the difficulties of processing a large variety and amount of information. But with computerized data processing, much more information about students can be handled, and not merely the achievement test data that has dominated evaluation up to now. For example, it should not be difficult with optical reading devices and other hardware, coupled with some ingenuity in devising coding systems, to accumulate anecdotal reports about student behavior in given learning situations that go far beyond present-day answer-oriented testing. Furthermore, this sort of information can contribute significantly to the empirical research observations needed to support research. With computers we can also include in our evaluation efforts a wider range of variables; for example, teacher and student background factors as well as performance data.

Evaluation based on objectives and norms defined on a more than local basis is nearly certain to be prominent. The developing National Assessment scheme is one example; suggested "behavioral objectives" defining the assessment in mathematics have already been published.[29] (I personally find this document unpromising but others disagree.) "Accountability" based on this or other evaluation schemes will also be a popular cause, and one fraught with hazards.

Learning Experiences

Given my gloomy estimate earlier of the actual learning experience of most school youngsters, it would be cheerful to report that over the next decade there will be fundamental changes in this experience, but under the restraint of my two minimal assumptions this seems quite unlikely. The real hopes for substantial and fundamental changes in learning experiences lie in becoming better informed through our research-evaluation efforts (as described in the previous section) and in achieving a fundamentally different and more positive pre-high school experience. But these are both massive undertakings and even if we were to attack them energetically forthwith, it would be near the end of the decade before they would bear fruit. (In fact, no such energetic attack seems yet begun.) However, there is still plenty to do in implementing on a widespread basis materials and good ideas that have been used successfully in a few places. The next decade will probably consist of such elaboration and implementation of trends and ideas already existent. Such elaborations are not unimportant, and we certainly have a lot to learn about implementing promising ideas, so that within the decade substantial (but not fundamental) improvements in the mathematics learning experience may be achieved while preparing the ground for more fundamental changes.

Here, then, is a list indicative of likely developments over the decade by way of improving school mathematics learning experiences. In making up the list we have in mind the two assumptions listed at the beginning of this section: (1) reform-minded activity will continue and (2) the school-school supplier establishment will absorb at least those useful things that require little dislocation of established patterns. Included in the list are likely developments in the several most important aspects of the child's actual learning experiences (textbooks, nonbook materials, teachers) at the various levels of his experience (early school, other pre-high school, high school). Except where noted otherwise by this list, it is assumed that those aspects of the existing scene included in the review above will continue into the next decade.

1. The mathematical models point of view is firmly entrenched in many enterprises in our society. (See Postscript 3.) There already exists considerable commitment to making the uses of mathematics a viable emphasis in the school experience. Hence, one is encouraged to believe that by the end of the decade school materials may at least make youngsters more aware of the ways in which mathematics becomes useful. We may even succeed in educating more students who can *use* what they have learned.

2. The high school college preparatory curriculum will continue to have substantial development efforts expended on it. There is plenty of scope there for excellent secondary school teachers and university mathematicians to experiment with new approaches to subject matter. The two most active curriculum reform projects at present are producing sophisticated new materials for that level.[30,31] For the geometry course, under fire for many years, new materials emphasizing various

approaches (e.g., transformations, linear algebra, vectors) are appearing in published and experimental materials here and abroad. For college preparatory courses, expository books are quite properly the main learning vehicle, and these are the easiest of learning materials to generate, produce, and distribute. For these and other reasons, activity in this area will be brisk over the next decade, and the results interesting.

3. We observed earlier that 80 to 90 percent of entering students in some high schools are assigned to remedial courses. This is such a visible scandal that efforts to correct it are sure to be prominent over the next decade. Several reform organizations have recently given attention to this problem[32] and the problem occupies the attention of many school system curriculum consultants. This last is significant, for there are very few things which school systems have bestirred themselves to do on their own behalf. Although the permanent solution is also the most unlikely one—a fundamentally improved K-8 mathematics experience for everyman—there are indications that the matter can be attacked successfully starting as late as the seventh grade, and this is the likely focus of stopgap measures over the next decade while we are working up to more fundamental solutions.[33]

4. "Individualization" of the mathematics experience will be a popular cause during the next decade. This will probably be based on published materials such as programs, workbooks, and the like rather than on the laboratory experiences and activity that would be far more fruitful. As in the past, an unstated component of many proposals for "individualization" of instruction will be a wish to take instruction out of the hands of teachers in favor of more "reliable" instruments. Computer *management* of instruction (utilizing standard materials) will increase as an aid to individualization, and by the end of the decade perhaps even computer presentation of materials. Even though individualized, the experiences will most likely still be overwhelmingly verbal and bookish in their nature. There may be some marginal improvement for youngsters who learn easily from such verbal materials in having them individually tailored and prescribed, but for many people (perhaps the majority) the individually prescribed but still bookish experience may be as unsatisfactory as ever. I see some danger that in the name of "individualization," small group and classroom group work may virtually disappear, with possibly serious consequences, including further isolation of children and dehumanizing of the educational process.

5. There will be better preservice teacher training in mathematics both for high school and elementary school teachers. Since schools have fairly rapid teacher turnover, by the end of the decade the average level of teacher expertness in mathematics should be higher than now at both the pre-high school and high school level. To a certain extent the reform will feed itself as those "college capable" students who benefited from better school materials graduate from college and enter teaching.

6. In the primary school grades there will be considerable adoption of activity-oriented curriculum materials. But since such materials are relatively unstructured they put even more demands on teachers than did the "new mathematics" textbooks. This could be a very positive development if only we could assume provision of consultation and creative services and retraining of teachers to assure that they are themselves at home with basic mathematics concepts as well as open-minded observers and helpers in activity-oriented situations. But such consultation and retraining would need to be provided for by the schools themselves, and this goes beyond the assumptions we made concerning what is *likely* within the next decade. Hence the quality of the experience resulting from adoption of activity-oriented curricula in the early school years will probably be low.

7. There are already available from sources here and abroad (especially Canada) a fairly large number of film and TV programs of high quality that would be very useful in mathematics instruction. With such rich resources available, it is possible that over the next decade we will find solutions to the distribution problems that have heretofore prevented their effective use. Solutions of these problems would in turn be a spur to further creation of materials. The net result by the end of the decade may be that the mathematics learning experience will at last include effective visual materials.

8. With the possible exceptions noted in (6) and (7) above, the mathematics learning experience will continue to be oriented to printed materials.

Other, Dimmer, Prospects for the Next Decade

The review just concluded suggests that within the next decade much will happen outside the schools that might provide the basis for substantial change sometime, but there may be little fundamental change in the actual school mathematics experience of most youngsters. However, an observer writing a similarly pessimistic forecast in the fifties would not have foreseen the explosion of activity that resulted in a fruitful decade of reform. Pressures similar to those of the early fifties are present in today's situation and may generate a response that would overturn our pessimistic forecast.

I will outline here some optimistic possibilities that are realistic extrapolations from the present-day situation. Any of these could easily become a part of mathematics education within the decade to come, provided only that one could assume greater effort along certain lines than it is really safe to predict.

Transformation of the Pre-High School Mathematics Experience. The key to making a fundamental and substantial difference in every-man's mathematical competence to deal with his world is very substantial changes in his early and middle school mathematics experience. The present situation is near the intolerable point, and the elementary school experience might just be given very substantial attention. If so, at least the following things are ready to happen.

The first requirement for fundamental progress is more mathematical expertness within elementary school staffs. This could happen in several ways. For example, there is at present both a surplus of technically trained people and a disposition among many young people to embark on social service careers. If increased attention to elementary schools also increases the probability that service there can be really fruitful, well-trained young people will be attracted. In addition, many gifted high school teachers are well aware of the serious inadequacies of early schooling and might be similarly attracted. These well-trained people could serve on school staffs as teachers, as producers of materials, as consultants, and as in-service teacher trainers. It must be observed, however, that at present there are no places available on school staffs for such people, so both tradition and reluctance to spend more money stand in the way. If these hurdles can be overcome it is likely that with such consultant help available many existing elementary school teachers could become perceptive users of good materials via willing collaboration with these more expert colleagues. With solution at last of the problem of insufficient knowledge within school staffs, a number of other things might naturally follow.

My experience in teaching elementary school teachers in a course that is a mixture of mathematical theory and of laboratory experiences persuades me that teachers quickly become converted to the attractiveness of laboratory, inquiry-oriented, experiences for children. Here their instincts agree with those of such mathematicians as Marshall Stone:

There is good reason to be quite explicit and emphatic in proclaiming that the early years of school mathematics must be as close to pure fun as the teacher can make them. The verbalization and drill can come later, when the child feels the need for them, as he will surely do if the teacher creates the right conditions in the classroom.[34]

With further training, continued help and consultation, and a reasonable teaching situation this particular reform of the early school situation would be quickly and widely implemented. But without these changes in their present situation, expecting teachers to put together genuinely mathematical experiences that are "pure fun" makes unreasonable demands in an already unreasonable situation.

With the changes just indicated and with the possibility of delegation of certain record-keeping and data processing responsibilities to human or computer helpers, an ungraded mathematics curriculum for the elementary grades would almost certainly be implemented. For this a wide variety of learning materials would be needed. Initially the goals would be in terms of subject matter now conventional for various school levels. Progress toward these goals would be evaluated, but children would proceed in various ways and at varying paces. As research efforts matured during the decade, more natural and more effective learning sequences might be formulated. Even with our present ignorance about how to accomplish what we want, however, the activity-oriented ungraded learning experience under the guidance of teachers who have a friendly feeling about mathematics would be a clear improvement, if only in making early mathematics learning a pleasant experience.

Another likely result of the changes indicated above would be coordination of mathematics learning with such other learnings as science, geography, art-aesthetics, and language. Sound recommendations have already been made with respect to coordination with the "new science" curricula.[35] Hardly talked of yet, hence less likely, is coordination with the other subject matters, but my conversations with experts in art education, geography, and reading reveal substantial overlap of basic objectives. Furthermore, when one talks of learning experiences designed to accomplish these basic objectives, it is easy to see how ideas very useful to mathematics intuition can be drawn from experiences in these other fields, and vice versa. With teachers equipped to be good and willing consumers of excellent materials, and with experts in mathematics and other subject matters on school staffs consulting with teachers, producing materials, and talking with each other, such integration could easily materialize within the decade.

The addition of more mathematical expertness to school staffs would obviously make much easier the gathering of empirical data basic to research and development aimed at long-range improvement of mathematics education. It would also facilitate school implementation of the results of this research and development.

School-University-Funding Source Alliances. There seems to me to be a pressing need for durable and continuing alliances among schools, universities or colleges, and funding sources. If it were possible to suppose that this nation would make a determined effort within the decade to improve schooling, it might also be possible to put such alliances together. These would facilitate the research efforts discussed earlier, and would help immeasurably in putting theory into practice. They would also make schools and colleges genuine partners in teacher training, replacing the uneasy arrangements that are now the rule. And they would give schools better access to funds for experimentation and research.

Many schools and colleges should enter into such coalitions, not just a privileged few. One way to accomplish this would be to have each institution now training teachers work closely with a few schools in its immediate vicinity—say one or more high schools and its feeder elementary schools. For example, there are enough excellent colleges and universities in the Chicago area that a considerable number of schools could be included in such alliances, including especially a number of very troubled schools and, for balance, a number of "average" and "good" schools as well.

In-service Mathematics Education Centers. With or without the above arrangements, in-service education centers should be established within the decade, patterned after the Japanese "Science Education Centers" that already exist.[36] The essential idea is to make it possible for teachers to leave their jobs for varying periods of time: to learn about new curricular ideas; to improve their own expertise; to work out some idea of their own; and so on. Teaching is a demanding job at best. It should not surprise us that after some years many teachers run out of energy and out of ideas and rely increasingly on past work and a codified set of survival techniques. One of the most positive things about the reform decade was the outlet it gave many teachers for their creative energy, as well as the sense of worth that came from participation in the reforms. We should surely find ways to institutionalize these things, and make continued learning and growth both an opportunity and a requirement for those who teach mathematics. The centers offer a way to do this. They could either be put together by universities (perhaps by contract with school systems) or, as in Japan, by the school districts themselves.

Task Force, Mission-Oriented, Research and Development Efforts. I have said that we are ignorant about a great many things and that in the normal course of events much of the decade will be gone before enough research results have accumulated to dispel some of this ignorance. But in this country we have spectacular examples in space, military hardware, medicine, transportation, and other places of very complicated questions solved in relatively brief periods of time simply by concerted efforts to find solutions. With or without the widespread formation of school-university coalitions as discussed above, it should be possible to select a few of the most pressing questions and work on them in at least a few places. For example, suppose a given question could be assigned to a few major universities, each in alliance with a few nearby schools. The first task would be collection of much empirical data, with a computer link for accumulating and analyzing the data. As these results accumulate to the point where theories can be formulated, they can be tested through the same network as produced the data. Teachers should be made genuine partners (with whatever would be appropriate as in-service training provided), for at our present state of ignorance teacher intuition may be a more valuable input than any other. Furthermore, with a direct link to schools and teachers, the gulf between theory and practice would be narrowed, and the process of finding ways to effectively implement findings would be considerably accelerated. While it may be that the analogy with other mission-oriented efforts that have sometimes achieved spectacular results is faulty, it seems to me that the main barrier is the lack of determination to launch such an all-out attack on some of our problems, and to provide the resources to do so.

There are a number of unsolved problems that should yield results rather quickly given such an attack. Examples include making the uses of mathematics a viable school emphasis; diagnosis and remediation of difficulties in learning mathematics; formulation and effective use of laboratory and other experiences to teach specific mathematical ideas; production and effective use of nonbookish materials. A more general question that might be amenable to such an attack is the basic unsolved problem of putting together a really effective primary school mathematics experience.

Some Miscellaneous Possibilities. Though laudable in intent, the provision of free textbooks (reissued year after year) has the effect of preventing children from using mathematics books as they should be used—to be freely studied and written in during a course, and as references afterward. It prevents creativity in producing books that are part exposition and part workbook, for students *must not write in the book.* It has the effect of sometimes forcing teachers to use textbooks which are poor or out of date, because it is expensive to get new books or because of state laws that require that a book once adopted be used some arbitrary number of years. A cure for this achievable during the decade would be widespread use of cheaply printed paperback textbooks, issued for youngsters to use and keep. (This is the practice in Mexico.) In addition, the output of high-speed printers (perhaps in conjunction with programs individually prescribed by computers) might well replace bound books for many purposes.

Marketing and distribution difficulties have up to now helped prevent effective use of many excellent learning materials (especially movies and TV tapes). It has been suggested that something like Chicago's "Merchandise Mart" is needed for mathematics education (and perhaps education generally). In such a one-stop center teachers and administrators in the course of a single day could examine, preview, and make decisions about a very wide range of materials and talk directly to distributors and manufacturers' representatives.

With only willingness and a little ingenuity school schedules could make time within the teachers' working week for in-service training efforts and cooperative staff curriculum development efforts. If, as suggested above, more mathematical expertness is available within school staffs the leadership for such efforts will exist already; otherwise, schools could contract with nearby universities and colleges for assistance. For example, it is probable that simply releasing the children from school one afternoon per week and arranging for staffs to engage in fruitful in-service training would yield more long-term benefits to the children than the few hours of schooling involved.

Perhaps within the decade schools will tackle problems of staff differentiation and delegation of function. Teachers now spend time in activities that obviously waste their professional training and talents and are a considerable drain on their energies. With large classroom groups, a given child frequently has very few genuine human contacts with adults during his school day and can seldom get help for problems he may have. These things indicate intelligent delegation of tasks to paraprofessional and volunteer help. On the other hand, promising proposals for school improvement are often ignored or poorly attended to because the requisite expertise is not available among the school staff. This indicates the need for more specialists. Finally, the matter of delegation of certain teaching functions to nonhuman devices such as computers needs attending to.

SUMMARY AND CONCLUSIONS

The messages of this chapter can be summarized like this: Sometime soon after World War II, and accelerating steadily since then, there has come a realization that better understanding of basic mathematical concepts and procedures is necessary not just for a few people but virtually for everyone. In contrast to this need, mathematics education succeeds with relatively few people. Since about 1958 a very fruitful decade of reform accomplished a necessary and substantial change of the content of school mathematics books—"The New Math." But in retrospect we have realized that whereas we thought this was the *basic* problem, it was only the easiest one. This has led to examination of many of the other assumptions underlying past and present mathematics education, with the additional realization that many of these are questionable or demonstrably false. Hence many mathematics educators are calling for building a more solid base for mathematics education practice by empirically based research and development.

This chapter summarized many aspects of present-day mathematics education in the wake of the reform decade. With this as a foundation forecasts were made for the next decade based on quite conservative assumptions. These conservative predictions include considerable activity from outside the school establishment resulting among other things in better basic knowledge about mathematics education; continued development of excellent curriculum materials published as books, especially for the college preparatory high school sequence; materials designed to "teach mathematics so as to be useful"; somewhat improved teacher training; and improved diagnostic and remedial procedures. Within schools we may see utilization of computers in management of instruction, if not in actual presentation of instructional sequences; continued attempts at "individualization" of instruction; and considerable (but possibly uninformed) adoption of activity-oriented curriculum materials.

The above would seem to be enough for one decade, and perhaps it is. Nonetheless, it is disturbing to observe that there is little in this "safe" prediction that would indicate that the mathematical experience of everyman will be much better a decade from now than it is today. If this is so, then at the end of yet another decade, the gap between the actual needs imposed by our world and the competence of everyman will be greater than ever, for the world moves on, even when education does not. There is, of course, the possibility that the decade will have produced in its research and theory building efforts the base for really substantial and revolutionary progress in the decade of the eighties. But the nagging feeling persists that we can no longer afford the luxury of poor mathematics education, even for just one more decade. One therefore hopes that the very necessity of improvement will generate such energetic responses as has sometimes been the case in the past so that some of the more unlikely prospects outlined near the end of this chapter will materialize. In particular, one hopes against all likelihood for a response that would truly equip teachers of elementary school mathematics for their task, and that would provide them with the means to give everyman the enjoyable and fruitful mathematics experience that would support formation of durable intuition and sure knowledge with respect to the mathematics essential to coping with the modern world.

POSTSCRIPTS

1. Samples from school mathematics instruction (each could be duplicated many times):

A. Once I was hired by a famous private school to help children who were going to be ornaments to society but couldn't learn arithmetic. One of the girls had been in trouble about fractions and decimals. One day she came to our appointment and she said, *"Now* I understand about percentages. Give me a problem and I'll do it."

I asked her to tell me how much was fifty percent of eighty-four. She wrote down, 84, and under it, .50. Then she said, "Nothing times four is nothing. I write it down. Five times four is twenty, write down the zero and carry the two. Five times eight is forty, add the two. Because it is percents, I move a point two places. The answer is forty-two."

I said, "Wait a minute. Let's think about this a little."

"Is it right?" she said. "Is the answer right?"

I said, "Yes, of course, it's right, but let's think about it a little."

She almost cried. She said, "Of all the children in the class, why must I be the only one who has to think?" (Catherine Stern, mathematician and psychologist, quoted in Martin Mayer, *The Schools,* Harper and Brothers, 1961.)

B. This anecdote concerns a child who could do arithmetic operations very well when told what to do. Since she passed standardized tests parents and teachers were satisfied, but she couldn't *use* her skills. Asked how she went about solving problems, she replied as follows:

"I know what to do by looking at the examples. If there are only two numbers, I subtract. If there are lots of numbers, I add. But if there are just two numbers and one is littler than the other, then it is a hard problem. I divide to see if they come out even, but if they don't, I multiply." (*The Guidance of Learning Activities,* 3rd Edition, by William H. Burton. Copyright © 1952–1962 by Appleton-Century-Crofts. Reprinted by permission of Appleton-Century-Crofts, Educational Division, Meredith Corporation.)

C. At this school I told my first lie to a person in authority. When we began arithmetic we worked with counters. But the more quick-witted soon began to discard their counters, and the day came when to ask for them would be to admit you were falling behind. I was among the first to do without the counters—not because I was quick at reckoning but because I discovered that rows of dots on the blue cover of our exercise book could be made to serve the same purpose.

Finally, of course, the day came when an injured spinsterly voice said to me, "Those specks we've found on your note-book cover, John—you haven't been using them as counters have you?" I think if she had phrased it, *"Have* you been using them as counters?", I might have said, "yes!" But it was the *"you've not"* that moved me to say, "no."

I suppose that was the moment when I realized what education was for. The object of it was not *intellectual* but *moral.*

I had put the specks on the cover to make it easy to add, but the question, worded as it was, taught me that the adding and subtracting didn't matter. The thing was the game and it had to be played the *hard* way. Making the dots make it easier was breaking rules and as such was *immoral.* (John Wain, *Sprightly Running,* New York: St. Martin's Press, Inc., Macmillan and Co., Ltd.)

2. An outline of the purposes, and eventual accomplishments, of "The New Math" curriculum reforms from The Commission on Mathematics "Nine-point Program for College Capable Students" (1959):

1) Strong preparation, *both* in concepts *and* in skills, for college mathematics at the level of calculus and analytic geometry
2) Understanding of the nature and role of deductive reasoning—in algebra, as well as in geometry
3) Appreciation of mathematical structure ("patterns")—for example, properties of natural, rational, real, and complex numbers
4) Judicious use of unifying ideas—sets, variables, functions, and relations
5) Treatment of inequalities along with equations
6) Incorporation with plane geometry of some coordinate geometry, and essentials of solid geometry and space perception
7) Introduction in grade 11 of fundamental trigonometry—centered on coordinates, vectors, and complex numbers
8) Emphasis in grade 12 on elementary functions (polynomial, exponential, circular)
9) Recommendation of additional alternative units for grade 12: *either* introductory probability with statistical applications *or* an introduction to modern algebra. (*See* Note 8.)

3. Some testimonies to the pervasive present day usefulness of mathematics

A. Since mathematics has proved indispensable for the understanding and the technological control not only of the physical world but also of the social structure, we can no longer keep silent about teaching mathematics so as to be useful. In educational philosophies of the past, mathematics often figures as the paragon of a disinterested science. No doubt it still is, but we can no longer afford to stress this point if this keeps our attention off the widespread use of mathematics and the fact that mathematics is needed not by a few people, but virtually by everybody. (*See* Note 1.)

B. It is a common observation that a change of an order of magnitude in a technology produces fundamentally new effects. . . . Computers have improved in speed by at least six orders of magnitude . . . [and] there has been a great increase in reliability of operation. . . . [T]he cost per operation . . . is something more than one-thousand times cheaper. It is as if suddenly automobiles now cost two to four dollars, houses twenty to sixty dollars. . . . At present I would guess that perhaps 10% of the experiments in the Bell

Telephone Laboratories are done on the computer rather than in the laboratory; I expect that in time the reverse will be true. . . . [I]t is time we began to adjust our educational system to these new ideas. (Hamming, R. W., "Intellectual Implications of the Computer Revolution." *The American Mathematical Monthly,* LXX (January 1963), 4-11.)

C. The use of mathematical language . . . is already desirable and will soon become inevitable. Without its help the further growth of business with its attendant complexity of organization will be retarded and perhaps halted. In the science of management, as in other sciences, mathematics has become a "condition of progress." (Battersby, A. *Mathematics in Management.* Baltimore, Md.: Pelican Books, 1966. © Albert Battersby, 1966.)

D. The application of mathematics to the social sciences has become a topic of great interest in recent years, although it is not, of course, completely new. Economists have worked with mathematical formulations of their theories for a long time, and econometrics is today a well-developed field in its own right. Psychologists have used mathematical tools in certain aspects of their work, especially in the development of tests and in psychophysics. What is new is the increasing development of mathematical models in disciplines that are now sometimes called the behavioral sciences, especially social psychology, sociology, and political science. The growth is best indicated by the rapid increase in the amount of available literature . . . including the new *Journal of Mathematical Psychology.* (From *Readings in Mathematical Social Science* by Paul F. Lazarsfeld and Neil W. Henry. © 1966, Science Research Associates, Inc. Reprinted by permission of publisher.)

NOTES

1. H. Freudenthal, "Why to Teach Mathematics so as to be Useful" *Educational Studies in Mathematics* (1968), 3-8. This first issue of a new journal contains the proceedings of the colloquium, "How to Teach Mathematics so as to be Useful," held in Utrech, Netherlands, August 21–25, 1967, and sponsored by the International Commission on Mathematics Instruction.

2. E. G. Begle, "The Role of Research in the Improvement of Mathematics Education" *Educational Studies in Mathematics,* 2 (1969), 232-44.

3. E. H. Moore, "On the Foundations of Mathematics," *Science,* XVII (March 13, 1903), 401-16.

4. The National Committee on Mathematical Requirements, *The Reorganization of Mathematics in Secondary Education* (Boston, Mass.: Houghton Mifflin Company, 1923).

5. The National Council of Teachers of Mathematics, *The Place of Mathematics in Secondary Education,* Fifteenth Yearbook (New York: Bureau of Publications, Teachers College, Columbia University, 1940).

6. M. Stone, "The Revolution in Mathematics," *The American Mathematical Monthly,* 68 (October 1961), 715-34.

7. J. Gardner, "A National Weakness," *The American Mathematical Monthly,* 63 (June 1956), 396-99.

8. A. W. Tucker et al, *Report of the Commission on Mathematics: Program for College Preparatory Mathematics* (New York: The College Entrance Examination Board, 1959).

9. W. Wooton, *SMSG: The Making of a Curriculum,* New Haven, Conn.: Yale University Press, 1965.

10. E. G. Begle, "Mathematics Curriculum: New Study," Letter in *Science,* 151 (February 11, 1966), 632.

11. *See* Note 2.

12. T. Husen, ed., *International Study of Achievement in Mathematics* (New York: John Wiley & Sons, 1967).

13. J. W. Wilson, L. S. Cahen, E. G. Begle, eds., *NLSMA Reports, V. 1-14* (Stanford: School Mathematics Study Group, 1968–71).

14. T. A. Romberg *et al.,* Mathematics Education Research, *Review of Educational Research,* 39 (October 1969), 473-571.

15. J. W. Wilson, L. R. Cary, eds., *Reviews of Recent Research in Mathematics Education,* Studies in Mathematics Volume XIX (Stanford: School Mathematics Study Group, 1969).

16. *See* Note 14.

17. E. G. Begle, "Curriculum Research in Mathematics," in *Research and Development Toward the Improvement of Education* edited by H. J. Klausmier and G. T. O'Hearn (Madison, Wis.: Dunbar Educational Research Services, 1968), 44-48.

18. *See* Note 2.

19. J. Kilpatrick, and I. Wirszup, eds., *Soviet Studies in the Psychology of Learning and Teaching Mathematics* (Stanford: School Mathematics Study Group, 1969).

20. L. S. Shulman, "Perspective on the Psychology of Learning and the Teaching of Science and Mathematics," Michigan State University, (Mimeo), 1967.

21. *See* Note 2.

22. J. B. Carroll, "A Model of School Learning," *Teacher College Record,* 64 (May 1963), 723-33.

23. S. Herriot, *The Slow Learner Project: The Secondary School Slow Learner in Mathematics* (Stanford: School Mathematics Study Group, 1967).

24. R. C. Atkinson, and H. A. Wilson, "Computer Assisted Instruction," *Science,* 162 (October 4, 1968), 73-77.

25. F. Keppel, in Introduction to *Goals For School Mathematics: A Report of The Cambridge Conference on School Mathematics* (Boston: Houghton Mifflin Company, 1963).

26. M. Stone, Review of *Goals for School Mathematics, The Mathematics Teacher,* 58 (April 1965), 360.

27. M. S. Bell, "A Survey of High School Mathematics Teachers' Backgrounds, Opinions, and Priorities" (University of Chicago [Multilith], 1969).

28. *Nuffield Mathematics Project* (London: Newgate Press Ltd., 1969). [Distributed in the United States by New York: John Wiley & Sons, Inc.]

29. E. L. Norris, and J. E. Bowes, eds., *Mathematics Objectives* (Ann Arbor, Mich.: National Assessment of Educational Progress, 1970).

30. H. Fehr, *Secondary School Mathematics Curriculum Improvement Study: Information Bulletin #5* (New York: SSMCIS, Box 120, Teachers College, Columbia University, 1970).

31. R. M. Exner *et. al., Elements of Mathematics Program* (Carbondale, Ill.: Comprehensive School Mathematics Program, 1969).

32. SMSG, *Mathematics for Disadvantaged and Low Achieving Students,* Newsletter Number 33 (Stanford: School Mathematics Study Group, 1970).

33. W. S. DeVenney, *Final Report on an Experiment with Junior High School Very Low Achievers in Mathematics* (Stanford: School Mathematics Study Group, 1969).

34. *See* Note 26.

35. Cambridge Conference on School Mathematics, *Goals for Correlation of Elementary School Science and Mathematics* (Boston: Houghton Mifflin Company, 1969).

36. B. Glass, "The Japanese Science Education Centers," *Science,* 154 (October 14, 1966), 221-24.

MARK M. KRUG
The University of Chicago

VI THE SOCIAL STUDIES— SEARCH FOR NEW DIRECTIONS

We might as well start the discussion with a few observations about the term "social studies." First, visitors to high schools across the land would be hard put to find a classroom where "social studies" are taught. He may find a "social studies department" but the members of these departments teach U.S. history, world history, civics, world civilizations, problems of democracy, and less often sociology, political science, psychology, anthropology, and economics. Thus, the term "social studies," unlike mathematics or biology, does not denote a specific high school discipline, a subject matter, but it is a covering term for a number of subject matters in the area of history and the social sciences.

The name "social studies" was adopted after World War I, to signify the introduction of a new subject of instruction which was to include a combination of history and geography infused with the accumulated research findings and methodology from the social sciences.

New developments in the state of human knowledge prompted this reexamination of the school curricula. The years after World War I saw a rapid growth of the social sciences, especially of sociology and anthropology. There slowly developed a general conviction that these new disciplines dedicated to the empirical study of man in society and of the human condition, had to be included in the school curriculum. A special commission established by the American Historical Association to reassess the teaching of history which was headed by Charles Beard, the distinguished American historian, issued a *Charter for the Social Sciences* in 1934 which stated that the fundamental purpose of instruction in the social studies was "the creation of rich, many-sided personalities, equipped with practical knowledge and inspired by ideals so that they can make their way and fulfill their mission in a changing society which is part of a world complex."

The trouble started with this well-intentioned, but ambiguous statement. What was meant by "practical knowledge"? What ideals are the young to be inspired with? What was the "mission" that the young were called to fulfill in a changing society? To what societal changes did the statement refer? Charles Beard himself was aware of the inexact nature of the fundamental objective that his Commission set for the social studies. "This is not a finding of exact science," he wrote, "it is a statement of an ethical ideal long inherent in Western thought; human beings are endowed with moral dignity, possess and present values in themselves, and cannot be used for purposes alien to humane ends."[1] This, of course, is a typical *obscura per obscurum* explanation. The explanation of the fundamental social studies objectives, offered by Beard, begs the question and raises more questions than it answers. Few, if any, historians of Western civilization and fewer philosophers would accept the ethnocentric assumption of the existence of an inherent ideal of moral dignity in Western thought and the suggestion, contradicted on almost every page of the history of the Western world, that this ideal was effective in preventing the Western man from using his system of values for "purposes alien to humane ends." The history of Western imperialism and colonialism and the history of African exploitation and of Negro slavery offer ample testimony to the repeated use by Western nations of their alleged ethical ideals to justify oppression, brutality, and exploitation of people in Asia, Africa, and Latin America. Of course, on the other side, Western ethical idealism also has a record of considerable achievement on the same continents.

Why are we debating here the views of Charles Beard who has long gone to his eternal rest and whose reputation as a brilliant historian is more secure today than it was even in his lifetime? Simply because the ambiguity and the confusion contained in the Beard Report in the *Charter for the Social Studies,* are still plaguing the field of social studies. One could cite hundreds of sets of objectives in social studies curricula now in use in high schools throughout the country that still glibly and ambiguously refer to the "creation of rich and many sided personalities" and to the training for adjustment to a complex society.

Even today, many decades after the publication of Beard's charter, some social studies educators advance the same exaggerated claims for the social sciences which Beard made in his celebrated book on *The Nature of the Social Sciences.* Charles Beard wrote what he wrote at the early stages of the social science investigations when it was premature to evaluate the impact of anthropology, sociology, or political science on the contemporary society. This is no longer true today when the scholars in social sciences engage in a searching and highly critical analysis of the worth and the influence and the directions of their disciplines.

In spite of the overwhelming evidence which points to the important limitations in the ability of social scientists to come to grips with the complex societal issues like peace and war, racial strife, or deeply rooted national animosities, many social studies educators still cling to Beard's inflated assessment of the nature and the function of the social sciences. Beard wrote:

The social sciences can furnish knowledge, an insight into the processes of social thought, and a method indispensible to the operation of formulating workable objectives. ... They disclose by examination and tabulation the objectives which American society ... has already proclaimed. They present facts and organizations of knowledge and thought corresponding, with more or less accuracy, to the realities of American society and world relations. ... They [the social sciences] describe the general trends or tendencies of society which provide the only available indications for *forecasting the necessities and probabilities of the future social situations in which children now in the schools will have to live their lives and discharge their obligations.* ... They describe the ethical and esthetic ideals which furnish guidance in determining what is desirable [and] which may be potentially realized. They describe qualities of human character that represent the ideal and are necessary to the maintenance and development of a society compatible with the realization of the ideal.[2]

In the perspective of 40 years since Beard made these statements, it is clear that some of his expectations for the social sciences were greatly exaggerated if not downright naïve. The social sciences have fulfilled the hope that they would bring more insight into the nature of man, his modes of behavior as an individual and in groups. Anthropology gave us a new understanding of the concept of culture, of the customs and mores of many civilizations, sociology has done much to explain man's behavior in society and political science has thrown much light on the sources and the use of political power in and by governments and other power groups, but none of the social sciences has had much success in, using Beard's language, "forecasting . . . future social situations" or in influencing changes in human or societal behavior or, most importantly, in helping to *solve* difficult and complex societal problems. In fact, we are now confronted with a situation in which a whole generation of college students who understand our society better with the help of sociology are revolted by it and reject our political system which they studied in political science classes, as iniquitous and unworkable. None of the social sciences has much to offer to the solution of the overriding dilemmas of our age, the elimination of war and the eradication of racial hatred and racial discrimination. Consequently, we are witnessing a rebellion of young social scientists who are charging, rightly or wrongly, the established scholars in their respective disciplines, of wittingly or unwittingly serving in the perpetuation of the status quo, in the American society.

The editors of a collection of essays written by dissident political scientists declared that modern political science was largely irrelevant because its research "was being used not to serve the interests of the poor and oppressed around the world, but rather to serve the interests of the U.S. government" which uses political science as its tool.[3] At the 1969 meeting of the American Political Science Association, Professor David Easton, the president of the association, said in his address: "For increasing numbers of us, it is no longer practical or morally tolerable to stand on the political sidelines when our expertise alerts us to disaster."

A number of sociologists and economists collaborated on a book entitled, *The Dissenting Academy,* whose major theme is the allegation that social scientists have limited their investigations to relatively unimportant issues and have neglected the crucial problems and crises facing our society.

However, in general, the infusion of the social sciences into the social studies curriculum has been beneficial in many respects, but it has failed to make a substantive difference in the area of values in

general and in citizenship education in particular. The general ineffectiveness of history instruction which too often consists of the teaching
of unrelated sets of "facts" or of "periods" or "ages" has long been
barren of opportunities to teach human and citizenship values. Since
many teachers look upon history as a definitive description of the past
to be transmitted to the young and do not look upon history as inquiry
into some aspects of the past by everchanging generations of historians,
the learners have few opportunities to engage in creative freewheeling
investigation of the past. In civics, an opportunity to mold attitudes and
to induce the formation of desirable values, is made impossible by the
insistence on teaching the static structure of government instead of
encouraging the study of the *process* of our government, and the fostering of an understanding of *how* the political system works and how it
could be changed and improved. No wonder that so many of the young
people have been "turned off" by American politics and are convinced
that the "System" is not susceptible to change or reform.

Professor Donald Oliver of Harvard has been deeply troubled by
the problem of effective citizenship education and value teaching.
Writing in 1957 on the issue, Oliver advocated the teaching of "direct
morality of cooperation and brotherly love."[4] To achieve this aim, Oliver suggested a curriculum which would concentrate on in-depth
inquiries and dialogues centering on the political and ethical conflicts
in the American pluralistic society. "The objective of social science
education," Oliver wrote, "is to introduce young people into the fire
and controversy that rages within a free society over ways of regulating
human affairs—ways that might presumably maximize the freedom of
the individual to pursue his own fulfillment. ...."[5] In the crucible of
these rational investigations of controversial issues, like freedom of the
press versus censorship, separation of church and state, and federal aid
to private schools, the citizenship values and attitudes of the students
would be forged.

In a book published with Professor James Shaver in 1966, *Teaching
Public Issues in the High School,* the authors while retaining the stress
on free inquiry of controversial issues and value conflicts, demanded
from teachers and students an a priori commitment to some of the basic
values in the American Creed, including free inquiry, human dignity,
and freedom of speech. They argued, with good reason, that their whole
approach would make no sense if it were not predicated on the prior
acceptance of the principle of rational inquiry and freedom of people

to think and to freely choose alternate modes of behavior or alternate solutions to value-conflicts and to public controversies.

Based on the rationale the Harvard Project published a whole series of units dealing with public controversies. These teaching units have been deservedly popular with many teachers. Criticism of the Harvard Project concentrated on doubts whether a whole social studies curricula ought to be built on public controversies and whether student interest can be sustained during the prolonged use of what basically is a single teaching technique. Professor Oliver in an impressive self-searching analysis at a session during the 1970 Convention of the National Conference for Social Studies, suggested that the feedback from teachers and students using the Harvard Project materials suggested an even more disturbing difficulty which can be defined in the following questions: Does a rational inquiry necessarily lead to rational and acceptable solutions of complex issues? How does one deal with the fact that many teachers and students find a rational inquiry burdensome and uncomfortable? and finally, and most importantly, *Is* it possible to conduct truly rational inquiries into value-laden problems in a society which is increasingly dominated by irrational forces and is rent by emotional conflicts and disputes?

At the same session, Professor Michael Scriven of Berkeley attempted to answer the last question by stating that since our society is saturated with indoctrination, and since so little in our culture is worth transmitting, teachers are duty bound to desist from transmitting the cultural values and mores of the society. In fact, Scriven contended that the teachers make the schools centers of active resistance to the existing values of the society. They must engage in a thorough and dispassionate examination of the society, through fostering free inquiry and autonomous judgments which may even lead the students to a total rejection of our form of government. "We can be saved," Scriven said, "not by a revolution, but by opening the possibility of revolution."

There is nothing particularly disturbing or frightening in this far-reaching proposal. One ought not to be afraid to give human minds a free reign. But the difficulty, it seems to me, lies in Scriven's exaggerated reliance on the power of reason to "solve" complex issues. Even less faith ought to be put in human beings as reasonable *actors* on the stage of life.

Rational discourse, critical inquiry, the use of the skills of autonomous judgment, are indeed precious tools for the examination of societal problems, of human dilemmas, of public issues and controversies or in the examination of values and they enhance one's intelligent judgment, but they do not carry with it a guarantee of behavioral change or even less of sound behavior which may lead to a greater happiness of the individual or the society. It seems important to emphasize that human beings either as individuals or as a society, do not necessarily act as reason or a reasonable discourse or inquiry suggests or even dictates. Human beings individually and in groups, societies, or nations, just as often act irrationally driven by impulse, emotion, pride, or passion. Even some of the splendid case studies in the Oliver-Newmann series suggest that a rational dialogue may well suggest several or even contradictory courses of action.

History is replete with examples indicating that the use of skills in critical thinking do not guarantee sound decisions.

Picture for a moment this scenario. Four men sit in the Oval Room of the White House, in the time of the Lyndon Johnson Presidency and debate a crucial decision on the Vietnam War. The group is composed of McGeorge Bundy, Walt Rostow, Robert McNamara, and General Maxwell Taylor. It is common knowledge that these men are sharp, bright, endowed with incisive minds, eminently qualified to conduct a critical inquiry into a complex issue. And yet out of this and other meetings and deliberations of this group came the wretched and self-defeating decisions that got us into the morass and the tragedy of Vietnam.

The Age of Reason produced the works of Diderot and Voltaire, the Declaration of the Rights of Man, but it also produced the unspeakable brutality and terror of the Committee on Public Safety which brought the heads of the makers of the revolution to roll off the guillotine platforms to the roars of joy and laughter of Parisian mobs.

The magnificent rational inquiry into the history of mankind by Marx and Engels in *Das Kapital* led directly to the Russian Revolution and to the murder by Stalin of the fathers of the Revolution and of millions of innocent Russians and the brilliant analysis by Hitler and Goebbels of the psychological mood of the Germans in the days of the Weimar Republic, led directly to the concentration camps and to the crematoria of Auschwitz and Treblinka.

And coming closer to our society, the truth must be said that the Civil Rights Revolution has been largely a failure. Logically and rationally and even legally, it is clear that we have committed and are committing a monstrous injustice toward the 20 million black Americans. We have examined and analyzed this injustice with all the tools of critical inquiry—we *know* what must be done, but who will deny that the blind, emotional, irrational fear of the blacks has, so far, vitiated all efforts to bring about true racial equality.

All this is not said here to indicate despair with the usefulness of rational inquiry or a critical examination of our society, but we must be clearly aware of the limitations of critical inquiry conducted by complex human beings of an even more complex human society. This realization ought to suggest that we have to put the objectives in social studies in a proper perspective and free them from exaggerated claims.

History and historians have learned an important lesson from history, namely that irrational factors are as important and as governing in the behavior of nations as the rational and the logical ones. That seems to be a lesson of history that so many of our young people and even some of our social studies curriculum builders wish to ignore. I wish it were not so, *but it is* and we have to live with this realization. Any rational inquiry into the past or the present which ignores the presence of the irrational, of the accident, of the complex and often inexplicable sources and motivations of human behavior is apt to be incomplete and lead to erroneous conclusions.

Finally, there is the question whether it is indeed immoral, as Professor Scriven puts it, to suppose that we have any rights to pass on values to our young generations and whether indeed as he suggests, it is far from clear whether they are worth passing on. In a sense the question is academic. All societies—tribal, primitive, partly and relatively advanced—have always and are now passing on their mores and values to the young. That is the essence of their culture and that is the cement that makes their survival possible. No other way has yet been found for a society to survive. The Eskimos have to teach their young how to hunt and how to build igloos and the Catholics in Ulster feel that they have to teach their young about their religion, their community, their history, their mores to survive in a hostile Protestant country. And the Protestants, for the same reason, follow a similar course. It is really immaterial in a sense whether these values or mores are good or bad, positive or negative—*that is all that the older society has to offer.* It is also rather doubtful whether the young generations, if allowed to ignore the values of the preceding generations, would develop mores and values that would be better, sounder and lead to more happiness.

All that we must be sure is that the young generation is offered an opportunity to examine these values with as much freedom as is possible in a complex, prejudiced, indoctrinated society. This leads me to an optimistic note about the bloodless revolution in the social studies. It was on the whole a very welcome revolution. To be sure, many of the projects made excessive claims, some had exaggerated expectations and a few tried to evolve or even impose a single ideal curriculum. These claims, of course, proved to be a disappointment. But the projects have released new energies, they have infused a new life into the teaching of history and the social studies, and have often brilliantly utilized the techniques and the accumulated research in the social sciences to illuminate hitherto unexplained aspects of human behavior.

It is through these new approaches, attached to the old, that we may hope that the transmission of cultural values may be more successful in the future than it was in the past.

It is important to emphasize that human experience must be passed on *in toto*—the good and the bad. The current very successful television series on "Civilisation" produced, written, and narrated by Sir Kenneth Clark, while impressive and instructive, is seriously flawed in that it presents a one-sided march forward of Western Civilization. It is one sided because it presents the glory and the splendor of the Chinese Wall and the beauty of Bellini's Fountain of Trevi without pointing out the sweat and blood of millions, and thousands who paid with their health and lives for these monuments to civilization. The glory of Greece and the spirit of freedom of the Athenians are part of Greek civilization, but so is the infamous judicial murder of Socrates.

Equally important is to begin to teach a New American History in place of the cleaned up, sanitized version of history which we teach today. This new history would not ignore the violence, both foreign and domestic in U.S. history. Much of the disdain or even contempt that our young people have for U.S. history courses is a logical consequence of their correct assessment that they are being taught an expurgated version of the history of this country. They, seldom if ever, are taught about the systematic policy of extermination of Indians, the suppression and oppression of blacks, and they are taught the myth of the melting pot and made to believe that this country did indeed—in the words of the famous poem of Emma Lazarus—welcome the wretched refuse of the teeming shores of Europe. In fact, most immigrants, Irish, Chinese, Jews, and Italians, were welcomed by boycotts, by nativist movements, the Know-Nothing Party and the white Anglo-Saxon immigration exclusion acts. The immigrants often succeeded, not with the assistance, but in *spite* of the dominant society.

In foreign policy, we have not always followed George Washington's injunction to deal fairly with the nations of the world. We must teach the immorality of the war with Mexico, the chicanery of the building of the Panama Canal, the unprovoked onslaught on Cuba in the Spanish-American War, and the tragedy of Vietnam. While it would be a mistake, as the late Professor Richard Hofstadter, in his recent book on the history of violence in America, states, to lapse into a state of maudlin and conventional anti-Americanism or to indulge in too much breast-beating, a thorough revision of our history courses, in high schools and in colleges, is long overdue. Americans have on the whole, had a unique history, filled with great achievements and a sustained, if not always successful, search for freedom and well-being of all its citizens. This fact will come out stronger if the weaknesses and blunders are not ignored.

John Dewey as we know, had serious doubts about the existence of eternal values and he was a determined opponent of indoctrination. Yet, Dewey recognized the importance, nay, the necessity, of passing on to the young, what he called the "consciousness of the race" or the achievements and values of the older generation, in order for the young to understand the contemporary society.

The growing peril to the survival of our society, the bewildering impatience of the young people to find new modes for political and social expression, make the shift of emphasis in the curriculum from the past to a new curriculum which would combine the past and the present imperative.

The discussion on the definition of the "social studies" seems never to end. One of the most recent formulations has come from the Marin Social Studies Project in California which was assigned the task of developing a new K-12 "Social Studies Curricula for a Modern World." It reads as follows: "The social studies is that portion of the general education curriculum the purpose of which is to make students more rational with regard to human behavior and social interaction."[6] Rationality, Sidney Lester of the staff of the Project, explained, was used as a criterion for the exclusion or inclusion of social studies material. Generally, the selected areas of study were those in which human beings have difficulty in applying a rational analysis. These include, law, religion, sex, economics, nationalism, patriotism, foreign affairs, race, and minority relations. "The rationale we offer," Lester wrote, "for our definition is based on the fact that there are today numerous threats to the survival of mankind. We feel that the development of greater degrees of rationality will enhance the opportunity of our youth to survive in a world worth surviving in." By *rationality*, the Marin Project staff meant the application of logical thought to the analysis of problems. The staff decided not to include education for citizenship in its definition because "if good citizenship" in a nation demands nonrational behavior on the part of its citizens, and certainly there are historical cases where this has been evidenced, then we must opt for rational behavior as opposed to good citizenship. To state it a different way, we would say that good citizenship in our nation must be dependent upon rational behavior.[7]

The Marin Project rationale is as full of holes as a sieve. Let's first take "rational thinking" as an educational objective. Such thinking is based on logical thought which supposedly in turn leads to rational behavior. But the fact is that sound logical thinking can lead to contradictory modes of behavior, both of which must be accepted as rational in terms of their respective frames of reference. Senator McGovern using logical deduction, concludes that the war in Vietnam is immoral, resulting in the killing of thousands of South and North Vietnamese and it therefore must be ended immediately regardless of consequences to South Vietnam or to the United States. The columnist, Joseph Alsop, using *his* system of rational analysis, asserts that a precipitous withdrawal from Vietnam would hand South Vietnam over to the North Vietnam dictatorship. This could constitute an immoral act which would eventually result in more wars in Southeast Asia. A rational inquiry, using principles of logical thinking cannot resolve this dilemma. In the final analysis, the personal, *subjective* preferences, feelings and biases of the student will decide the issue for him. Even more complex is, for instance, the question of abortion laws. The best rational analysis will be for naught when confronted by a stand on abortion dictated by religious faith. In truth, historians have been trying to make this point for years, that much of the behavior of individuals and nations is dictated, in addition to a rational analysis, by self-interest, by irrational factors like, ambition, quest for power, anger, or momentary aberration. This reality is well known to all men facing family problems and career decisions. What appears logical and rational at one point in one's life, becomes clearly a bad or a foolish decision in the reflection of a few years. Therefore to postulate that education for citizenship is not an acceptable objective for social studies because sometime rational behavior is opposed to good citizenship is to assume that we *know,* in complex issues, what "rational behavior" is, or is not. Was Truman's decision to drop atomic bombs on Hiroshima and Nagasaki an example of rational behavior or of bad citizenship? A logical and rational argument can be and has been made for both points of view. Would the teachers in the Marin Project undertake to make the *final* decision?

What is needed when we talk of attitudinal value training in social studies is caution, modesty, and perspective. All that can be said is that we can try to encourage rational thought and critical thinking as *one* of the avenues to a better understanding of our complex society. In this task the role of history as an inquiry into the past must be emphasized. History, if taught as a series of investigations conducted by historians into the fragments of the past, can well present to the students a variety of ways in which men reacted to the challenges of their times and their particular situations. The students may see and benefit from these examples of rational and irrational modes of behavior.

While we have made little progress in the crucial area of teaching values and citizenship education, which some postulate as *the* most important objective in the social studies, we have done considerably better in improving the curriculum in social studies. Here the instructional materials published by many history and social science projects financed by governmental or foundation monies have been most helpful.

One book contributed more than any other factor to the "new social studies." It was *The Process of Education* by Jerome Bruner. Bruner's influence was profound because it provided social studies educators, confronted with an amorphous subject matter and a discipline which really was not a respectable academic discipline like mathematics or biology, with a new conceptual framework. Bruner postulated that every academic discipline is basically a set, a structure of concepts and generalizations defined or discovered by its scholars. These concepts are arranged sequentially and are logically connected. Obviously then, according to Bruner, the best way to teach a discipline is to teach sequentially its structure of concepts and generalizations.

Bruner's views were accepted with enthusiasm by social studies educators. They promised order and a sense of purpose in a disorientated, diffuse and largely demoralized field. Unwisely, and uncritically, efforts were made to find *the* structure in history to build curricula based on the sequential set of historical concepts and generalizations. It soon became apparent that it was futile to search for *the* structure of history because history, which in fact consists of a great variety of historical writings by historians who wrote in various times and in various lands, has no one unified structure like physics or mathematics, and its concepts have little sequential interrelationship. As for great generations or predictive laws, few academic historians were willing even to attempt to find them and even less ready to attempt to find a consensus on them with their colleagues.

In spite of these disappointments and the exaggerated expectations, Jerome Bruner had a profound and beneficial influence on the new social studies. While the search for *one* structure had to be abandoned, the search for structures or substructures in historical events or movements, like the French Revolution, Reformation, and imperialist rule in colonial possessions, proved to be useful and methodologically rewarding. Social studies innovators, using Brunerian ideas, were disappointed in their attempt to find great generalizations or predictive laws in history, but they have greatly revitalized the instruction of history which suffered from an undue emphasis on the recitation of unrelated facts, by the often successful attempts to illuminate historical events or movements by the use of such concepts as elite, class struggle, social mobility, and class alienation.

There is no question that the search for structures and the use of concepts brought much needed vitality and a new sense of purpose into the social studies classrooms. Even more importantly, the "new social studies" made it possible to relate past events to the present, to make use of the abiding interest of many students in contemporary societal issues and to make instruction more "relevant."

The single, most important indirect contribution of Jerome Bruner for history teachers was that he reminded them of something that most of them have forgotten or overlooked, namely, that history was not a summary of "known" facts about the past but an *inquiry into the past.* Bruner postulated that one of the best ways to teach children any discipline was to lead them through the steps of scientific inquiry and investigation followed by the scholars of that discipline. Many teachers of history are now providing their students with opportunities and guidance to engage in historical inquiries into small segments of the past, in a way in which such inquiries are pursued by professional historians. The success of this teaching technique is, of course spotty, but the successes achieved more than justify the efforts. All in all, the orderly revolution in the social studies, inspired by Bruner's ideas on the nature of the disciplines and on the process of teaching and learning, opened a new era for high school social studies.

There is little doubt that the Anthropology Project, headed by Mrs. Malcolm Collier and enjoying the cooperation of the American Anthropological Association, has been eminently successful in introducing anthropology into the high school social studies curriculum. Mrs. Collier and her staff of academic anthropologists and teachers have, since 1960, tested and re-tested, through a rigorous program of experimental use in a variety of schools, a number of anthropological units. The original units "The Study of Early Man" and "The Great Transformations" have been completely revised. Portions of these units will be incorporated into anthropology curricular materials which are scheduled to be published by two commercial firms. Two case studies of considerable merit, *The Great Tree and the Longhouse: Culture of the Iroquois,* by Hazel W. Hertzberg, and *Kiowa Years: Study in Culture Impact and Profile of a People,* by Alice Marriott, have already been published.

The central concepts in anthropology, the concepts of culture and cultural change, are dealt with, in a detailed outline for a three-week course in anthropology entitled, "History as Culture Change." This course is designed to be supplementary to a regular history course and to allow the students to perceive the evolution of culture patterns from the primitive societies of Bushmen in the Kalahari Desert in Africa to a comparison of the impact of modernization in Hasanabad, a village in Iran, with a village in today's Mexico. The emphasis is on the difficulties and actual sufferings faced by rural areas in the underdeveloped countries which face the inroads of cultural changes due to improved communications and advanced technology. The unit is an excellent example of how the use of insights and concepts from a social science can be used as a new lens to illuminate hitherto unexplored aspects of the history of mankind.

The leaders of the Sociological Resources Project for Secondary Schools have been refreshingly frank in describing the difficulties that they have experienced in preparing sociological materials for the use in schools. These confessions, far from damaging the reputation of the sociology project, especially when contrasted with the claims made by some other social studies enterprises, testify to the high professional standards of the sociologists working for the S.R.S.S. The difficulties may also be an indication of the growing realization that in spite of its magnificent advances, sociology is, as yet, not ready for a mass packaging of its products and that we are still far from a real knowledge of basic principles or laws that govern the interaction of groups in our complex society.

Nevertheless, the S.R.S.S. after a long period of trial and error experimentation produced a variety of excellent materials. The first paperback produced by the project is entitled *Cities and City Life* and includes 20 chapters on such topics as "Where You Live," "Segregation Where Whites and Negroes Live," "The City Man's Neighbors and Friends," "The Slum: Who Has to Live There and Who Chooses to Live There," and "Cats, Kicks and Color."

The most interesting materials are the sociological episodes or relatively small units of study which have been carefully tested in schools and then revised and published by a commercial publisher. *Images of People* is an interesting and instructive analysis of stereotypes and images and how they affect societal behavior. *Leadership in American Society: A Case Study of Negro Leadership* explains to the student the concept of leadership not in terms of the nature and personal qualities of leaders, but it emphasizes the interrelationship of the leader with the group or society that he is leading. With this background, the unit explains the careers of Booker T. Washington and Stokely Carmichael. The discussion of the rise to leadership of these men, in the context of the status and aspirations of the black communities of their times, is novel, insightful and instructive.

The S.R.S.S. *Newsletter* of Autumn, 1969, includes two papers which analyze the episodes which were revised on the basis of the feedback from students and teachers who were using them. The conclusions reached have a bearing on our discussion on the teaching of social sciences in secondary schools. The evaluators, both staff members of the S.R.S.S., Graeme Fraser and Thomas Switzer, conclude that "ponderous academic sociology just doesn't go over." What does go over are sociological episodes that are "novel, fresh, surprising and improbable." Most of the episodes that I have read fall into this category. Furthermore, the critics found that each episode must treat one limited issue in depth and that "though sociology is an abstract generalizing discipline, high school students learn more readily from concrete picturable material." This is not exactly news to classroom teachers, but it is good to see the known confirmed. One can only hope that the few rather confused and misguided social studies curriculum makers who want to teach abstract concepts and generalizations without appropriate content would take heed and desist.

The Geography Project has made a significant contribution in preparing an excellent curriculum aimed at the freshman year in high school. This new geography curriculum includes units on "Geography of Cities," "Manufacturing and Agriculture," "Cultural Geography," "Political Geography," "Habitat and Resources" and "Japan."

And yet in spite of the accumulation of the new teaching materials, relatively little progress can be observed in the social studies classrooms. The difficulty seems to be with the social studies teachers. The task of a social studies teacher who is trying to teach the New Social Studies is formidable, if not impossible. In most schools, the new materials in sociology, anthropology, geography, and economics have been grafted into the existing curriculum which is centered on the United States and world history. Social studies curricula, across the country present a veritable hodgepodge of history, social sciences, courses of study based on the search for a structure in history and in the social sciences, on concepts, or on a search for broad generalizations. Still others, postulate skills of inquiry and critical thinking (whatever is meant by these ambiguous terms) as their main objectives. Obviously, the field has gone far beyond the simplistic definition offered in 1937 by Edgar Wesley who said: "The social studies are the social sciences adapted and simplified for pedagogical purposes." No teacher would today attempt to simplify or adapt modern sociology or anthropology for instructional purposes. If he did, the justified wrath of academic sociologists and anthropologists would descend on his head.

Barth and Shermis have some time ago made a valiant attempt to make some sense out of the various goals in social studies curricula. They suggested that generally speaking, some curricula look on social studies as citizenship education, others, treat social studies as social sciences, and still others interpret the essence of the social studies as reflective inquiry.[8] One may add a bit cynically that many curricula mix either two or even all three approaches. This makes for a garden variety curriculum which confuses students and teachers alike. Another serious difficulty results from the lack of professional preparation of many teachers to effectively use the materials published by the various social studies projects. To teach on the basis of units prepared by the an-thropology, geography, or sociology projects, teachers need more, not less, grounding in the social science disciplines and a great many new teaching skills. And yet, few schools, or school districts have made provisions for the training or retraining of teachers before the new social studies curricula have been introduced. The result of this failure is that many teachers make halfhearted attempts to introduce some project materials and then abandon the effort because of total un-familiarity with the material, or because of the formidable methodologi-cal problems encountered. In many cases, it was much easier to return to the well-trodden if ineffective ways of traditional teaching. It would be unfair to fault the classroom teachers for this debacle. Their responsi-bility must be shared by the project directors, the school leaders in all levels for the failure to provide adequate in-service training.

WHAT OF THE FUTURE?

Most of the major projects have arranged for the publication of their materials by commercial publishing firms. This step was inevitable in order to assure wide distribution. There are, however, some obvious drawbacks in this development. Control by the publishers will mean an end of experimentation and the decisions whether to republish a unit or an entire curriculum series will depend almost entirely upon whether they are profitable. In a few years the next texts or study units will not be republished and will disappear from circulation.

There are already authenticated reports that many of the new project materials which were put on the market are not selling well and there is a growing feeling in the profession that the interest in the discipline-orientated curriculum innovations has already peaked and is on the decline. It is now suggested by some leading spokesmen in social studies that the newest social studies revolution will move in the direc-tion of an interdisciplinary social studies curriculum which would oblit-erate the boundaries between history, sociology, and anthropology and draw on exciting concepts, research, and methods from all of the social sciences. Furthermore, the new social studies curricula would center more on the affective domain, the realm of values and attitudes and would evolve around the individual and his interaction with society, war and peace, ecology, and the interests of students. A survey of the field which included interviews with leading social studies educators concluded that "there is a pronounced movement away from materials based on single disciplines—their cognitive content—toward multi- and cross-disciplinary studies, with emphasis on modes and processes of inquiry, values and value conflicts."[9] The authors of the survey conclude on the basis of the interviews that, "The reaction away from single discipline materials is engendered both by a demand on the part of the schools and a realization on the part of curriculum developers that an integrated humanistic approach to social studies education is more realistic and more effective than a fragmented program based on single-discipline courses."[10]

Thus, long before the materials and the new curricula produced at such a heavy investment of human resources and money, by the anthropology, history, sociology, economics, and geography projects have been widely used and tested, the volatile and insecure field of social studies is moving away from them. Only a few years ago, the same leaders in the field who are now ready to pronounce the final benediction over the projects, hailed the method of discipline teaching through Bruner's theory of structure and discovery as the most significant breakthrough in social studies instruction. Without waiting for an orderly and scholarly testing and evaluation of the new curricula and new approaches they are ready to move on to new,   even less charted territories in response to what is perceived as the mood of the times. There are several even more perturbing implications in this new direction. Much of the difficulty with the use of project materials related to the deficiencies in discipline competence and the limited ability to use inquiry methods of many social studies teachers. If this was the case with materials centered on one social science discipline, how much greater will be the obstacles with interdisciplinary materials. Who will be responsible for developing the new integrated, humanistic interdisciplinary materials? Academic geographers and academic anthropologists were willing to sit down with geography and anthropology teachers, respectively, to work on a geography and anthropology curricula, but there is a serious doubt whether the academic scholars would be amenable to the planning of interdisciplinary curricula when such integration efforts are at the very initial stages on the university level. Finally, the new curricula would put the heaviest emphasis on the teaching of values and that happens to be the one single area in social studies in which the rate of success has been the least significant.

Historians have long been impressed with the complex nature of man, with the erratic behavior of nations, and with the role that the unexpected and the accidental plays in the affairs of mankind. They are naturally reluctant to spend too much time on predicting the future. This writer shares in this reluctance. But within these limitations it may be safe to venture a few prognostications:

1. In spite of the difficulties referred to above, social science curricular materials, particularly those from sociology, political science, economics, geography, and anthropology, will be used in an increasing measure in social studies classrooms. Similarly, modes of inquiry from the social sciences, particularly, polling, questionnaires, field study, and interviews will be incorporated in the teaching techniques in social studies. This development is inevitable and ought to be warmly welcomed because insights, research findings, and research techniques from the social sciences may be of great help to social studies teachers to close the gap between social studies classroom instruction and the outside world which in fact is less and less on the "outside." The revolution in communication has largely erased the former isolation of schools from society. It makes little sense for some social studies educators to make exaggerated claims for the social sciences as "solvers" of current societal ills and problems but there is no doubt that the *study* of the major issues in our contemporary society would be, or ought to be, unthinkable without the wealth of new information which has been accumulated by anthropologists, sociologists, and other social scientists. Hopefully, boards of education and school districts will finally recognize the need to provide the necessary training which would enable social studies teachers to make the best of this new opportunity.

2. History will remain the central core of instruction in the social studies. This will be so primarily because, in spite of the assertions of some social studies educators to the contrary, it seems unthinkable to a vast majority of parents, legislators, *and students,* that they may graduate from high school without some basic knowledge and understandings in the history of our country and of the world. In spite of all the harangues (some of them justified) against history and history teaching, there is a widely held view in our society which holds that there is an intrinsic value in the study of history and that there is a large measure of continuity of historical experience which makes the study of the past not only useful, but essential to the understanding of the present. All the detractors of history cannot, for instance, weaken the conviction of

the general newspaper reader that the fighting between the Catholics and the Protestants in Ulster has its roots in the history of that small country and that an understanding of this conflict makes the study of that history a must. The same is true of the Middle East and of the struggle between East and West Pakistan.

One must make a clear distinction between the past and history. Both those that denigrate and those that defend history must be clear about this distinction. It is history—the books and monographs and articles written by historians—that is sometimes pedantic, that often puts too much stress on facts and dates without paying proper attention to connections, general meanings, and movements. On the other hand, the past itself is dynamic, colorful, a living force, and is always an intrinsic part of the present. Any distinction between the past and the present is artificial and unrealistic. One can claim that some of the written history is irrelevant to the present, but the *past* is always relevant to today because it is part of the present.

History teachers must heed the complaints that some of them teach the history which does not exist. They must try to teach an inquiry into the past use of historical writing, including textbooks, as only one of the tools of an inquiry into past experiences of men. If they do this they will find that the past is indeed a rich mine for presenting and teaching varieties of human experiences and even greater varieties of human modes of behavior. They and their students will find in this study not "solutions" to new situations and problems, but excellent tools for the understanding of modern societal issues.

Again, it must be emphasized that modern historians and history teachers must teach "new history," a history that does not ignore the story of the blacks, the experiences of the Indians and that benefits from the new insights into the past that can be revealed to us by the application of the work of sociologists, anthropologists, and other social scientists.

3. The current widespread conviction of American young people that the American political system is seriously flawed or even that it is unworkable must eventually result in a strong pressure to scrap the existing ineffective civics courses and to develop a meaningful program of citizenship education. Such a program would stress instead of the study of the structure of government, the *process* of the working of our government system. The emphasis will have to be teaching our young that our political system is basically right, but that it is in need of

constant improvement and perfection and that it is susceptible to change. Schools may well in the future become laboratories from which the President, the Congress, and even the judicial system may draw on ideas for the needed reforms to make our government more efficient and ready to respond to the changing needs of the people and of society.

NOTES

1. Charles Beard, *The Nature of the Social Sciences* (New York: Charles Scribners' Sons, 1938), p. 179.

2. *Ibid.,* p. 181.

3. Marvin Surkin and Alan Wolfe (eds.), *An End to Political Science* (New York: Basic Books, Inc., 1970), p. 4.

4. Donald Oliver, "The Selection of Content in the Social Studies," *Harvard Educational Review* (1957), p. 271.

5. *Ibid.,* p. 278.

6. G. Sidney Lester, "Redefining the Social Studies Curriculum," mimeographed paper, p. 8. Prepared for delivery at the American Historical Association Meeting, December, 1970.

7. *Ibid.,* p. 12.

8. James L. Barth and S. Samuel Shermis, "Defining Social Studies: An Explanation of Three Traditions," *Social Education* (November, 1967), p. 744.

9. Michael A. Radz and C. Frederick Risinger, "A Revolution Comes of Age: Social Studies Curriculum Development in the Seventies," *Social Science Education Consortium Newsletter,* Boulder, Colorado (May, 1971) p. 3.

10. *Ibid.,* p. 4.

KEVIN RYAN
University of Chicago

VII
TEACHER EDUCATION—
REALITIES AND PROSPECTS

For several decades now the epigram, "teachers are born and not made" has hovered over a discussion of the education of teachers. It has been the rallying cry of two groups attempting to influence teacher education: first, those who believe that all one needs to know is a good deal about what he is teaching and the rest will follow naturally; and second, those who believe that teaching is an art which defies scientific analysis and is thus highly intuitive and individualistic. By and large more serious thinkers have dismissed these points of view. The assertion that individuals cannot be substantially aided in the process of becoming a teacher flies in the face of all we know about learning and human behavior. It has all the credibility of "surgeons are born, not made."

Nevertheless, the education of teachers has been a serious problem in this country for over 100 years. From the time our nation made a commitment to mass public education it has been faced with the task of taking large numbers of people with average intellectual endowments and turning them into competent teachers. While there have been periods of time when there was no shortage of teachers, such as the Depression and the present, the quality of the nation's teaching force has been an abiding source of concern. Besides a plethora of learned volumes, and high-level conferences, 11 major studies of teacher education in the United States have been conducted and reported to the people in the last 50 years.[1] While the recommendations emanating from these studies are striking in their disparity one from the other, the studies appear to have one attribute in common: They have had relatively little impact on the manner in which teachers are educated and trained in this country.

Any consideration of the curriculum of teacher education and its future directions must be considered in light of the massive size of the teacher education apparatus. In 1971 the nation's colleges and universities will graduate 275,000 young people eligible to teach. One out of every three college students go through teacher education programs and are eligible for certification upon graduation.[2]

Teacher education is carried on in over 1,000 full four-year institutions.[3] The sheer size of the teacher education enterprise and the manner in which it is intertwined with the rest of the undergraduate curriculum make fundamental change most difficult. Nevertheless, recently there has been renewed call for reform in teacher education.[4] The possibility for sustained attention to reforming teacher education would appear to be enhanced by the growing dissatisfaction with the nation's public schools. The old but rather compelling argument that the quality of classroom teaching depends on the quality of teacher turned out by the teacher training institutions is being given fresh attention.

This chapter will attempt to describe the predominant modes, both formal and informal, of training teachers, some of the recent trends, some major obstacles to improvement, and, finally, some speculation about desirable directions for the future.

THE CURRICULA FOR BECOMING A TEACHER

There are two curricula for becoming a teacher. One is overt; the other is covert. One is formal, and is the officially sanctioned means by which someone becomes a teacher. The other is informal and, as such, unsanctioned. In fact, this informal curricula is rarely acknowledged as a contributor to the professional development of a teacher.

Formal Curriculum

The formal curriculum in teacher education is controlled by universities and leads to certification by state departments of education. The curriculum for elementary and secondary school teacher trainees began to take shape approximately a century ago when the universities took on the responsibility of educating pre-collegiate teachers. From all the options available to these pioneer teacher trainers, they chose the obvious. Instead of identifying the unique knowledge qualities, professional skills and strategies possessed by good teachers, and then building the programs to allow people to acquire these attributes, the early curriculum designers imposed on teacher education the dominant university modes of instruction: lecture courses. The only significant exception here is student teaching. (These special courses plus the standard courses in the arts and sciences became the training program for teachers.)

The typical four-year program for teachers can be broken down in the following way. First, the prospective teacher takes a pattern of general education courses which is normally required of all students regardless of major or area of concentration. Second, if he is a prospective high school teacher, he will take a sequence of courses that will provide depth in his teaching field; or, if he is a prospective elementary school teacher, he will take a wide spectrum of introductory courses in science, mathematics, English, art, music, the social studies, and physical education. Often these courses are geared specially to prospective teachers. Third, he will take a pattern of courses frequently called "the professional sequence." These would include foundation courses in educational philosophy, sociology, psychology, and history. Included in this professional sequence are methods courses designed to bridge the gap between educational theory and classroom practice. Often these courses give students an opportunity to design teaching units and plan instructional approaches. Fourth, there is a student teaching experience which typically takes place off campus in a public school. After a period of observation, the student teacher takes over a major portion of the teaching responsibilities in the class. This fourth component of the teacher education program varies in length between a semester and six weeks. It occurs normally in the late stages of teacher training. If the student has passed all the necessary courses and has done acceptably in student teaching, he is recommended for certification upon receiving the B.A. degree. Thus, the formal curriculum for entrance into teaching is over.[5]

The Informal Curriculum

The informal curriculum of teacher education is the experience that is common to the great mass of Americans. However, the effect of this covert curriculum becomes most apparent when people assume the formal role of teacher. The informal curriculum, then, consists of four components: socially learned teaching habits, extended teacher watching, mass media models, and initial, "real world of the school" teaching experiences.

Socially Learned Teaching Habits. Man has survived on our planet because he has had a special capacity. He has been able to pass skills and knowledge on one to the other. Thanks to this ability to teach, no man has to discover everything for himself.

Our evolution as a species was accelerated when early man learned how to pass on to others the tool-using and hunting skills he had acquired through personal experience. Teaching, then, became a habit of the race, a habit that was and is motivated by the desire to survive. From the time a child can crawl he is exposed to the "teaching habit." He is taught how to efficiently put food into his mouth. He is told what is good behavior and what is bad behavior ("Good baby" and "That's a no no"). He is warned not to play with matches. Children not only learn what to do and what not to do from these exchanges, but they learn the *teaching habit.* And, they learn it quite young. Observation of children two-, three-, and four-years old would reveal that much of the "play" activity of children is devoted to imitating their parents. The child teaches to his little playmates or his stuffed animals and dolls what he has learned from his parents. These lessons are complete with elaborate scoldings and affectionate praising.

This socially learned teaching habit, acquired early in life, is deeply engrained in the very character of the race. We spend an extraordinary amount of time telling one another what we know, correcting one another, moralizing and responding to the behavior of others.[6] When someone enters the classroom as a teacher, these habits are very much with him. In fact, he is given a fresh field of operation. If these teaching habits are not always legitimate in adult social life, they would seem to be legitimized when dealing with the young in school.

Extended Teacher Watching. As mentioned above, observation in public schools is a part of the formal curriculum for teachers. It is infinitesimal, however, compared with the amount and intensity of observation in the informal curriculum. By the time the prospective teacher has graduated from college he has spent 16 or 17 years observing from 60 to 70 different teachers. Since most schools in this country are teacher-centered, the student spends a good deal of his day watching and listening to his teacher. Although much of this is casual observation, frequently, the student's academic survival depends upon his skill at teacher watching. "Psyching out" the teacher is a major preoccupation of students. Many students would argue that being able to predict the "moves of the teacher and knowing what he wants" are far more important than mastery of subject matter. The precise effect of these years of teacher watching on the prospective teacher is unknown. However, when we consider all of the time and energy students devote to the analysis of their teachers' personalities, instructional methodologies, command of their subject, their motivations and general effectiveness, the suspicion grows that the impact is great. He has acquired standards for what he thinks is good teaching and bad teaching. He has observed a great range of teacher behaviors and chosen from among them ones he approves of and with which he would be comfortable. He has stored away methods and instructional approaches. He has decided on what constitutes acceptable and unacceptable student behavior. He has stored away techniques for handling students who violate the behavior norms of the classroom. In short, 16 years in the classroom has taught him a great deal about what it is to be a teacher.

Mass Media Models. Until not too many years ago the teacher aspirant could learn the teacher "moves" and attitudes only from his flesh and blood teachers. The mass media almost totally ignored the schools and the profession of teaching except for presenting characters like Mr. Peepers and Miss Brooks. However, this is all changed in the recent past. Schools and teachers very much preoccupy the American people. Seven years ago television pioneered with a series on a high school English teacher, "Mr. Novak." There has been a succession of school-oriented series on since then. The current fare is the "Bill Cosby Show" and "Room 222." The movies have also demonstrated a fascination with teachers and schools. In recent years we have been offered *The Blackboard Jungle, Up the Down Staircase, To Sir, With Love, KES,* and *Getting Straight.* What these television series and films have done is to provide the prospective teacher with a new set of teacher models. In the heightened atmosphere of a dramatic situation, we see the media teachers responding to an array of school situations. Experiencing these media teachers is different from regular teacher watching in a number of ways. First, the media teachers are young and immensely attractive human beings. Frequently, the media viewer gets to know their personal lives and educational philosophy in much greater detail than that of his own teachers. Second, the media teachers (normally after some initial uncertainty) end up to be, what would be normally considered, exceptionally good teachers. Third, what we learn about teaching from the media teachers may be heightened because it is embedded in a dramatic situation. Fourth, media teachers may be observed with a greater degree of objectivity. The viewer does not have to "psych out" the hero of a TV series. He can learn, freed from many of the complications which attend the normal student-teacher relation.

Besides the conditions of experiencing these media teachers, they also deliver a message. Although the exact message the prospective teacher takes from them is difficult to discern, a few tentative generalities are offered. First, the media teachers play down the information dispenser role of the teacher and emphasize the role of question asker. Second, the media teachers deal directly with life situations or work hard to relate academic content to the lives of their children. Third, media teachers deal with much more than the intellectual lives of their children. They respond openly to the emotional and social needs of their students. Fourth, media teachers present teaching as an attractive, important, and totally involving occupation. In summary, the media teachers provide the prospective teacher with a dramatic picture of what he should be like in the classroom and what he might become.

Initial Real World of the Schools Teaching Experiences. In spite of all the informal learning and having completed the informal curriculum, the process of becoming a teacher is not over until the individual has been tested and shaped by the realities of school life. Few people leave teacher training as polished professionals. Although the difficulties and traumas of the first year of teaching have long been appreciated, what the beginning teacher actually learns during that year is just beginning to be appreciated. Anthropologists such as Estelle Fuchs and Elizabeth Eddy have applied anthropological concepts to the experiences of first-year teachers.[7] They have compared the sense of disorientation and physical and emotional exhaustion which is experienced by so many beginning teachers to culture shock. They assert that the beginning teacher, particularly when he is teaching students of a different social class or ethnic background than his own, experiences the same phenomenon as travelers or immigrants to a foreign culture. This unaccustomed sense of disorientation and vulnerability, and the accompanying quest for equilibrium make the beginning teacher a ready pupil. What the beginning teacher often learns is to behave as the students expect him to behave, that is to act like the other teachers. Frequently, this means the beginning teacher must put aside what he calls his "idealistic notions" and "those ivory tower educational theories." This learning is frequently a painful experience for the beginning teacher. The anthropologists, Fuchs and Eddy, refer to this as "the rites of passage," and compare them to the ritualized trials of adulthood undergone by aspiring adolescents in more primitive cultures.

The initial teaching experiences, then, are more than a testing period for the young professional. He learns an immense amount about himself and his craft. He finds out what he can do and cannot do with children. He develops the beginnings of his "bag of tricks." His attitudes about himself as a teacher and about his students take shape. And most important, he makes the decision whether or not he will persevere as a teacher. Once he has gone through the rites of passage and emerged intact his training period as a teacher comes to an end.

The Relationship between the Formal and Informal Curricula

Teacher educators who formulate and are responsible for the formal curriculum of future teachers give very little attention to the informal, hidden curriculum. They tend to treat prospective teachers as *tabulae rasae* on which they write what a good teacher should think and do. They fail to realize that much of the formal curriculum demands on the part of their prospective teachers a massive behavior change and rejection of past teaching models. For instance, teacher educators tell their students that they should be questioners rather than talkers. They urge them to stimulate a spirit of inquiry rather than a pursuit of short-range answers. While these are admirable dicta, they run headlong against what the student has learned from the informal curriculum. What the student has learned from the informal, hidden curriculum he learned at an early age and he has learned over a very long period of time. It is frequently what seems to "work" in the schools. Expecting to severely redirect the prospective teacher's orientation with a few courses and student teaching seems to be programming disappointment and failure.

We are just emerging from a decade during which the most frequent word on the lips of teacher educators was "innovation." There was much talk of new teaching methods. Prospective teachers were taught about the virtues of self-directed learning and the vices of teacher-dominated classrooms. Individualized instruction has been championed. However, these innovations (often ancient ideas in new garb) and others do not appear to be practiced in any sustained manner in the public schools. Perhaps the reason is that, while teachers intellectually understood these innovations and their virtues, they never became part of their personal teaching repertoire of skills.

Teacher educators, who are serious about effecting change in their students and thereby affecting public school education, must think of teacher education in terms of the informal and the formal curricula. Teacher-training programs should help their candidates understand and suppress the dysfunctional teaching behaviors learned from the informal curriculum, such as moralizing, and continually giving students the answers. Second, teacher educators must be certain that the teaching candidates not only understand what they *should* do as teachers, but indeed be able *to do* it in a classroom with children. Until these happen teacher educators will continue to be preoccupied with the formal curriculum that has limited transfer of learning.

RECENT CURRICULAR TRENDS IN TEACHER EDUCATION

In the United States the decade of the sixties began with a burst of vitality and new hope. After much turmoil and disappointment, the citizenry closed the decade somewhat dispirited and seemingly more sophisticated. A similar pattern of rise and fall, although less pronounced, can be seen within the teacher education community. In fact a good deal of the optimism that characterized teacher education in the sixties stemmed directly from the ebullient spirit of the federal government. The energies and talents spawned by the "New Frontier" and "Great Society," coupled with the new input of federal money, had its effect on teacher education. During the sixties, then, the curriculum of teacher education was the focus of a great deal of professional attention. Four curricular trends, in particular, will be examined: academic upgrading; clinical experiences in teaching; training in teacher behaviors; and sensitivity training.

Academic Upgrading

The sixties began with the education community under great pressure to improve the quality of subject-matter offerings in elementary and secondary schools. The general community's uneasiness with Russian scientific and technological feats took hold of Dr. James Conant's recommendations in his 1959 study, *The American High School Today*. Conant urged more and better academic training in the American high schools. This in turn set off a flurry of curriculum revision in the elementary schools. Dr. Conant's message was reinforced by Dr. Jerome Bruner's *The Process of Education*. "The structure of the discipline" became a new key to our educational nirvana. While this set off interesting discussions among disciplinarians concerning *the* structure of their discipline, in subject fields like English, which draws upon the discipline of rhetoric, linguistics, and communications, it caused deep consternation and much confusion.

However, this renewed interest in the disciplines and reforming the subject-matter curriculum of schools was not without its influence in teacher education. In some states the required number of education courses needed for certification was decreased, especially for secondary school teachers. Within the training institutions themselves there were changes. The hostilities between academics and educationists abated. Teacher education programs became more flexible in that the required number of education courses was lessened. In many institutions a major in secondary education was all but abandoned, and the prospective high school teacher was either required or urged to major in his teaching field. The future elementary school teacher still majored in education, but he was urged to take more academic courses rather than the so-called professional content courses such as "social studies for the elementary school" and "elementary language arts." Although the balance shifted within the training institutions, this emphasis on greater depth in subject field did not bring about any fundamental change in the undergraduate training program.

Graduate Programs in Teaching. The first Master of Arts in Teaching program began at Brown University over 75 years ago. However, not until the late fifties and sixties did this approach to the training of teachers flourish. Spurred on by a felt need to implement the curriculum reforms underway, many universities and colleges began Master of Arts in Teaching and other graduate programs for what was to be a "new breed" of classroom teachers. The MAT programs, in particular, attempted to recruit new kinds of people into the teaching field. Two groups were targeted: liberal arts graduates with strong majors in academic fields and well-qualified people who were ready to make a career change. This latter category included college-trained housewives and retired military personnel.

Although there was and continues to be a great deal of difference from one MAT program to the next, in general the programs shared three curricular principles: first, advanced graduate study in the prospective teacher's subject-matter field; education courses, frequently of an innovative type, such as those which focused on problems and drew on a number of disciplines for solutions; third, a well-supervised teaching internship in which the intern takes on all but complete responsibility for the conduct of his classes.

In the last 15 years the number of MAT programs has grown from a small handful to over 250.[8] While this is, indeed, a dramatic growth, the number of teachers prepared by MAT and other graduate teacher-training programs is still small. In 1967 such programs prepared only 15,000 or 7 percent of the teachers eligible for certification. It is difficult, however, to predict with any degree of certainty the future of graduate programs in education. It does seem certain, though, that an alternative to undergraduate teacher preparation has been widely and firmly established. A basic *tenet* of MAT programs, that future teachers should be as well grounded in liberal arts education as other college graduates, makes a great deal of sense to college students and those that hire beginning teachers. There are, however, three factors that may affect the growth of MAT programs, particularly in the years ahead. First, the initial enthusiasm for these programs is beginning to wane. There are fresher, more "innovative" programs, such as the National Teacher Corps in the spotlight. Second, the decade of the seventies seems to be starting with a reaction against the purely cognitive, overly academic curricula which made graduates of MAT programs so attractive to the schools. Third, the current surplus of teachers is making the internship component of MAT programs difficult to maintain. School districts faced with the opportunity to employ experienced teachers find it difficult to justify turning classes over to interns. Also, the scarcity of teaching jobs may cause potential MAT candidates to think twice before enrolling in these graduate programs.

Clinical Training for Teachers

A strong current of discussion and action during the sixties has been the need for clinical experiences in teacher training. The basic idea behind clinical training in education was borrowed directly from medical education, occurred just as the medical profession is becoming disenchanted with the efficacy of their clinical training. The idea, however, has been to put the teacher trainee in contact with a variety of "live" teaching in school experiences. These school-based experiences, in turn, become the material for careful analyses. The clinical training movement within education has a number of different manifestations. Perhaps the most well known is the institutionalization of clinical professorships.

Clinical Professors. In 1963 James B. Conant addressed a persistent tension in higher education: the status of the university supervisor of teachers.[9] By definition, the college supervisor should be an expert in the process of teaching and in the content of instruction at a particular grade level or within a particular teaching field. However, because of the very clinical nature of his work, a supervising teacher is usually a marginal person in a university or college. The duties and status of the college supervisor and the attending rewards have not attracted the best qualified people to this important work. Conant urged the establishment of what he called "clinical professorships" for the individual who is to supervise and assess the work of student teachers. He urged that the clinical professor's status be analogous to that of the clinical professor in certain medical schools. Further, he suggested that institutions training secondary school teachers should have clinical professors for each field or a combination of closely related fields. Conant's recommendation influenced a number of institutions. At present several institutions—such as Northwestern and Harvard—are experimenting with the clinical professorship plan.

Approaches to Clinical Training. Response to the need for clinical training has been strong but somewhat diffused. It ranges from increased emphasis on observation of classrooms to the internship concept discussed above. At its core, however, this approach attempts to facilitate the bridging of educational theory and classroom practice. It aids the prospective teachers and their teacher (clinical professor, methods instructor, foundations professor) in focusing actual problems of teaching and learning. This is done in a number of ways. One method has been to build the curriculum for particular education courses directly on the perceived problems of the teacher education students. The problems they observed or experienced in student teaching become the focus for examination. Although frequently effective learning devices, such courses often tend to become platforms for simplistic "experience-based" solutions. A variation of this approach is the conducting of university methods and other education courses in a school setting. This and the addition of audio- or videotape replays of the student teacher's or intern's performance is credited with bringing a greater degree of realism to the attempts to bridge theory and practice.

The movement toward clinical training in teacher education appears to be gaining strength. The school-centered quality of the National Teacher Corps programs has given it impetus. The desire of many, both faculty and students, to be "relevant" and "where it's at" has encouraged early teaching experiences and an array of school-based teacher-training activities. Fundamentally, however, the clinical training movement seems to lack real substance at this time. It is a reaction against formal courses which do not enlighten or enhance the practice of teachers. The plan for clinical professors, while attractive in its possibilities, is very expensive. Nevertheless, the trend toward clinical training is still very much alive. Further, it has contributed directly to the emphasis on teacher behaviors.

Teacher Behaviors

During the last decade the curriculum of teacher education was affected by a new interest in teacher behaviors. This interest in what teachers actually do in classrooms was developed from two different sources. The first, a growing line of research on the language of classrooms and systems of categorizing such language came together with a renewed interest in directly training teachers for their classroom tasks. The reason for the renewed interest in training was stated by B. O. Smith:

Almost all teachers are now prepared in programs that provide little or no training in teaching skills. These programs consist of courses in the sociology and philosophy of education, learning theory and human development and in information about teaching and the management of the classroom. These are taught apart from the realities that a teacher will meet and are considered preparatory to student teaching. While student teaching usually comes after the formal courses, it frequently has little relationship to them and is ordinarily inadequate preparation for the responsibilities given the beginning teacher. The trainee studies theories that lead nowhere, then does his teaching with little theoretical understanding of the situations he meets.[10]

The research interest in the language of the classroom provides a vocabulary for the teacher educator. Further the emphasis on breaking down the global concept of teaching into describable events that could be categorized encouraged the identification of teaching skills and strategies. These in turn became the subject of training.

Interaction Analysis. Interaction analysis is a case in point. For a number of years educational researchers have been working on instruments that could be used to measure and categorize the language and other social behaviors of the classroom.[11] Some of these tools of the research proved effective in the instruction of the dynamics of teaching. The next step was to train teachers in the use of these observation instruments and, more specifically, to teach them so that they could manipulate their own behavior to get certain kinds of ratings from these *instruments.* The most widely used is a technique for interaction analyses developed by Professor Ned A. Flanders. Flanders' system breaks classroom interchanges down into 10 categories, 4 which contain types of teacher talk of an indirect influence, 3 categories exemplifying teacher's indirect influence, and 3 categories for student or unclassifiable responses.[12]

An interaction analysis system like Flanders' provides the teacher trainee with a way of conceptualizing and thinking about teaching. His future interaction with his students can be seen as human behavior which in turn can be classified in a number of ways. This categorization, further, allows him a standard against which to manipulate his own teaching behavior. The teacher can have his classes taped and apply the interaction analysis instrument to the behavior that has been recorded or someone else can use the instrument on his "live" class. The completed instrument then becomes a form of feedback which the teacher can use as a means of greater understanding and possible future improvement.

Interaction analyses and other classroom behavior systems are being used in a variety of places in the teacher education curriculum. They are being used in methods courses, courses in educational psychology, and in particular, in student teaching. In this latter situation, the supervising teacher observes the student teacher and applies the instrument to the classroom behavior he is observing. The results are used as input for the supervisory conference that follows.

Interaction analyses techniques and other instruments for analyzing classroom behavior are, as mentioned earlier, research instruments. However, there is a tendency for those who work with them to think of them in value terms. Frequently, those who use them believe that teacher behavior in some categories is "good" and teacher behavior in other categories is "bad." For instance, many of those who have used Professor Flanders' interaction analysis system have attempted to teach teachers not to use "direct" statements rather than aiding teachers in gaining greater control over their teaching behavior. The teacher trainer often lacks caution in applying research tools to training situations.

Microteaching. Microteaching is a method that grew directly out of a concern for training individuals in teaching behaviors. Its origins are much more practical than interaction analysis. The microteaching approach was developed in response to a problem. The problem was that while student teaching and other direct teaching experience had certain values, there were few assurances that people were learning any effective teaching behaviors. The two causes for this failure are a lack of specificity of the goals (what the teacher should do) and little or no knowledge of results or feedback on performance (how he actually did). Microteaching is an attempt to establish a training setting that will remedy both these deficiencies. The normal complexities of the classroom are reduced and the possibilities of growth-producing feedback are maximized. A typical microteaching session would proceed as follows: first, a teacher trainee would receive some initial introduction about a specific approach or strategy or teaching skill. For example, he may be trying to master the skill of asking probing questions. After seeing a demonstration film or videotape, and reading about how and when the skill is most appropriately used, he would prepare a brief lesson to be taught to four or five children. The primary purpose of the lesson is as a vehicle for the trainee to practice a particular skill or approach under study. The content is important, but primarily it is a means to practice and gain mastery of the teaching skill or approach. After the brief lesson, feedback forms on the skill are handed out to the student and the supervisor. Everyone, including the trainee, fills out a form. The purpose here is to get immediate feedback on the performance of that skill. Although not essential, the microteaching procedure is really enhanced if the lesson can be videotaped. When the students complete their forms, the trainee and the supervisor enter the critique phase. Normally, they would review both the written feedback forms and parts of the videotape of the lesson. The critique sessions are not aimed at an across-the-board improvement of the trainee's performance. Rather, the intention is to focus on specific areas. At the end of the critique period, the trainee goes off for a short period of time to reflect on his performance and the feedback he has received. He, then, returns to teach the same lesson to a different group of students, this time with the benefit of practice with the feedback.

The training potential of microteaching rests on three strengths: (1) in microteaching the normal complexities of the classroom (number of students, subject matter, and time) are reduced; (2) the amount of feedback on performance is greatly increased; and (3) microteaching focuses the attention of the trainee and the supervisor on the performance of specified skills, rather than "general teaching excellence."

Microteaching is only eight years old, and in that time it has been discussed widely in the educational literature as a new addition to the curriculum in teacher education. Although it appears to be practiced widely, it is practiced thinly. Many teacher trainer institutions do a little microteaching. Besides the normal resistance to new practices, microteaching deviates markedly from the normal course structure of teacher education. It involves coordinating the efforts of elementary and secondary school teachers, supervisors, teacher education students, physical locations, and equipment. Its future depends very much on the degree of flexibility and amount of resources available to teacher education programs in the years ahead.

Simulation. Since World War II the curriculum for the training of military men has relied heavily on a technique called simulation. Simulation can be broadly defined as a representative format of a realistic setting or situation that provides the participant with the opportunities to make decisions or solve problems and further provides or allows feedback for the evaluation of actual or potential performance, i.e., role playing in an administrative situation or participation in a structured teacher setting.[13] For example, military men engage in "war games" which are designed to equip them to perform specific tasks under conditions of battle.

Simulation has been introduced into teacher education only recently. However, interest in it is great and its potential appears to be quite high. It differs from microteaching in a number of ways. Most essentially, however, microteaching is a constructed, but real teaching encounter between a teacher and some students. Simulation, on the other hand, occurs among adults, usually teacher trainees, playing different roles. Also, while microteaching focuses directly on the acquisition of skills, simulation aims more at the understanding and solving of classroom problems.

Simulation can be applied to the problem of running an entire high school or a teacher dealing with an angry parent. Essentially, a problem and certain conditions surrounding that problem are established. Individuals assume specified roles, such as a teacher, administrator, and student. Each person is given information about his role and in some cases a little information about the problem situation. One commercially available set of materials simulates an entire elementary classroom.[14] Information is provided on the socioeconomic background of the community, on the characteristics of a particular school, and on the teacher's students, such as records, test scores, and reports of past teachers. In this set of materials there are over 20 common problems encountered by teachers, ranging from evaluation to student misbehavior. Once a particular problem is chosen, the teacher education students are assigned different roles, given the necessary background and information and the game begins. Sometimes, the problem is introduced by means of a short film. Once a problem has run its course, the class, led by the teacher educator, analyzes the problem and the manner in which the teacher tried to solve it. Alternate interpretations of the problem and alternate teacher responses are discussed. Frequently, the problem is reintroduced and the teacher trainee has an opportunity to respond with a different set of teacher behaviors. Although the problem situations are not real, teacher trainees realize that these are the problems that they will be confronted with once they begin teaching. As a result, they almost invariably take the problems and their response to them quite seriously.

Simulation of the type above has normally been practiced in principles of education courses preparing people for student teaching. However, as a technique, simulation can be used quite widely in teacher education in methods courses and human relations training. Like early teaching experiences, it can be used to introduce prospective teachers to some of the problems and issues of the schools. Later in training simulated experiences can be used as a check to see if teaching candidates have acquired the desired teacher behaviors. Another use of simulation is to open up discussion on specific issues. For instance, a class studying teaching by inquiry can begin with a simulated inquiry lesson. This event, then, is used for analysis of the underlying principles of inquiry. One major disadvantage, however, is that simulation can be badly misused. Its virtue is in presenting the problem and the real conditions surrounding such a problem. However, the interpretation of the problem and the teacher behaviors that go toward a resolution of the problem are left to the teacher educator and the students to work out. While this can be a great virtue, it can also lead to simplistic solutions and inappropriate teacher behaviors.

Performance-based Teacher Education Programs. A quite recent development in teacher education is the total training program devoted to teacher behaviors. As indicated earlier in this chapter, a major difficulty in most teacher education programs is the lack of clear goals. Frequently neither the trainee nor the teacher trainers know exactly what the trainee should be able to do as a result of having gone through the program. Performance-based teacher education programs are designed to establish the behaviors the teachers should possess at the end of their training. Once the terminal behaviors of the programs are specified, then, instructional training and experiences are established so that the prospective teacher can acquire those behaviors. Successful completion of the program is not indicated by the normal paper and pencil test, the amassing of credits or survival in a student teaching situation. Successful completion depends upon a demonstrated mastery of the teacher behaviors which were the goals of the program.

The movement toward the development of performance-based programs has been greatly stimulated by financial supports from the U.S. Office of Education. A number of different models for performance-based programs are currently in the early stages of implementation in universities and colleges around the country. If this performance-based method proves to be as successful as many of its advocates are suggesting, and if the idea continues to have the backing of the U.S. Office of Education, the whole complexion of teacher education could radically alter in a very short time.

Resources for Mediated Teacher Education. Not long ago the education of teachers was almost exclusively a matter of the verbal exchange between a teacher educator and his students. This approach limits the amount of attention that could be given to teacher behaviors. What an elementary or secondary school teacher actually did in class had to be conveyed through words, either written or spoken. Since people's interpretation of words vary so widely, the actual behavior of teachers keeps slipping through the fingers of discussion. Recently, however, this problem has been lessened through the use of motion pictures, audiotapes, videotapes, and multimedia systems. In the latter part of the sixties two kinds of materials began to become available, protocol and training materials. Protocol materials are actual reproductions of human behavior, behavior that has been captured live rather than especially staged. Further, they are free of interpretation. In effect, protocols present "what is" for analysis. These materials, which can be audio- or videotapes or films are used in the instruction phase of teacher education. As such, protocol materials can be appropriately used in a wide array of education courses from foundations to methods. The other kind of mediated teacher education is used for training purposes. Training materials are used to present examples of teacher behavior that clearly represent desirable or undesirable behavior. The aim here is not analysis by the trainee, but the acquisition of specified behaviors. For instance, in the standard microteaching situation, short model films are used to clarify the skills to be practiced in the microteaching setting.

The development of mediated teacher education resources is quite new, but the audience is already large. Recently the major professional organization in teacher education has encouraged their use with the distribution of a bibliography of available resources.[15] The teacher behavior emphasis in the curriculum of teacher education would appear to be in for a period of rapid and intensive growth.

Sensitivity Training

Teacher educators and schoolmen have long believed that the teacher's personality is crucial to his professional success. The teacher's ability to relate to children and colleagues and his ability to accept himself as a person have much to do with his effectiveness as a teacher. By and large, however, very little attention has been given to the teacher's acquisition of human relations skills and to his affective development generally. The general attitude in pre-service training about the future teacher's human relations skills has been that he either "has it or doesn't have it."

During the latter part of the 1960's sensitivity training became widely talked about as a phenomenon of the culture. Although difficult to precisely describe, sensitivity training has its roots in a gestalt psychology, nondirective therapy, awareness training, and a number of other activities to extend man's sensitivities.[16] Sensitivity training had its initial impact on in-service training. Many school districts employed sensitivity training sessions to help their teachers more effectively deal with racial tensions and the growing student unrest in the schools. The aim of sensitivity training is to help teachers become more sensitive to themselves and others and the way they interact with others. To accomplish these rather straightforward objectives, a variety of techniques, some quite unorthodox, are employed. Typically, people become members of a training group which has a designated, and usually trained, leader. Through a series of exercises and games which attempt to break through superficial communication, individuals gain a greater understanding of the way they are usually perceived by others. They also become involved in helping other group members see themselves and adapt more fruitful methods of communicating. Again, it is difficult to speak with any precision about a sensitivity training movement because it is so new and so diverse. Also, its effectiveness depends both on the skill and "sensitivity" of the trainer and the mental health of the individual group members.

While there is no data available about the extent of sensitivity training in pre-service teacher education programs, the suspicion exists that it is more widely talked about than practiced at the present time.

Recently, the whole area of the affective development of the teacher has been given support by the publication of the American Association of Colleges of Teacher Education, *Teachers for the Real World.*

The prospective teacher's attitudes and feelings are too important to leave the shaping of them to the accidents of human association or to the interests of individual instructors. A definite plan for identifying personality problems and attitudes should be developed in every program of teacher education. These problems and attitudes should be identified in the early stages of each trainee's preparation. And a systematic program of remedial situations should be worked out and followed through.[17]

While there is a certain undeniable faddish quality to much of the sensitivity training movement, the problem of the teacher's inability to relate to others and to deal with his own or his students' affective world remains a very real one. It would appear, too, that though it is unclear the exact form the sensitivity movement will take, the teacher education community has committed itself to addressing the underlying problems of human interaction.

PERENNIAL PROBLEMS IN THE EDUCATION OF TEACHERS

The curriculum of teacher education is constrained by a number of issues. Some of these issues have all the characteristics of problems in that they constrain the development of positive ideas and tendencies. None of the problems that will be addressed here are new. They are discussed because their presence affects the climate of discourse in teacher education. Also, these problems need to be thoroughly understood by those individuals concerned with curriculum planning for teachers.

The "Is or Ought" Conflict

At the present time the prospective teacher spends rather limited time in professional preparation for teaching. The curriculum decision-makers in teacher education, therefore, must make difficult choices about what their students should learn. Underlying these decisions is the "is or ought" dilemma. Should the prospective teacher be prepared for the schools as they are—warts and all—or as the schools should be and may be in the future. Said another way, should teacher education be survival training for the school jungle or should it prepare people to inherit the new educational Jerusalem. From this question some very practical questions flow. How much emphasis will we give in teacher preparation to discipline problems and techniques of controlling human behavior? How much training should we give upper elementary, junior high, and senior high teachers in reading instruction so that they can cope with their students' limitations in this area? Do we instruct the new teacher in how to use the most advanced curricula or do we teach him to be an amateur curriculum builder, using the limited materials (the only ones) he will find in his future school? Those trained for survival in the jungle often turn out like grim guerrillas, fighting hard but with no enlightening vision of what can be done. Those trained for the ideal school often are crushed by the realities and limitations of daily school life. One proposed solution is to prepare "change agents." However, such a person would need all of the survival training and preparation for new modes of education plus special social skills and a thorough knowledge of how to bring about institutional change. If we were prepared to give such training, it would take many more resources than are presently devoted to teacher preparation.

Low Commitment of Trainees

A large number of people entering teacher education enter with hesitancy and confusion about their plans to be a part of the teaching profession. Fully one quarter of those who are trained and qualify for certification do not teach. Many of those who do enter the schools only teach for a year or two. Fully 12 percent of all teachers leave the schools at the end of each school year.[18] This high dropout rate among teachers has something of a paralyzing effect on teacher educators. For one thing though students do not have the same intense desire that is evident among other prospective professionals such as doctors, architects, and lawyers, many young people take a program leading to certification as part of their undergraduate program, viewing it as an occupational insurance policy: "I can always *teach!*" On the other hand, the high dropout rate and the inferred low commitment of many teacher education students makes it difficult to get support for the kind of thorough, intensive education programs which might nurture a commitment among some and attract the commitment of others.

The All-purpose or Specialist Teacher

The curriculum builder in teacher education is not only faced with the question of training for "what is" or "what ought," but also, the problem of providing all candidates with relatively the same kind of training. The educational community has not found a way to use the differing talents and commitments of people.

All teachers of a particular grade level or subject field are given generally the same responsibilities in schools. Therefore, the demands of the educational marketplace force the curriculum builder of teacher education to spread his resources thin and provide candidates with a little training in many areas. Instead of carefully training teachers in evaluation and test construction, they are normally given a few principles and some mechanical rules. Instead of giving them thorough training in an array of teaching modes, such as individual tutoring, group work, teacher-led discussions, and lecturing, these different teaching modes are simply and briefly discussed. Although the major difficulty here is attempting to develop all-purpose teachers with limited resources, there are excesses in the other direction, also. Frequently teachers are trained as subject-matter specialists and their teaching assignment does not correspond to their highly specialized training. It is not uncommon for someone trained in European history to be teaching American government or history. An English teacher with training and interest in creative writing may end up teaching British literature. In brief, the curriculum in teacher education is often out of phase with the demands the teacher encounters in the classroom.

The Setting for Teacher Education

As discussed earlier, for the last 100 years teacher education in this country has more and more become a university responsibility. Although tax-supported universities can become greatly enthused about the mission of training teachers during the time they submit their budgets to the state legislatures, normally, there is little enthusiasm for teacher education within universities. Teacher education is done, but done grudgingly, and to the embarrassment of many of the academic community. Often, the educationists responsible for teacher education feel like a minority of marginal men. They have not cut out the clearly autonomous role of professors in other professional schools, such as law or medicine. Since teacher education is usually part of the undergraduate training, they must work with academics in the arts and sciences departments. Given teacher educators' uneasy status in the university and the general lack of enthusiasm for their specialty, few daring curriculum innovations are proposed. Teacher educators tend to adopt the modes and styles of instruction of general education. This abdication severely limits the curricular potential of teacher education.

The Knowledge Base in Teacher Education

Teacher education has been a discernible activity since the 16th century. It is only until fairly recently that teacher education has begun to transcend the earlier modes of instruction by description, exhortation, and personal example. The demand for more effective and systematic teacher training has led to a greater codification of what is known in education and also toward a greater impetus for genuine research. While there is much that we do not know, the knowledge base in education has been growing rapidly. However, it is in a form that makes it difficult to use. For example, in 1963 the *Handbook for Research on Teaching,* an important and valuable addition to educational literature, was published. However, the teacher educator or teacher who read through the over 1,000 pages would find little information that would form and direct his practice. There are two problems here. First, what we know about teaching and learning is not in a form that is readily usable by teacher educators. While many creative teacher educators are able to transcend this difficulty, the majority are not. Second, much of the knowledge base in education is descriptive, providing data and occasionally insights into current practice. However, it does not answer the teacher's question, "What should I do tomorrow?"

Directions for Teacher Education

This section is about future curricular trends in the education of teachers. Although it is based on discernible trends, it is best described as the author's wishful thinking. The projected trends are based on the assumption of a relatively stable future. They preclude major war or pestilence. Further, they do not take into consideration the radical educational alternatives such as Ivan Illich's plan for de-schooling, by which I understand him to mean the dismantling of the public school system to bring about a more efficient, equal distribution of educational opportunities.[19] These projections also preclude the wholesale mechanization of the school with computer-assisted instruction and other advanced technologies. They are based on a future in which the relationship between superior public education and the common good is more clearly seen, and in which effective teacher education is viewed as immediately instrumental in bringing about *improved education.*

Conditions for Change

At present teacher education and public elementary and secondary education are linked in something of a producer-consumer relationship. Teacher preparation institutions must abide by one reality condition: their graduates must find jobs. This condition has kept teacher education from developing especially innovative programs. There are, however, two educational movements which are gaining momentum and public attention. If they become part of the mainstream of American education, they will have a profound and salutary effect on teacher education.

Differentiated Staffing. As noted earlier, a persistent problem in teacher education is having to prepare the "all-purpose" teacher. Generally speaking, all teachers come out of the same mold and go into the same slots. The beginning teacher fresh out of a teacher education program has exactly the same responsibilities as the teacher in the next classroom who has been teaching for 30 years. They have the same responsibility to teach the same curriculum. Except for differences in grade level or subject matter, the schools make very limited use of the teachers' differences in talent, interest, and experience. Teachers simply conform to the specifications of the job.

The concept of differentiated staff is basically a reorganization of the human resources on a faculty. It takes into consideration the differences in talent, interest, and experience. Also, it tries to reorganize these qualities in light of new educational needs of children. To do this, it breaks down the present monolithic role of the teacher into a cluster of roles encompassing such discrete functions as team leader, formulator of detailed objectives, instructional sequence planner, script writer, presenter of information, evaluator of pupil responses, designer of supplementary pupil experiences, and a variety of other roles.[20] A differentiated teaching approach would require more specialization and a greater focusing of training. The implications for teacher education are many. First, however, the beginning teacher can be better trained to engage in a smaller spectrum of teaching skills. He would not be required to be an omni-competent Sylvia Ashton-Warner when he first enters the school. The very fact of breaking up the "all-purpose" teacher model would allow pre-service teachers a more gradual entrance into work in the schools, perhaps working on teams and performing special tasks. It would give pre-service teachers and beginning teachers a good opportunity to learn on the job from their more experienced colleagues.

The effect of differentiated staffing on teacher education curricula would be to allow it to focus more directly on specific roles and related skills. The new clarity about what a beginning teacher should be able to do in the schools would clarify to teacher educators what they should be doing to prepare teachers.

University-School Collaboration. As mentioned earlier, the university as the setting for teacher education has many deficiencies. Individuals disenchanted with a university-based teacher education frequently suggest that teacher education occur in the schools and be the responsibility of the schools. Such a suggestion ignores the fact that presently the schools are struggling to cope with their primary task, the education of children. They have neither the resources nor the energies to train the nation's teachers. A third alternative is being explored at present. That is a close collaboration between teacher-training institutions and public schools.

The school-university collaborative approach to teacher education hopes to bypass a history of mistrust and conflicting ideologies, and instead to build on the strengths of both institutions. Some of the public schools strengths are that they have real children, rare commodities in colleges and universities. Schools have skilled practitioners dealing with complex learning problems. Schools have settings in which teacher trainees can learn through doing. Teacher-training institutions, on the other hand, have new ideas about what should be taught and how it should be taught. They have young adults who can provide a variety of services for the schools. Besides offering in-service training for experienced teachers, universities can provide a retreat where classroom teachers can refresh themselves intellectually and acquire new teaching skills.

When close university-school collaboration is effected, teacher education takes place in both settings. Also, the education goes in many directions. Not only do beginning and experienced teachers have new training opportunities, so do teacher educators and school administrators. University professors have many legitimate opportunities to work with young children, thereby testing their ideas and keeping themselves experientially abreast. Such in-school experiences allow teacher educators to have an immediate relevance check on their ideas and instructional approaches. It enables university academics to search within their discipline and rediscover which content is most valuable to children at different stages of growth and development. The teacher trainees, of course, experience these same benefits of relevance checking and exploration within the discipline.

At present there are over 40 universities and school districts that are attempting to work out collaborative programs in teacher education. Sponsored by the Office of Education's Trainers of Teacher Trainers Program, schools, communities, arts and science, and teacher education faculties are attempting to bring about a new mix of resources in the preparation of teachers. Underlying such relationships is a spirit to share responsibility and resources. For the teacher trainee the effect is freer movement between school and university and a greater opportunity to merge educational theory and practice.

Proposed Curricular Elements in Teacher Education

Both of these trends, differentiated staffing and university-school collaboration, will help teacher education, especially the curricular trends here projected. The greater clarity of goals for teacher education, the opportunity for clinical training, a closer relation between teachers and teacher educators will aid in establishing a cycle of inquiry about teaching and learning within the education community.

Philosophical Understandings. Even before James Conant downgraded the philosophy of education course, it was steadily losing favor.[21] Typically this course has been a review of several philosophical positions and the drawing out of their implications for classroom instruction. This approach to the philosophy of education would appear to be too remote for the future teacher. He is more interested in practical questions, like "Will I survive in the classroom?" And, "What do I need to know to be a success?" Nevertheless, the beginning teacher must, by the very nature of his work, deal with these issues of a philosophical nature.

In his recent book, *Crisis in the Classroom,* Charles E. Silberman speaks of this issue.

The central task of teacher education, therefore, is to provide teachers with a sense of purpose, or, if you will, with a philosophy of education. This means developing teachers' ability and their desire to think seriously, deeply and continuously about the purposes and consequences of what they do—about the ways in which their curriculum and teaching methods, classroom and school organization, testing and grading procedures, affect purpose and are affected by it.[22]

A philosophy of education, then, is needed if the teacher is to be more than a sterile technician. His professional work must be linked to the larger questions of man and his relationship to his fellowman and his universe. A method which shows great promise of aiding the prospective teacher in the application of philosophical concepts to practical problems is the case study method. The case study method has been used for many years in business, law, and other professional education. The case method can engage the prospective teacher in the real-world problems of schools. Problems touching on the rights of students, the value of a particular curriculum, and a teacher's relationship with a student raise questions about the nature of authority, knowledge, and man's relationship to one another. In working on a particular case the future teacher must analyze the situation, take action, and be ready to justify his action. In working out solutions to practical problems, the future teacher realizes that these practical problems have philosophical implications and philosophy is practical in their solution. However, no matter what the method of instruction, the goal is clear. Teacher education must help its students acquire the habit of asking themselves such questions as "What am I doing?" and "Why am I doing it?" It must help the prospective teacher see not only that teaching is a purposeful activity, but it would help them gain answers to these questions.

Besides a clear sense of purpose, the future teacher needs command of the skills of critical thinking. In his daily work he will be called upon to make a large number of decisions. He had to decide about what to teach and how to teach it. He must choose a text. He must make sense of experiences in his classroom. Daily he must analyze a great deal of human experience in light of school policy. In order to do this and do it well, the beginning teacher needs to acquire a core of critical thinking skills, ways of analyzing events and coming up with sound decisions. Once having initially been exposed to these critical thinking skills, the case method could be a valuable means of training future teachers in them.

Skill in Teaching. Besides knowing why he is teaching and what he is teaching, the prospective teacher must learn how to teach. As indicated earlier, a good deal of attention is being given to the "how to teach" component. More and more it is being realized that two previously distinct trends of the teacher education curriculum must come together and work in closer harmony.[23] One strand provides the beginning teacher with theoretical knowledge about learning and human behavior while the other helps him gain control of those teaching skills which facilitate learning. The theoretical knowledge comes from psychology, sociology, anthropology, and a number of other disciplines. In the past, if the prospective teacher was exposed to this knowledge it was in the form of specialized courses. However, since the goal is the ability to apply this theoretical knowledge to actual classroom situations, a different tack is suggested. In order to get future teachers to understand the classroom, classroom phenomena should be analyzed as directly as possible. To do this, a great variety of protocol materials, which are essentially slices of raw behavior from schools, should be used. At present, these protocol materials are in the form of film or videotape. The purpose of these protocols is simply to present real situations for analysis. Once the future teacher is presented with real situations, the concepts drawn from the disciplines become the valuable tool of analysis. It must be stressed, however, that the purpose of these protocols is not to present the future teacher with exemplars of "how to teach," but rather a sophisticated understanding of what occurs in classrooms and the effects of different kinds of teacher behaviors on the events of the classroom.

Once the beginning teacher gains an understanding of what is occurring in the classroom, he is ready to gain control of certain technical skills of teaching. Simply understanding or knowing does not ensure that the future teacher *can* do in the classroom. The prospective teacher needs to develop a repertoire of teaching skills. In contrast with the theoretical knowledge components of a teacher's preparation where the focus is on the situation to be examined and understood, the teaching skills component focuses on the future teacher's own behavior which will be observed, analyzed, and modified. While educational researchers have not yet identified the teaching skills which produce the most salutary impact on student learning, nevertheless the collective wisdom of the profession, as faulty as it is, and the research, as slim as it is, suggest the value of acquiring certain skills. Some of these are: the ability to ask different kinds of questions, each of which requires different types of thought processes from the students; the ability to effectively reinforce certain kinds of student behavior; the ability to diagnose student needs and learning difficulties; the ability to continually vary the learning situation in order to keep the students involved; the ability to define objectives of particular lessons and units in terms of student behaviors; and the ability to relate learning to the student's experience. This brief, suggestive list is far from complete. However, the skills listed represent the kinds of behavior that should be the objectives of the training program.

The means of acquiring these teaching skills is training. "Training" is an activity to which many teacher educators object. The objection is that training a teacher somehow makes him perform as a robot and prevents the release of his creative energies. This position contradicts what we know about training in other occupations. For instance, surgeons and airplane pilots are trained to perform certain operations until they can demonstrate the skills proficiently, and indeed, almost automatically. This level of mastery enables them to turn their energy to tasks more worthy of their creativity. As B. O. Smith says, "a trained individual has relaxed control which frees him from preoccupation with immediate acts so he can scan the new situation and respond to it constructively. Training and resourcefulness are complementary, not antithetical, elements of behavior."[24] The actual method of training needs to vary with the complexity of the skill and its place in the sequence of training. Some of the methods of skill acquisition, such as microteaching and simulation exercises, have already been mentioned. Many technical skills and strategies can be practiced in teaching groups made up of peers. Also, a good portion of the in-school, clinical training of teachers should be devoted to skill acquisition. It should be clear, however, that the "skill at teaching" strand of the curriculum will be severely limited unless strong links of collaboration are forged between university and school.

Subject-Matter Preparation

Up to this point this chapter has avoided discussion of the general education or liberal arts curriculum for teachers. Since the specifics of subject-matter preparation will be dealt with in other chapters, only very brief remarks about subject-matter preparation will be made here. It must be clear, however, that the acquisition of knowledge and control of subject matter is of the *utmost* importance to the teacher. Although the teacher is nothing if he lacks the skills to help others acquire and use knowledge, he must first possess command of his subject field. Therefore, with respect to subject-matter preparation of teachers, two points will be made. One deals with the degree of general education of a teacher and the other with the qualities of that training.

Teacher education in America is still evolving from its normal school origins. Although the general education of teachers has improved at a dramatic rate in this century, prospective teachers are not as well prepared in this area as their fellow university students. The need to take specialized education courses and student teaching cuts deeply into the future teacher's general education program. Since the acquisition of knowledge is so fundamental to the teacher's role, we must assure that his general education is as strong, if not stronger than his university peers. Besides the teacher's obvious need for subject-matter competence, there is a pragmatic reason for quality general education programs. The teaching profession will attract few individuals of high-academic competence if they must sacrifice a sound general education in order to fulfill the requirements for teaching. If this means extending teacher education into a fifth year or requiring summer work for prospective teachers, so be it. However, much more can be done to combine the learning of subject matter and professional education. Charles Silberman has recently written to this point.

If colleges and universities were as they should be, teachers would acquire much of that knowledge and insight in the process of learning subject matter itself. One of the significant differences between education for teaching and for other professions is that every subject a student takes in the course of his liberal education can and should be a professional course as well. Any course, that is to say, be it in history, literature, chemistry, physics, or mathematics, should also be a course in teaching methods, epistomology, and the philosophy of education.[25]

Silberman's assertion that each subject-matter course should, among other things, be a course in epistomology, takes us to the next point.

In order to adequately deal with the subject matter of instruction, the prospective teacher must have an understanding of the discipline or disciplines which support his teaching field. This should be acquired through general education and academic specialization. However, the teacher needs not only to possess knowledge, he must also possess knowledge about knowledge.[26] As a teacher he is immersed in both his subject matter and the process of instruction. In a sense, he needs to be able to stand outside and above his subject matter if he is to have full control of it. As B. O. Smith has said:

Knowledge about knowledge in general enables the teacher to gain this higher and more comprehensive perspective. This sort of knowledge is built upon more particular knowledge of the elements of subject matter and the relations among them, the uses of the disciplines' knowledge and the ways their information is manipulated and its dependability decided.[27]

Few teachers would appear to have this kind of knowledge about knowledge. In the university it falls between the academic professors and professors of education. When the teacher has left the university and is in the classroom, then he begins to get questions about his subject field's elements, its uses, and its relationship to the needs of pupils. Unfortunately, he rarely has the training or the luxury of time to pursue these questions. It seems that this understanding must be part of his teacher preparation. One way to facilitate this is to make teaching a regular part of learning one's subject field. It has long been recognized that nothing reveals our inadequate grasp of knowledge as much as a request to teach it. As the distinguished physicist Gerrold Zacharias has stated of such a proposal, "not only would the student get a feel for teaching and learn the problems, possibilities, and pitfalls of the classroom, but he would also learn a great deal about his subject matter. He can't help learning more when he has to know both his own and his pupils' understanding."[28] Such methods of instruction would indeed be a radical change in many universities. However, the movement within teacher education itself, toward earlier teaching experiences and the emphasis on clinical training could greatly facilitate the type of mastery of the subject fields suggested by B. O. Smith.

CONCLUSION

Teacher education, by its nature, does not lead. Its task is to prepare individuals for teaching positions in the schools as they exist. While it is tempting to prepare teachers for utopian schools (and certainly some universities and schools should), the teacher education community must be responsive to the realities of today's schools. Nevertheless, while teacher education does not lead, it most certainly can influence. For instance, the preparation of a generation of teacher-scholars will certainly make the American schools more scholarly. Or, if teachers are trained in human relations skills and chosen for their generosity of spirit, the American schools will undoubtedly be more humane. Today, the performance of teachers and their schools are coming under greater scrutiny. Educators, parents and, increasingly, students themselves are articulating their dissatisfactions with public schooling. People are calling for a new interpretation of what it means to be an educated man. Therefore, while teacher education must prepare teachers for the reality conditions of the American schools, it must also prepare teachers who can bring about a renewal of the schools. Like the teacher it prepares, teacher education must exist in tension.

NOTES

1. Charles E. Silberman, *Crisis in the Classroom* (New York: Random House, 1970), pp. 414-15.

2. The National Education Association, *Teacher Supply and Demand in Public Schools, 1968* (Washington,·D.C.: NEA Research Report, 1969-R4).

3. The American Association of Colleges for Teacher Education, *Teacher Productivity—1967* (Washington, D.C.: The American Association of Colleges for Teacher Education, 1968).

4. B. Othanel Smith *et al., Teachers for the Real World* (Washington, D.C.: American Association of Colleges for Teacher Education, 1969); and Charles E. Silberman, *op. cit.*

5. Walter K. Beggs, *The Education of Teachers,* in the Library of Education Series (New York: Center of Applied Research in Education, Inc., 1965), chap. 2.

6. J. M. Stephens, "Research in the Preparation of Teachers: Background Factors That Might Be Considered," unpublished paper delivered at the Ontario Institute for the Study of Education, April, 1968, p. 3.

7. Estelle Fuchs, Teachers Talk: Voices from Inside City Schools (Garden City, N.Y.: Anchor Books, Doubleday and Co., 1969); and Elizabeth Eddy, Becoming a Teacher, (New York: Teachers College Press, 1969).

8. American Association of Colleges for Teacher Education, Teacher Productivity—1967 (Washington, D.C.: The American Association of Colleges for Teacher Education, 1968).

9. James B. Conant, The Education of Teachers (New York: McGraw-Hill Book Co., 1963), pp. 64-65.

10. B. O. Smith et al., op. cit., pp. 69-70. See N. L. Gage, The Handbook of Research on Teaching (Chicago: Rand McNally & Co., 1963), chaps. 6 and 13.

11. Essentially these are paper and pencil instruments applied by a trained rater to various teaching-learning situations.

12. Edmund J. Amidon and John B. Hough (eds.), Interaction Analysis: Theory, Research and Application (Reading, Mass.: Addison Wesley, 1967). Dwight W. Allen and Kevin Ryan, Microteaching (Reading, Mass.: Addison Wesley, 1969).

13. W. C. Meierhenry (ed.), Mediated Teacher Education Resources (Washington, D.C.: The American Association of Colleges for Teacher Education, 1970).

14. Donald Cruickshank, Teaching Problems Laboratory (Chicago: Science Research Associates, 1967).

15. Meierhenry (ed.), op. cit.

16. Max Birnbaum, "Sense about Sensitivity Training," Saturday Review, (November 15, 1969).

17. B. O. Smith et al., op. cit., p. 92.

18. Ibid., p. 22.

19. Ivan Illich, De-schooling, New York Review of Books.

20. Henry M. Brickell, "Local Organization and Administration of Education," Implications for Education of Perspective Changes in Society, ed. Edgar L. Morphet and Charles O. Ryan (Denver: Designing Education for the Future, January, 1967), p. 227.

21. James B. Conant, The Education of American Teachers (New York: McGraw-Hill Paperbacks, 1964).

22. Silberman, op. cit., p. 472.

23. B. O. Smith et al., op. cit.

24. Ibid., p. 80.

25. Silberman, op. cit., p. 490.

26. B. O. Smith et al., op. cit., pp. 112-13.

27. Ibid., p. 113.

28. Gerrold Zacharias, "A Portmanteau Proposal," paper given to the Tri-University Project in Elementary Education, New Orleans, February 1-3, 1968 (mimeographed).

National Council of Teachers of English, 3, 15, 27; censorship, 119; professionalism, 24; resource materials, 29
National Defense Education Act (NDEA): language programs, 119, 120; teachers institutes, 6-7, 17, 35
National Long-Term Study of Mathematics Achievement, 156
National Science Foundation, 151, 164; teacher training, 161
National Teacher Corps, 217, 218
Nature of the Social Sciences, The, 187
"New Mathematics," 147, 150-153
New Worlds in Literature series, 18
Northwestern University Project English Center, 4-5

Oliver, Donald, 189, 190
Oppenheimer, J., Robert, 54-55
Oregon Curriculum Center, 4

Paraprofessional, 23
Parker, William Riley, 118
Photography, 72
Physical science, 89-90, 91, 96
Piaget, Jean, 25, 34, 95, 157
Pillet, Roger A., 113
Political science, 188
Postman, Neil, 27
Process of Education, The, 3, 7, 196, 215
Professionalism: english teachers, 21-24, 35; foreign language teachers, 122
Programmed learning, 28; mathematics, 159
Progressivism, 2
Project English, 3, 4, 35
Prospective Scientists stream, 88-89, 91-92, 93, 94
Protocol materials, 224, 234

Read, Herbert, 78
Related Arts movement, 69-71
Research: foreign language studies, 127; mathematics, 155-157, 167-169, 176-177
Rhinelander, Philip H., 46
Rilke, Rainer Maria, 1

Roberts, Paul, 18
Roberts English Series, 8, 25
Rogers, Carl R., 27
Rosenberg, Harold, 59, 75, 76
Rotating unit approach, 13-14
Ryan, Kevin, 207

School Mathematics Study Group, 151; achievement study, 156; textbooks, 152
Science Alpha sequence, 89, 91
Science Curriculum Improvement Study, 95-96
Science education, 85-110; core programs, 89-90, 95; mainstream units, 102-103; social problems, 103-105
Scientific inquiry, 107-109
Scientific literacy, 96-98
Scientific Literacy stream, 88-89, 91-92, 93-94
Scriven, Michael, 190, 192
Second Language Learning, 116
Sensitivity training, 225
Sequential curriculum, 4, 25; mathematics, 149; social studies, 196, 197
Shaver, James, 189
Shermis, S. Samuel, 200
Shugrue, Michael, 17
Shuman, R. Baird, 1
Silberman, Charles, 27, 31, 34, 75, 233, 236-237
Simon and Schuster, Inc., 18
Simulation, 222-223
Situation Ethics, 48
Smith, B. O., 219, 235, 237, 238
Smith, C. M., 59
Smith, R. A., 59
Social sciences, 186, 187, 188
Social studies, 185-205
Sociological Resources Project for Secondary Schools, 198, 199
Specialization: art education, 45-46; english teaching, 12-14; teacher training, 228
Sputnik I, 2; language study, 115, 119
Squire, James, 26
Student, 14-15; foreign language studies, 130
Student teaching, 209-210
Studio workshop, 65

THE BOOK MANUFACTURE

What Will Be Taught—The Next Decade was composed at Datagraphics in Phoenix, with printing and binding by Kingsport Press, Inc. The paper is Perkins & Squier Company's Glatfelter Special Book XL. Interior design was by the F. E. Peacock art department. Cover design was by Evelyn Hansen. The type is Caledonia.

B&T 854